Sir Geraint Evans has written his autobiography with the help of Noël Goodwin, a freelance writer and broadcaster on music and dance, contributing to *The Times* and to arts publications in Britain and the USA. He was Music and Drama critic for the *Daily Express* for 22 years, 1956-1978, during which time he took particular interest in the careers of British singers at home and abroad. He first heard Geraint Evans sing Figaro at Covent Garden in 1950, and later wrote about most of his major performances in Britain and on the Continent. Noël Goodwin has written histories of the London Symphony Orchestra (with Hubert Foss) and of the Scottish Ballet, and he edited the Royal Opera and Royal Ballet Yearbooks, 1978-1980. He was also executive Editor, *Music and Musicians*, 1963-1971, and has written major contributions to *Encyclopaedia Britannica*, *The New Grove Dictionary of Music and Musicians*, *Encyclopaedia of Opera*, and other works of reference in Britain, the USA and Germany.

SIR GERAINT EVANS
with Noël Goodwin

SIR GERAINT EVANS:
A Knight at the Opera

Futura

A Futura BOOK

Copyright © Geraint Evans 1984

First published in Great Britain in 1984
by Michael Joseph Ltd

This Futura edition first published in 1985

ISBN 0 7088 2741 1

Printed in Great Britain by
The Guernsey Press Company Ltd,
Guernsey, Channel Islands.

Futura Publications
A division of
Macdonald & Co (Publishers) Ltd
Maxwell House
74 Worship Street
London EC2A 2EN
A BPCC plc Company

*For Brenda
and for Alun, Huw and Susie,
in love and thanksgiving*

Contents

ACKNOWLEDGEMENTS

I should like to express my thanks to Noël Goodwin, for keeping my variable memory on the right track while we shaped these reminiscences, and for compiling the Chronology of Roles and the Discography; to Jill Lloyd-Roberts, my secretary, for typing and re-typing the results of our labours; to *Opera* magazine, for references to past performances and to the Archives of the Royal Opera House, Covent Garden, for assistance and verification of certain details.

G.E.

Illustration credits

At home with Brenda and their two sons, Alun and Huw
Michael Murray

Backstage in Salzburg with Olivera Miljakovic *Foto Felicitas Timpe*

Geraint as Dr Bartolo in *The Barber of Seville* in Chicago, 1969
David H. Fishman

As Tonio in the Zeffirelli production of *I pagliacci* at Covent Garden,
1959 *Houston Rogers*

Falstaff: Sir Osbert Lancaster's design for the Glyndebourne
production, 1958 *Photo Pic*

Dressing for the part *John Downing, Daily Express*

Debut at the Met, 1964 *Anger International Photos*

Figaro with Graziella Sciutti in Milan *Erio Piccagliani*

Figaro with Evelyn Lear in Salzburg *Photo Ellinger*

Bottom in *A Midsummer Night's Dream* at Covent Garden *Tony Evans*

Working with Herbert von Karajan on a recording of *Die Meistersinger*
in Dresden *Siegfried Lauterwasser*

L'elisir d'amore for HRH Prince Charles following a performance at
Covent Garden *Donald Southern*

*Every effort has been made to attribute illustrations correctly. We
apologise for any errors or omissions; they will be remedied in
future editions.*

CHAPTER ONE

A Look Far Back

School ended for the day with the ringing of the bell at four-fifteen, and I, like all the other kids, couldn't get out quickly enough.

As we were running down the hill towards our homes the hooter from the colliery started bellowing intermittent blasts.

'Accident at the pit!' cried one of the boys, and we ran like the wind, curious to know what had happened, and wanting to see all we could.

To us that hooter was a fact of life. Day in and day out it sounded over the village at regular times, calling the men to work and measuring out the shifts. If it blew at other times it usually meant something was wrong, and that was another fact we grew up with.

We reached the top of the colliery in a few minutes. Edging our way past the stables (I can smell it even now, there were a lot of pit-ponies still working down the mine in those days), we crept stealthily along, black mud over our ankles, until we were within fifteen to twenty yards of the 'cage' which took the miners down to the bowels of the earth and brought them back up.

Hiding behind a discarded dram, as the trucks carrying waste from the pit were called, we watched the commotion around the cage. There wasn't long to wait before it came to the surface and some miners came out, two of them carrying a stretcher on which lay a body covered in an old blanket.

Nothing much to see there, we thought. But as the stretcher-bearers trudged through the mud to the Ambulance Room, something fell from the stretcher.

A severed arm.

Our eyes popped. I felt sick. Ashamed to show it, I stepped aside to vomit, but when I looked back at my pals I saw they were nauseated too. We'd had more than enough, and ran away to the stream on the common where we could wash the tell-tale black mud from our legs and clean our shoes before we went home, because we knew full well the row we would get if it was found we'd been anywhere near the pit-head.

1

When I got home, all my grandfather said was: 'Ble r'wyt ti wedi bod? Mae wedi mynd amser te'. ('Where have you been? It's past tea-time'.) Welsh was our family language. I spoke it before I learned English.

From the way my grandfather spoke I knew he wasn't very annoyed with me, only concerned that I'd broken the fixed daily routine. Always it was breakfast at eight, the midday meal at one o'clock, tea at four-thirty and supper at eight. My grandmother took no notice of him and went on getting my tea ready: as far as she was concerned I could do no wrong, so my home was a haven of safety and warmth.

We lived at 55 William Street, a terraced house in the Welsh mining village of Cilfynydd, two miles from Pontypridd and twelve miles from Cardiff. I was born in that house on 16 February 1922, under a picture of Lloyd George, the hero of Wales at that time, resplendent in his robes as Chancellor of the Exchequer.

I was the first child of William John Evans and Charlotte May Thomas, the first grandchild on my father's side of the family and the fourth on my mother's side.

Sadly, I have no memory of my mother, as she died in childbirth only eighteen months later, bearing a daughter who didn't long survive her. She was twenty-two years old.

Years later I was told that she had been among the most popular girls in the village. The funeral procession was one of the longest seen there, and some mourners were still leaving the house when the head of the procession reached the top of the mountain road that led to the cemetery. It seemed the whole village had turned out in spite of pouring rain, and amid all this my shocked and bereaved father had to stay at home, ill with pneumonia, unwillingly confined to bed on doctor's orders.

Family councils now decided that I should be brought up by my mother's parents in William Street, no mean task when they were then both over sixty years old. My father went back to live with his own parents at the top of the village. Like most of the men in Cilfynydd, he was a miner, and the long hours he worked meant that I didn't see him very often. So it was a great thrill for me whenever he called, or took me out, carrying me high on his shoulders.

Music was my father's abiding passion. I'm sure this is what brought him and my mother together. Apparently she had a lovely mezzo-soprano voice and my father was a fine baritone. Both were involved in all the musical activities in Bethel, the Welsh Methodist chapel they attended regularly.

I am told that my mother would sit and sing to me for hours. Could it be that she instilled in me a love of music from my early infancy?

My father's interest in music went deeper: he wanted to learn more of the theory of music and in the little spare time he had he took a correspondence course from one of the London colleges. He was appointed conductor of the Handel Glee Party, a choir which became very well known at the various *eisteddfodau*, the singing competitions in Wales. It was particularly noted for its pianissimo singing, although how he ever got them to sing that softly I'll never know. As a boy I used to sit in on an occasional rehearsal and I remember him shouting at the top of his voice, 'Piano, piano.' Indeed what fun we had, my cousins Aeron, Alun and I, imitating the grimaces and mannerisms of various members of the choir.

I suppose my father fulfilled any ambitions he ever had. He conducted oratorios and operettas for various mixed and male voice choirs in the locality, and when he retired he was conductor of the Pontypridd Male Voice Choir.

All my grandparents were from west Wales, from the small town of Newcastle Emlyn and from the seaside town of Aberaeron. So on both sides I was a 'Cardi', as the Welsh used to call those of Cardiganshire stock – before the boundaries were all re-drawn into what is now the county of Dyfed.

Like many from this area, my maternal grandfather had grown up to the sea and looked first to that for a living. He went to sea in the old sailing ships, travelling the world and rising to the rank of First Mate before he 'came ashore'. Seamen have the best stories of all to tell, and many were the adventures he told to me as a boy.

Once ashore, he came south to the Glamorganshire valleys, where the coal-mines afforded at least some assurance of a regular wage.

He was a tall man, just over six feet. I remember him best sitting by the hearth at home, wreathed in clouds of blue smoke from his pipe filled with Franklyn's shag tobacco.

He was quiet and reserved in his manner, but with an inner strength to his character. He spoke firmly and to the point, and if he gave an order it was instantly carried out. How well I remember breaking the commandment 'Thou shalt not steal', and feeling his heavy hand on my buttocks.

It was my turn in our small gang to buy a tuppenny packet of Woodbines from the slot machine outside the grocer's shop. Try as I did, I could not get that money from anyone. But I had seen sixpence lying on the mantelpiece at home and it seemed to loom larger and larger as time went on. I was getting quite desperate, and finally I took it! Not only did I buy one packet of cigarettes, I bought two, but I can't say I really enjoyed that surreptitious smoke on the common.

The time came to return home and my grandfather was there, waiting. I tried to appear as nonchalant as I could, but by his look I knew that *he* knew. Then the dreaded words came, but in Welsh, 'There's sixpence missing from the house. Did you take it?' I denied it instantly. He asked the question again and still I denied it. The third time he asked I dissolved into tears.

According to my grandfather and the Good Book, the cock had crowed three times.

Down came my trousers! But I never stole again!

Up the mountainside he had an allotment where he grew fruit and vegetables to supplement our otherwise pretty plain diet. Often he'd take me there with him, and we'd share a packet of sandwiches and drink cold tea from a bottle with a screw of paper for a stopper. I enjoyed those occasions – as we sat outside the stone hut where he kept his gardening tools, I felt as though I was in a man's world.

From my grandfather and his sister, my great-aunt Jane, I learned a little of the family disgrace their father had brought about by marrying a gipsy. 'A real Romany', my great-aunt said she was, dark and striking to look at; but my great-grandfather was virtually disowned by *his* father, a respectable land bailiff at Borth, near Aberystwyth, for marrying as he did. When my great-aunt and her two brothers were bidden to tea at the bailiff's house, their mother wasn't allowed inside; she had to collect her children at the gate when the visit was over.

Such was the prejudice over this rash marriage, my great-grandfather could get no work in the district, and with his wife they scraped a living together by gathering cockles on the seashore, filling great baskets which they then humped on their backs many miles to market. The Romany strain came out again in later generations. Uncle Will, my mother's brother, had exactly the piercing eyes and dark looks of a gipsy, and perhaps there's something of it in my own appearance. At any rate, I've been told that I strongly looked that way in some of the operatic roles I played.

Despite this background, my grandfather was fair with blue eyes, and an elegant couple he and my grandmother made when they went to chapel or ventured out together on a rare and special occasion.

Best clothes were kept for Sundays and holidays. The Monday morning ritual was to brush, fold and put away the clothes for another week and, as the drawers and cupboards were opened, the room reeked with the smell of moth-balls.

On high days and holidays my grandmother, Mamgu, was always immaculately dressed with her short fur cape and silver-topped cane, and in the summer out came her black straw hat with what I thought looked like an evil-looking bird with shiny wings stretched across the brim.

She was as close to me as my mother would have been and doted on me. She was very ambitious and hoped that one day 'ein Geraint bach ni' (our little Geraint) would become a celebrated preacher. I suppose this was because my cousin Menna and I would stay at home with her on alternate Sunday nights while the rest of the family went to chapel. Mamgu always wanted me to read the Bible to her and to break the monotony I would mimic the 'hwyl' of the old Welsh ministers, shouting and gesticulating. I wonder now what she would have thought about my ending up on the stage, that 'den of iniquity'!

In later years she became bed-ridden and blind and one of her greatest remaining pleasures was to listen to the wireless she was given by the Blind Institution. This was very fortunate for me. Not many people in our village possessed a radio at that time and after my grandparents had retired I used to tune in, late at night, to the foreign stations.

I heard my first Wagner this way. I wasn't conscious at the time I was listening to Wagner – all I knew was that it was wonderful and I wallowed in every phrase.

Dadcu was not as appreciative of music. In later years, after I had started to broadcast, he wanted to listen to no one else but me and, if I were singing a duet with a soprano, however beautiful her voice, he always wanted to know, 'Pam mae'r hen fenw 'na yn screchan?' (Why is that woman screeching?)

My grandmother died just before I was fifteen and I felt that my world had come to an end, even though there had always been other members of the family around me as a child. Mamgu Oaklands, my father's mother, so called because she lived in Oakland Terrace, was always kind. She also had a lovely sense of humour even until she died at ninety-six.

Aunty Blodwen was a dedicated member of the St John's Ambulance Brigade, so whenever I felt ill or hurt myself, Aunty Blod was sent for.

Aunty Bessie was a strong-minded, self-taught woman, well known in the district and a deaconess in Bethel Chapel. She was the first to make me aware of poetry and of the arts. It was to her I was sent to perfect the verses and poetry I was to recite in school. She had the greatest influence of all in my up-bringing and I am deeply indebted to her.

But although I had great love and attention from all the family, from a very early age everybody had some say in what I did. My grandparents, so anxious that everything should work out correctly for me, sent me to ask advice from one or the other on practically every issue. Sometimes my father would give advice, but often that would be out-voted by the rest of the family. I really didn't know who I should turn to or to whom I was responsible, especially as they all, including my father, had other children of their own.

As a small boy, there were moments when I felt so frustrated that I would walk to the cemetery on the top of the mountain, sit on the wall and carry on an imaginary conversation with my mother. I always came home feeling that somehow things had been sorted out.

All the menfolk in the family worked underground, and even my father's grandmother, Mamgu Rees, had worked down the mines as a girl. She was sent there when she was about eleven years old to work as a doorgirl, opening and closing the doors that controlled the draughts to and from the coal-face, banished for long hours in the dark and the dust.

Virtually all the working life of Cilfynydd revolved round the Albion Colliery at the edge of the village. The mine and all its workings have long since disappeared, the shaft is filled in and grown over, but in my boyhood it ruled our lives and indeed cut many of them short. Young men would scarcely grow to be thirty years old before they were gasping for breath as they walked up the hill to their homes, coughing from the depths of their stomachs to rid themselves of the black coal-dust that clogged their lungs. What we now know as pneumoconiosis and silicosis was to them a touch of 'coal-dust on the chest'.

Nor was it only the dust they had to contend with. Injuries occurred frequently, and miners regularly became so accustomed to pain that they sometimes failed to realise how serious their injuries were. Washing my father's back on one occasion, as he leaned over a tub of water in front of the fire, he warned me to be careful. 'I've a cut on my back,' was all he said.

As I washed the pit dirt away I was horrified to see a great gash, perhaps fifteen inches long, the flesh open almost to the bone. To my father it was just another painful injury. When we told him how serious it looked, he calmly put his clothes on, got on a tram and went to his doctor, who put in more than twenty stitches to help it heal.

Another day I passed one of the deacons from our chapel going home from work in the middle of a shift. I gave him a respectful 'Good afternoon, Mr Humphries,' as I passed, and couldn't figure out why, although he replied with a cheerful 'Hello, bach,' he kept his head held back with one hand covering his nose with a very soiled handkerchief. 'Bit of an accident,' he told his wife. When she cleaned his face, she saw the cut had almost severed his nose. She took him to the hospital and it mended after treatment, but for the rest of his life he carried the miner's tell-tale blue scar across his nose.

With so much depending on the mine, the year of the General Strike, 1926, brought great hardship to our village, as it did to all the mining communities. I was four and a half years old, but I remember being taken by the hand to the soup-kitchens that provided some sort of sustenance, and even helping my grandfather and my uncles pick over the coal-waste at the tip for some fuel to make a fire in our home.

They were harder times than I could possibly understand. But of course parents in the valleys sacrificed as much as they could to make sure we children did not go without the necessities, and they struggled fiercely to make the best of what they had. However short of food and money they were, the house would be kept spotless. Every Friday it was cleaned from top to bottom, the floors spread with newspaper and the doorstep scrubbed and 'stoned'. The floors stayed covered until after the midday meal on Sunday, when the newspapers would be taken up to show them polished and shining for the week to come.

Cilfynydd, pronounced Kill-vun-ith, nestled in the side of a narrow valley, and the name stems from Cil-y-mynydd, meaning the niche in the side of the mountain. It had a population of around 1800, a community where everybody knew everyone else, where doors were never locked, except perhaps at night, and where people helped each other in times of distress. If anybody was taken ill, there would always be a voice at the door, offering to do the washing or the shopping. Life was warm and friendly in those rows of houses clinging to the mountainside, dark grey stone under roofs of blue-black slate, glistening on a rainy day like black diamonds against the rugged green of the hillside beyond.

For reasons I never discovered, most of the streets in our village had Christian names like May, Ann, Richard, Howell and William, but there were so many Joneses, Evanses or Williamses around that street names were often added to differentiate between one family and another. Then, if there were too many with the same surname in each street, people became known by their nicknames: Davies Tea Caddy (the grocer), Jones Tailor, Ianto Gas, Benny Top Shop, Dai Up-and-down (a pit accident had left him with a limp), Tommy Cantwr (singer). My father was known as Bill John Stripes because he wore a black jacket and striped trousers.

Many of our grandparents were self-taught, and having left school at an early age they read widely to 'better themselves'. Almost every house would boast a large Welsh Bible and a number of the classics translated into Welsh, as well as religious books, and the Miners' Library in the Workmen's Hall was in constant use. The ideals of self-education in turn influenced our parents who taught, nurtured and encouraged any talents their children showed.

Sometimes I think Cilfynydd had more than its share of talent, and William Street most of all, as was depicted in a broadcast some years back by D. Gwyn Jones, a Director of Education who recalled his contemporaries in our street.

What other double row of eighty-two village houses can claim more than a dozen teachers and luminaries of the teaching profession alone? One was Dr Gareth Owen, now Principal of the University College of Wales, Aberystwyth. There was also Merlyn Rees, the former Labour Government minister who, although he wasn't born there, lived there for some time. Then there are the three men who have sung principal roles at Covent Garden: the tenor Stuart Burrows, my younger half-brother John (who later gave up singing) and myself.

Our games followed the seasonal patterns of marbles and conkers, bowling hoops or whipping tops, and we also got up to our own special kinds of mischief. We 'rode the drams', those trucks carrying pit-waste and hauled by cable to the top of the colliery tip. It was illegal and dangerous, and we risked a stinging clip round the ear from the village policeman, Sergeant Gayler, if we were caught. Then we would get our own back by scaring his chickens, until one day he hid in wait for us in the chicken-coop, and when he came roaring furiously out he sent us running faster than the chickens.

I have no idea who first discovered it, but a favourite sport on a windy night was to crumple up some old dry newspaper and stuff it into the bottom of a drainpipe that ran down the side of a house. When the paper was lit, the wind would send the draught up the pipe with a mournful sound just like the colliery hooter from a distance. Anybody sleeping upstairs might be deceived into thinking just that, and our wicked hope was, of course, that they would be roused to get up and perhaps even dress before discovering they were actually hours adrift.

We spent many happy hours tickling and catching trout in the two streams which ran past the edge of the village, the Cold Stream and the Warm Stream. At a point where they met, some of the unemployed men of the village decided to build a dam and make a swimming-pool. It could not have been better placed, with woods of fir on one side and greenery all around, and the 'baths up the cwm', as we called it, gave us something to enjoy for many years to come.

As was the case all over South Wales, the main ball game for the men was rugby football, not 'soccer'. My father and uncles played regularly for the village team and many was the time I watched them on a Saturday afternoon. Sometimes they came on to the field straight off a shift from the pit, still grimed with coal-dust except perhaps where they'd had time for a hasty wash of face and hands. Their game was as hard as their muscles and, in village rivalries, no quarter was asked or given.

One such occasion was the only time I've seen a rugby scrum collapse *upwards*. The visiting team had a notoriously 'dirty' player among their forwards, while Cilfynydd had my Uncle Will, who was always known in the village as Will Aber, packing in the front row. He played hard but fairly, but even he began to resent some of the opposing forward's dirty tricks. Whereupon our captain called to him: 'Go on, Will Aber! Sort him out!'

'All right, boy!' growled my uncle, and waited his chance for the next scrum.

When that happened, Uncle Will got down in it, one arm round the hooker but the other kept free. No sooner had the ball gone in than there was an agonised scream, the front rows suddenly shot up into the air and collapsed all round. Only afterwards did I find out that my uncle's free and massive hand had reached out and squeezed the opposing forward in the crotch, right where it hurt most.

I played rugby myself as a schoolboy (and later in the Services), but I suffered from asthma when I was young and when I had an attack, my grandmother made me wear a waistcoat of Welsh flannel lined with thermogene, which was impregnated to generate heat. I was just getting over one of these attacks when I was chosen to play for Pontypridd Schoolboys, a very important match for me, but Mamgu made me promise, on my word of honour, that I would not take off the waistcoat during the game.

As I perspired with the effort of the game, the thermogene burned so badly I felt my chest glowing like a furnace. I played like a boy possessed, forgetting all the finer points of the game.

I have always derived tremendous pleasure from watching the game, the Welsh team in the big international matches in particular, especially when it included my brother-in-law, Glyn Davies. In later years, of course, I've been thrilled to watch my own two boys play rugby. Glyn and I used to fantasise about our futures and think how marvellous it would be if, one day, I were to take Brenda to watch him play for Wales at Twickenham, and he were to accompany her to Covent Garden to hear me sing in an opera. Never for one moment did we think that both would one day happen.

The core and pivot of village life remained the chapels, where we attended regularly on Sundays, beginning with a young people's prayer meeting before the morning service; choir practice at one o'clock before Sunday school at 2 pm; and the evening service as well. A full day indeed! Sundays meant no games of any kind; no whistling, no reading except the Bible or a Welsh newspaper. My grandparents believed firmly that Welsh was the language of God so it was all right to read the *Welsh Gazette*! But this was a domestic discipline that I had to accept as a way of life.

It was not only my grandparents who thought that it was the language of God. On one occasion I flew from Los Angeles to New York and I thought I recognised the back of a fellow-passenger as he passed me during the flight. When he returned I saw it was the actor Hugh Griffith, so I greeted him in my deepest rich voice: 'Bore da, Hugh Griffith.'

As he heard this he raised his eyes heavenwards and lifted his arms in the air, as if thirty-five thousand feet had brought him that much closer to God, calling out: 'Duw! Duw!' (My God! My God!) Then, pulling himself together and looking about him at the other passengers, he enquired, 'Who said that?'

But whatever else they stood for in our religious faith, the chapels also meant music. There was the joy not only of singing together on Sundays, of hymns and folksongs and children's solos, but also of the music that flowed through our lives at other times. There were the choir practices and concerts; the constant competition between choirs and soloists at the regular *eisteddfodau*, the festival of hymn singing known as *Cymanfa Ganu*, usually at Easter and Whitsun, and the oratorios, plays and children's cantatas that each chapel managed to put on every year. Whether we liked it or not, whether or not we had the talent, our parents made sure that we took part.

I recall one local *eisteddfod* at the Workmen's Hall at Cilfynydd when I was given the task of presenting the winner's medal to the champion soloist. For this the winning singers in each category – soprano, alto, tenor, bass – competed against each other in front of the three adjudicators who, on this occasion, declared the contralto to be the winner.

Came the moment when my young self, all of nine years old and tongue-tied with it, was about to hand over the medal to the contralto when suddenly there was a noisy disturbance and the defeated soprano charged on to the stage. She was a large bosomy woman, dark like an Italian opera singer, with black hair tied in a bun, and her equally big and generous voice had thrilled the audience when she sang. Everybody expected her to win, but apparently the adjudicators had picked the contralto on grounds of musicality and interpretation as much as vocal quality. Now they sat mesmerised as the soprano elbowed me and the medal out of the way, pointed an accusing finger at them and shouted: 'If I had a gun I'd shoot the bloody lot of you!'

And with that she stamped away, loudly applauded by the audience, and leaving me in appalled embarrassment.

Until this time I had taken it for granted that I had to compete. I had won my first gold medal when I was only four and when I was six I won first prize for the best singing-actor in the Children's Action Song Competition at the Pontypridd Town Hall. But this incident made such an impression on me that I never wanted to compete again, and neither did I except for one occasion when, during the early stages of the war, the *News Chronicle* held a singing competition. I was in the RAF when I entered and got as far as the semi-final when unfortunately I was posted.

To obtain the best visiting soloists for the big oratorio performances, competition was often fierce, and as a boy I heard many of the leading British singers of the day. Any one of their names – such as Eva Turner or Heddle Nash – was enough to fill a hall or chapel, and I sat listening in wonderment to these voices, never dreaming that a decade or so later I would be sharing a platform with them myself.

At that time I was content to listen, although we could never listen for long enough. What I didn't realise was that one way and another, music was gradually exerting a hold over me.

One of the weekly comics of those days, *Wizard* or the *Hotspur* or some such greatly prized reading for kids of ten or eleven, had a feature on 'How to build a one-string violin'. I followed the instructions avidly.

I acquired an old cigar box from our local barber, a piece of mahogany from Bob Owen, our local undertaker, and spent a couple of shillings on an A string and an old bow from a pawn shop. The result wasn't the most musical sound to listen to, but at least it worked.

Our local barber, known as Dai Barber, contributed more than an old cigar box towards my musical education. We as children hated to go there to have our hair cut, because we knew we would be there for hours. There were always lengthy discussions about the Bible and about local history between him and some of the older men of the village. But Dai Barber had an excellent tenor voice and, if there had been an oratorio or a concert the night before, there was no knowing how long you would have to wait. So many times during the hair-cut, Dai Barber would stop, poised with scissors and comb in mid-air, and demonstrate how beautifully a phrase had been sung, or even how it should have been sung.

Many a boy, not daring to move in the high chair, toppled in a faint, unable to stay the course.

About this time my father married again and moved with his new wife to Hopkinstown, where he worked as a fireman at the Ty Mawr Colliery. It was a village on the other side of Pontypridd, near the mouth of the Rhondda valley, and when I was ten years old it was arranged for me to leave my grandparents and live with my father and my new stepmother.

The move could hardly have come at a worse time for me, because it meant leaving a familiar school and starting somewhere strange just as I was coming up to the crucial examination called 'the scholarship', which in those days determined whether one was bright enough to go to a grammar school for the next stage of one's education.

So far I'd done pretty well at school. I hadn't been top of the class, but I was usually close to it, in the first three or four as a rule. The change of school caused me to slip back badly. What's more, as a new boy there I had problems with some of the others. One in particular was a hero in his little gang and was goaded into bullying me, but one day I decided I'd had enough and I fought him. Thank goodness, I won. I suppose I had to prove myself and from that time the 'new boy' was accepted.

Home life wasn't very happy either. My stepmother suffered from a heart condition which often made her fractious and irritable. Because of her illness I had to help look after my half-brother John and half-sisters Margaret and Mair, and cope with household chores instead of having enough time to do my homework and perhaps go out to play with other boys.

No doubt I was difficult too at times, but this was all very different from the life I had known with my grandparents and it was very unsettling.

The scholarship time came, I sat the examination, and I failed. I can never describe what a blow this was to all the hopes I had. Now both the grammar school and the secondary school in Pontypridd were out of my reach. Most of my pals got through. There were others, of course, with no scholarly ambitions who were content to leave school at fourteen and look for a job, but that wasn't what I wanted. Besides, my family and my teachers had all expected me to do well.

After the results came through and left us all shocked and dismayed, the headmasters at both my primary schools, in Cilfynydd and Hopkinstown, wrote to the education authorities on my behalf, as did the Minister of Bethel Chapel. I don't know what they thought they could do, but it was good to realise they thought I wasn't that dull. However, no exceptions could be made and the rest of my schooling was to be at Lan Wood School in Pontypridd, where I would stay until I was fourteen and then go to work.

The shattering effect of my scholarship failure stayed with me for many years, and it lingered as a sense of inadequacy or inferiority even after I started my singing career. Sometimes it's put to me that I might never have had the career I did if I'd actually gone to grammar school then. Who can tell? I believe that music would have led me the way it did whatever my schooling, but in spite of everything that's happened since, I *do* regret missing the chance and what it might have meant to me, and that feeling has stayed with me, always. I still maintain that the grammar school was the backbone of education in Britain.

My father could see I wasn't happy in Hopkinstown and when I was about thirteen he suggested I might prefer to go back to Cilfynydd and to my grandparents, but I refused. I told him I wouldn't go back there without a proper reason so that I would not cause any embarrassment. Gradually I realised that if I could find work when the time came for me to leave school (and this was in 1936, when the effects of the Depression were still all around us in South Wales), my earnings would supplement my grandparents' small pension. With this in mind I eventually moved back to Cilfynydd, making my home again in William Street.

Pontypridd itself was a lively place compared to the villages. The town grew up at the meeting of two rivers, the Rhondda and the Taff, and Taff Street was its main thoroughfare of shops and offices, with the Town Hall and the busy Market Square in the middle. The railway station was a junction for lines to the Rhondda, Merthyr and Aberdare, and one of the great historic sights in Wales was, and still is, the single-span stone bridge built over the river in the eighteenth century.

Pontypridd could also boast that the Welsh National Anthem ('Mae Hen Wlad fy Nhadau'), was composed by Evan James and James James, a father and son who lived in Mill Street.

'Ponty', as we referred to it, was the market town for the locality, where tradespeople had their premises and where professional people practised. There was also a works where anchor chains were made for the large sea-going liners.

It was the obvious place to look for a job for a Cilfynydd boy who had no intention of going down the mine. So here I went after the school doors closed behind me and thought myself lucky to be accepted as an errand boy at the Maypole Dairy, a grocery shop in Taff Street.

Just across the street in 1936 a Mr Theophilus displayed his 'High Class Ladies' Fashions' and a few days before I was due to start work at the Maypole Dairy, a friend of my father's stopped me in the village and told me that Mr Theophilus was looking for a bright boy to work there. 'It might suit you,' he said. 'You were good at art in school, weren't you? Maybe you could get the chance to learn the trade, become a window-dresser and that sort of thing.'

Intrigued by the possibilities this conjured up, and not mentioning my impending engagement at the Maypole Dairy, I thanked him for the tip and went off to see Mr Theophilus, who gave me the job. 'Start tomorrow morning,' he commanded. 'Nine sharp!'

So here I was with *two* jobs starting at the same time, only one of which I could possibly take up. I decided I preferred the ladies' outfitters and Mr Theophilus, and I turned up the next morning as ordered.

My first task was to clean the windows, outside, and in full view of the Maypole Dairy. I kept my head down, hoping I wouldn't be noticed before lunchtime, when I intended to go over to explain and to thank the Manager. But I hadn't cleaned very much window before he saw me and rushed across the street. 'Evans!' he shouted, 'You're cleaning the wrong windows!'

I tried in my embarrassment to explain how the other job had made me change my mind and that I wouldn't now be working for him, but he was furious and quite rightly so, telling me what he thought of me in very forthright terms.

Nevertheless, I stayed where I was, and for seven shillings and sixpence a week (less than forty pence, but by no means out of scale with wages then) I cleaned the windows at Theophilus's, made the tea, delivered the hats and gowns to his customers at the end of the day, and generally tried to make myself useful. There was one time of day, though, when I made sure I had something to do inside the shop, and that was when the grammar school boys and girls passed on their way home. I just didn't want them to see me.

In a sense I suppose I was cut off from my friends, but I tried to make up for it in other ways. I joined the YMCA not far from where I worked and it became a kind of social centre. I played the violin in the YMCA orchestra, and when I was about seventeen I enrolled in the dramatic society and took part in a couple of plays. I found I had no inhibitions about performing on stage and fancied myself right away as an actor with a future.

More than anything, I think, I enjoyed the opportunity this provided of losing my daily self and becoming somebody else. I sang in the Schubert musical *Lilac Time*, and was cast for the Pontypridd Operatic Christmas pantomime in the Town Hall. It was just by chance that a friend persuaded me to go to a read-through of *Ali Baba and the Forty Thieves*. By the end of that meeting I found myself cast for the part of Casim Baba, the villain of the piece.

Part of the pantomime tradition was to work in a number of well-known ballads and other popular songs of the time, whatever the main story-line. Presumably that's why Casim Baba that year was to be heard giving a rousing version of 'On the Road to Mandalay'. Afterwards I was told by a former opera singer, Bert Gregory Evans, that I had a very good voice. He was a singing teacher, an elegant and distinguished-looking man with a waxed moustache, who spoke with a singer's deep resonance. It was the first time anybody professional had commented on my voice, and I was naturally pretty thrilled.

Another singer who heard me sing in the pantomime was Teifion Williams, a well-known local baritone. He complimented me on my voice and added, 'You ought to have it trained. I could do that so you could sing at concerts, and if you can't afford to pay me [which I certainly couldn't] you can give me ten per cent of your concert fees.'

It was a tempting offer but one which I never accepted. Instead I had a pleasant surprise when soon afterwards my father told me I could have weekly singing lessons with Idloes Owen, a respected musician and teacher in Cardiff. What I didn't know then was that my father borrowed the money to pay for my first quarter's lessons. All I could afford to pay was the train fare to Cardiff and back each Thursday afternoon, the early-closing day at the Pontypridd shop.

Even so, I still wasn't thinking of a future as a singer at that time, but nor was I very happy at the long hours and, as it seemed, lack of future in my job at Theophilus's after being there more than a year. Fired, I suppose, by my grandfather's example and the stories he told me, I had it in mind to take myself to sea and sign on as a merchant-seaman.

I went one day to Mr Theophilus, ready to give in my notice and to ask him for a reference, but he forestalled me. 'Would you like to learn window-dressing?' he asked. 'If so, find me another errand boy to take your place, and you can go on windows.'

It actually took some time to find Mr Theophilus another boy that he approved of, but I eventually did so and was able to become an apprentice window-dresser to the head dresser, Trevor Evans. He took a great pride in his work and told me it could make a good career if I went about it properly and learned all I could. I was keen to learn as well as work, and I enrolled for evening classes at Cardiff Technical College, taking Colour and Design, and Textile Merchandising. It often meant running three-quarters of a mile or so after the shop closed to catch the Cardiff bus twice a week, but I kept going to the classes for a full year and what I learned came in useful.

The manager of the store was Tim Richards, nephew of the owner. He was very interested in art and painting and indeed was a brilliant window-dresser, a perfectionist. He was most encouraging and I learned a tremendous amount from him.

I still remember the first window I put in. What a disaster! It was a sale window and it was so awful I was made to take it all out and start again. But I persevered and gradually learned the skill. I had no idea then how it might help me later on, when it came to dressing a stage, for instance, or adjusting a costume.

When the head window-dresser decided to leave, the applicants for his job were given a practical test of skill. I applied, and the only time I could be given was the following morning, before the shop closed early for the half-day. That meant there was only time to dress a hat window, and although it was summer, we were preparing for the autumn fashions.

I had to think fast because there wasn't much time for preparation. But that night, I went up the mountain to collect stones, ferns and moss. After carting them back I was up until four in the morning starching the ferns and threading wire through the stems, tinting the leaves, moss and stones to reflect the colours of autumn. My grandfather, who was now in his eighties, helped me by painting the stones and the somewhat shaky hand of age he brought to them gave just the effect I wanted.

By the time we finished there was no point in going to bed. I piled everything into a wheelbarrow and at about six in the morning I wheeled this all the way to Ponty and left the contents in the shop doorway. Then I pushed the barrow home again, had breakfast, tidied myself up and went back to the shop by nine to dress the window.

Fortunately, it turned out to be an excellent window, but alas, it didn't last. Within a few days all the ferns and moss died from the heat of the lights and I had to re-dress it. But my efforts weren't in vain. The job was mine and I was an established window-dresser. It was my first real success. I'd proved I could achieve something, and that gave a marvellous feeling of satisfaction.

From then on I continued working for Mr Theophilus happily enough, with no further thought of going to sea. People often admired the window displays and one day a stranger who stopped and looked asked me if I'd like a job at Liberty's, the fashion store in London's West End. Liberty's? I hadn't heard of it then, the name meant nothing to me. But somehow I didn't fancy uprooting myself to London and I refused his offer.

Besides, I was enjoying more and more musical activities. I was now a member of the Lyrian Singers, a glee party which broadcast regularly, and I was starting to sing at local concerts.

Then the BBC in Cardiff offered me a solo broadcast. I was to take part in a programme called 'Welsh Rarebit', in the slot known as 'Youth takes a bow'.

I went along to face a microphone on my own for the first time. Word went around the village that I would be on the wireless, and it frightened me to think that so many people I knew might be listening.

Although I was very excited, I was also acutely embarrassed by the whole affair. Even worse was the feeling when I left the studio to catch the bus home from Cardiff. I felt that people in the street knew about that programme and were looking at me. Of course it was nonsense, but the feeling was so strong that I bought an evening newspaper and hid behind it in the back of the bus, not reading a word, and then when I reached Cilfynydd I went home up the back lane, praying I wouldn't meet anybody.

Such was, I suppose, the start of my singing career: the first professional engagement outside my immediate neighbourhood, for which I earned the princely sum of one guinea.

It was a long, long time before I learned to overcome the awkward feeling of shyness whenever I sang in concert, whereas I could shed my inhibitions more readily if I dressed in costume and hid behind make-up and wig, becoming a different character. The Pontypridd pantomime had been a start in this direction, and not long after the Cardiff broadcast I had another opportunity.

Bethel Chapel in Cilfynydd decided not just to give its annual concert performance of oratorio, but to perform it in character. Oratorios seldom went beyond the alternation of Handel's *Messiah* and Mendelssohn's *Elijah*, so that you might almost think their composers had become Welsh by adoption. On this occasion it was to be *Elijah* in costume, and I was asked to dress up and sing the role of the prophet.

Had I thought about it, I might have realised that the musical demands were really beyond a youth of seventeen with only a few

17

voice lessons to his credit, especially as there was to be more than one performance. But doing it in costume was the magic ingredient so far as I was concerned. I would wear a theatrical wig and beard and flowing robes, and become somebody else. I was delighted to take it on.

We rehearsed in the vestry at the chapel, but the performances were in the Workmen's Hall where the first night was a tremendous success. Inexperienced as I was, I'd sung out at rehearsal and gave everything I had to the first performance. By the second night I was already suffering from a sore throat.

I realise now, of course, how much I must have flogged my young voice that evening. I must have been mad, and my father strongly disapproved, but I performed with all the determination and enthusiasm of youth.

At the time the only remedy was the well-tried local treatment of goose-grease rubbed into the neck and a woollen sock wrapped round to protect the throat. By the time the prophet Elijah reached his great aria, 'It is enough', it was as much a statement of fact as an expression of the musical situation. Somehow I pulled through and, as a result of general enthusiasm and local write-ups, we even managed an extra performance for those who hadn't been able to get tickets earlier.

I often visit Mrs Howells, a grand lady in her nineties, who conducted that production of *Elijah* and who, under her former name of Madame Harrison, taught me to play the piano and the violin. We spend hours reminiscing about that great occasion and the professional performance we achieved, using only the amateur talent from our village.

Life was great! I was very happy and, I believe, successful in my job. People were constantly coming into the shop to compliment me on my display stands and window-dressing.

I was at the same time getting more and more involved with the musical activity in the town and every Thursday afternoon I still went to Cardiff for my singing lesson. I met up with all my friends at the local Youth Club, and like all young men of that age, I started taking out my first girlfriend.

I wonder now how I managed to cope with everything I did, but all this gave me a good feeling of security and fulfilment. And I almost burst with pride when Mr E. R. Thomas, the headmaster of the grammar school, stopped me in town to congratulate me on a concert I had done and added 'because I always consider you to be one of my boys'.

Then, in the midst of all this, war was declared.

As young men we listened to this announcement with a peculiar kind of excitement, hardly realising what it was all about and wondering what the future had in store for us, indeed if there would be a future at all.

I waited impatiently for my eighteenth birthday. Many of my friends had already been called up and most of them had joined the RAF. It was the glamorous thing to do.

My birthday came and even before I received any call-up papers, I was at the recruiting office in Cardiff volunteering for the RAF. When I got inside I began to feel a little apprehensive, and the twenty or so boys sitting with me probably all felt the same. I chatted with two university students and after one of them had been for his interview he came back to sit with us.

'What did they ask you?' his friend asked. 'Oh, I had to do some mental arithmetic and intelligence tests, then they asked what was Ohm's Law?'

Ohm's Law! I had never heard of it, so I said quite nonchalantly, 'I've forgotten about that, what is it?'

'E=IR,' he replied. What that meant I had no idea, but I kept repeating it to myself like a talisman.

It came to my turn to go in. I answered all the questions I was asked, and then it came, 'What is Ohm's Law?'

'E=IR'

'And what does R equal?'

I took a wild guess and I was in the RAF!

I came out feeling quite excited. I was already using Brylcreem and could quite imagine myself wearing 'wings', but that was not to be. I failed my medical. I was Grade 2.

Although I had been accepted by the RAF, it was many months before I was called up. At that time people were putting on concerts to support the war effort and I went with the Lyrian Singers to sing at some of the hospitals where the wounded from Dunkirk were being cared for. The first flush of excitement was dampened quickly by stark reality when we heard the stories they had to tell.

When eventually I was called up, I was posted to Weston-super-Mare to do my 'square-bashing' and it was embarrassing indeed to be put through our paces on the promenade using only wooden 'rifles', while crowds of curious holiday-makers looked on.

After this initial training I was posted to St Athan, not as a radio mechanic as I had been told, but as a flight mechanic, which was something quite different. I suppose the axiom 'theirs not to reason why' had already registered, and I accepted my posting without any question.

St Athan was a good place to be. It was near home and I managed to get the occasional pass. Also there was an excellent padre at the station, Padre Madoc-Jones, who was very concerned with our welfare and took a keen interest in organising entertainment at the camp. Almost immediately I was taking part in the concert parties and Padre Madoc-Jones tried to arrange that I should be attached to the RAF Band there, but to my regret it didn't happen.

Towards the end of the sixteen-week period it was discovered that I was on the wrong course and I was detailed to join the radio mechanic course at 'Brummagem'. The order came through late in the evening and by the time I had collected various clearance chits from all over that vast camp, it was one o'clock and the boys in the billet were fast asleep.

Six o'clock in the morning saw me waiting at the local halt for the Cardiff train, and two WAAF officers got into the same compartment. They knew me because I had been singing with the concert party, and now seeing me with full kit one of them asked, 'Where are you posted, then?'

I replied, 'Brummagem, Ma'am.' Seeing a frown on one face, I realised I wasn't the only one who didn't know where Brummagem was. But then the other one said 'Birmingham? That's a good place to be posted.'

When I reported to the duty sergeant at my destination, he took my particulars and said quite blithely, 'Right, we don't want you until Monday morning.'

Monday morning! This was Friday afternoon and I wasn't needed until Monday! To make matters worse, I had very little money. I wondered if I was to spend the next forty-eight hours stretched out in the canteen, or a YMCA. Then I remembered that my Aunty Blod and Uncle Will had moved to Birmingham and were caretakers in the Methodist chapel in Kingstanding on the outskirts of the city. I had no idea how big Kingstanding was but, after I got off the bus, I walked and walked, making enquiries here and there until I eventually knocked on their front door at about one o'clock in the morning. I stayed there for the weekend and then had a lucky break by getting myself billeted with them for the whole time I was in Birmingham.

Although I wasn't very electrically minded, I was able to cope with the radio mechanic course. We were tested every two weeks and I seemed to be doing very well until I started singing with a dance band, at the invitation of the pianist, who was Clifford Farr, cousin of the boxer Tommy Farr and very proud of it too. He'd been a schoolteacher in Birmingham and was now posted back there on the same course.

So when we should have been studying, most evenings found us with the band, he playing the piano and I crooning 'Who's taking you home tonight', or some such popular song of the time, for ten shillings a session, a welcome extra to our meagre pay.

It put us so very behind with the set work that eventually we two, together with a few others, were called up in front of the C.O. I had the audacity to tell him that I really wasn't very interested in the course, not being mechanically minded, and I suggested I might become a P.T. Instructor.

He blew his top. I had wasted ten weeks of valuable time. Without any further discussion I was ordered to train as a radar operator and this was what I did for the rest of the war.

One person I remember very vividly from my training time in Yatesbury was a fellow called Jones. He had some difficulty in obtaining the correct pay due to him, and although he had been making enquiries and complaining for weeks, he was still getting only five shillings a fortnight. Then came one more pay parade. When his name was called, he walked to the table where all the money was laid out, hoping once more that his difficulties had been sorted out.

The officer called, 'Jones 359. Five shillings.'

Jones put out his hand in disgust, took the money and slowly turned away from the table, instead of taking two steps back and saluting as he should have done.

The officer shouted, 'Jones, you salute for your pay.'

Whereupon Jones turned disgustedly back to the table and, throwing a shilling to each of the three officers in turn, said, 'A shilling for you, a shilling for you, a shilling for you and b—— the rest of you.'

And as he made that last remark he caught hold of the edge of the table and lifted it in the air. The money went rolling over the NAAFI floor, and those of us who were standing in line surreptitiously tried to cover each coin as it rolled our way, before picking it up discreetly in the commotion that followed and putting it in our pockets. The RAF police stood rooted to the spot in disbelief, then suddenly descended on poor Jones, put him under arrest, and that was the last we ever saw of him.

My first posting as a radar operator was to West Wales, to a station called Folly. For many of us it was our first operational unit where we worked exceptionally hard, but it was a great station.

Our commanding officer was a Canadian, and Harrison Grey (who for years compiled the crossword in a leading newspaper) was our adjutant. They certainly knew how to handle men and get the best out of them.

21

There was a great deal of talent at that camp. We had two excellent pianists, Emlyn Davies from North Wales and Gareth Thomas, who later became Registrar of the University of Wales. We formed a choir, ostensibly for our own amusement, and I was the soloist. Soon people in the vicinity came to hear of this choir and we were invited to their churches and chapels to sing. The concerts were usually arranged when the moon was full so that the farmers and their families, who formed most of the audience, could travel home by horse and trap in the blackout without having to use any lights.

After the concert the farmers' wives would prepare supper for us and the food was so marvellous that more and more people from the camp wanted to come to the concert. We were in danger of having more servicemen than locals in the audience, the food being a greater attraction than the concert for most of them.

We were about two hundred airmen and WAAF at Folly, the first time that so many of us had been together for any length of time. So it came as a shock when orders came through posting about half the camp elsewhere. In our nostalgia we organised a gala in the NAAFI the night before we left. At the end of the evening, no doubt helped by the alcohol we consumed and my singing of 'Bless this House', it all became very emotional.

I was posted to a small mobile radar unit of about thirty men. We spent the next two and a half years together as a close-knit group, and a marvellous bunch of men they were, on-duty and off. We spent most of our time under canvas on the east coast, plotting the enemy planes and the dreaded V–1s as they came over. These rocket weapons were nicknamed 'doodlebugs', but when Jimmy Weaver in my unit wrote home to his mother that we'd been troubled by a few doodlebugs he was not a little taken aback to receive from her a parcel containing a well-known brand of flea-powder and some insect-killer.

We must have been a pretty 'crack' unit because we were often sent out to help other units in emergency. We were also filmed at work, and this film was used to demonstrate to other units how things should be done.

We still found time for other things. I called on some of my artistic skills to decorate the cookhouse marquee, painting a scantily clad portrait of Miss Blandish, of 'No Orchids' fame, and another likeness of General Montgomery, as he then was, on the inside canvas. We also made up a small choir and sang in the pubs in the evenings. Even to the boys who didn't drink, the pub was at least a warm place to spend an evening, because living under canvas was no joke in the country in the middle of winter.

We were always welcome at any of the pubs in the area because word would get around where we would be singing and the locals would crowd in to listen. This, of course, meant free beer for the boys, and one pub in particular always showed extra appreciation by providing free sausage rolls as well.

It was an agricultural area and people were always kind enough to ask some of the boys to their homes. We were at a dance one evening when I was invited by a good-looking girl I danced with to go on to her twenty-first birthday party nearby. I explained that I had come on the 'Liberty Truck' with some other boys from the camp and her parents immediately asked them to come along too. Their large Victorian house was warm and inviting and the table was laden with good things to eat and drink. In due course I asked my way to the bathroom. Everywhere was blacked out and, in the usual way then, the only light bulb in the hall was painted blue, which was no help at all as I went upstairs.

I opened the bathroom door and groped around for the light switch, but try as I did I couldn't find one. I felt the bath, I felt the wash basin, but do you think I could find the toilet?

By this time matters were getting desperate and I decided the only thing I could do was to turn the taps on in the bath and make use of that. Which I did.

As I was leaving the bathroom, feeling my way out, I felt a string or cord in front of me and thought it might be the light-switch. I gave it a tug and the light came on, showing me a large old-fashioned bathroom with a huge bath and a marble washbasin, and the toilet tucked behind the door.

Being a gentleman, I wanted to make sure that the bath was unsullied, and was shocked to discover that it contained numerous glasses of trifle, obviously put there to set in the coolest place. My embarrassment was so great that I crept out of the bathroom, down the stairs and walked the entire nine miles back to camp.

Eventually, like thousands of other servicemen, our unit was posted to a compound on the south coast. We knew from all these preparations that Something Big was about to happen, and soon enough we heard news of the D-Day landings across the Channel – although our unit was not sent over until some weeks later.

We crossed the Channel on an LCT, a flat-bottomed boat, crewed by Americans. They treated us so well, giving us all they could, that we began to worry we might not be expected to come back.

Naturally we were nervous, and Jimmy Weaver tried to divert us by reading aloud some of the poems he had written. Gruesome as they were, he at least kept us occupied for a short time.

On our second day in France, all the units were gathered together for a religious service 'in the field', conducted by our padre, the Reverend Phil Bowen, a Welshman from Carmarthen. After the service he said that if anyone would like to take Communion, he was holding the service at a little church belonging to the château which was quite close by.

I went along with about twelve others. The padre gave Communion to each one in turn, and when he came to me he changed automatically to Welsh. Whether it was fear, whether it was listening to the service in my native tongue, I don't know, but at that moment I had the strangest feeling, a kind of contact, and I think I understood then what people meant when they said the hand of God had touched them.

I had this same experience once more, a few years later, when I was up in the Trossachs, on my own. The Covent Garden Opera was touring Scotland and I drove to the Trossachs one day to get away from it all for a while. It was a winter's day and it had been snowing. The beauty of the valley and the ruggedness of the mountains, the very stillness were all so overwhelming and I felt that strange sense of contact once again, but this time with a difference: there was no thought of fear.

Our unit was lucky. We travelled through northern France and although we saw the awful ravages of war, we were never actually in contact with the enemy. We were in Brussels when the city was liberated, amid tears of joy and a wonderful excitement all around us.

We moved on to Dehaan, on the coast not far from Ostend, where a sackful of mail which had been chasing us from place to place finally caught up with the unit. Among the welcome letters from home was one I wished had not been there. Aunty Bessie wrote to say that her son Alun, who was more like a brother to me than a cousin, had been killed in action at Caen some months before. She wrote with grief, yet with a strength of spirit that only her faith could have given her, but the effect on me was devastating. I wanted only to get my hands on the enemy and take my revenge for Alun's death, but time is always a wonderful healer.

It was from Dehaan that I had my first home leave, by way of a nightmare train journey to Calais, though we would have endured anything for the sake of a home visit. For me now that meant 23 William Street instead of number 55. My grandfather, getting on in years, had gone to live with his daughter, my Aunty Bessie, so that she could look after him in his old age.

As soon as I had seen my family I went down to number 78, where

Brenda Davies lived. It was always a very hospitable house and a lot of us young people would gather there to talk, to have a sing-song around the piano or to listen to records, but this time I went to thank Brenda for writing to me while I was abroad, something she did to many of the boys from the village.

I was home on leave for about two weeks and I saw quite a lot of Brenda in that time. One night a crowd of us went to the Old Boys' Dance in Pontypridd. It poured with rain on the way home and we were soaking wet. Brenda's boyfriend was there as well and, as he was due back to his squadron the next day, Brenda and I stayed up all night drying and pressing his uniform.

I had known the Davies's from childhood and had always been a casual friend of Brenda, her sister Marion and her brother Glyn, but talking together throughout that night made me realise that Brenda and I had a great deal in common. When I returned to Belgium our letters began to be more frequent and by the time I returned home from the Services, I knew she was the girl for me.

Our unit was stationed in Groningen when the war in Europe came to an end. We managed to get a bottle of beer each to celebrate, and that was all, so we went in search of something more to drink in the town. At our little bar, 'la patronne' demanded that we sang 'Tipperary' before she would serve us, because at night-time our air-force blue looked too much like the German field-grey for her to be sure of the difference.

From here the unit was next moved to Oldenburg, where my service life now took another turn. At this time the British Forces Network in Hamburg would broadcast invitations to servicemen who had any talent to write for an audition. Eddie Peters, a boy in our unit, was a marvellous pianist but very diffident about applying, so Jimmy Weaver wrote on his behalf for an audition, mentioning my name at the same time.

I knew nothing of this, and when Eddie asked me to to go with him I said I would go along for the ride, not intending to audition myself. We were met by Sergeant Arthur Langford who worked in the music department of the radio station. He listed to Eddie then asked, 'Where is this singer you have?'

Eddie pointed to me, but I explained that I hadn't come to audition and had no music with me anyway. Arthur wouldn't take no for an answer and produced some ballads and one or two oratorios from the small library they had there. I remember singing 'Arm, arm ye brave' and 'Honour and Arms', as well as Vaughan Williams's 'The Vagabond' among other items.

Eventually a signal arrived, inviting Eddie Peters to do one or two broadcasts, and I was asked to become the soloist with the BFN Chorus. This was great, even though it meant that I had to travel to Hamburg and back every weekend. There was always an argument as to who was going to be my driver because it meant that he could have a good weekend in Hamburg while I was working. It was a six-hour drive each way, and sometimes we had other duties too.

Sent with the truck to collect some equipment from a warehouse on the outskirts of Hamburg one day, we found our way with the help of a German waitress in the NAAFI, who lived just across the road from the place we had to find. We always carried some cigarettes and coffee for bartering, so after loading up I went across to the girl's house and gave the family something for her kindness. Next time we were in the vicinity they invited the driver and myself to have some of the coffee we'd given them.

As we chatted I told them that I lodged during my weekend visits to Hamburg in a 'transit hotel', which was no better than the term suggests, and which I hated. 'Why not stay with us?' they suggested, and I accepted gratefully, sleeping on a settee in their living-room. A few weekends later, they offered me a bed upstairs, and after trying rather unsuccessfully to learn a German card game, I decided to turn in early, making my apologies.

It was a wonderfully comfortable large bed and I was just drifting off to sleep when I felt somebody pulling away the bedclothes. Turning to grab them back I was startled to see the daughter of the house climbing into bed with me. I started to stammer something, but all she said was, 'I only come to keep you warm. We do not make love.'

So there I was, taken aback and wondering, lying alongside her hardly daring to move, when the door opened again and in trooped the girl's mother and her aunt. They walked unconcernedly past the foot of the bed to reach, as I discovered, their own bedroom on the other side.

The girl was as good as her word. She kept the bed warm. But I didn't sleep all night, wondering about the situation in which I found myself. Next day I discovered that the family, who were kindness itself, came from a part of Germany where sharing a bed with a guest in the interests of warmth and hospitality was an accepted custom. They were in fact giving me, a stranger, who not long before was an enemy, an ultimate gift of hospitality, even if it seemed cruel enough to me, as a healthy male in an intimate situation. But I certainly couldn't have coped with another such night and, after that one occasion, I decided it would be safer to stay elsewhere, even the transit hotel.

After a while the journey to and from Hamburg every weekend began to tell, but luck was again with me. A vacancy occurred in the music department and Captain Trevor Harvey, the Head of Music at BFN, managed to arrange for my transfer. Little as I knew it at the time, that move to BFN changed the whole pattern of my life.

As well as singing with the chorus I now became involved in producing music programmes, taking part in drama series, reading poetry and making myself generally useful.

There were some extremely talented people working at BFN Hamburg: Trevor Harvey, who had been Chorus Master for the BBC before the war; James Gibb, a concert pianist, who is now Head of Piano Studies at the Guildhall School of Music; Barney Colehan, the television producer (of Wilfred Pickles's 'Give him the money, Barney' fame) who originated the 'Old Tyme Music Hall' programmes; Jeff Webb, who wrote the script for the Dick Barton series; the producer Trevor Hill, and his wife Margaret Potter, author of many children's programmes; Robin Boyle, who is still a presenter on BBC; Cliff Michelmore; Joseph Cooper, who often came there to broadcast and could turn from the classics into swing at the turn of a finger; and a lovely Irish girl, Paddy Flynn, with whom I worked on many programmes. It was most exhilarating. We worked very hard from early morning till late at night but this was work that we loved doing, and that made all the difference.

Being in Hamburg gave me the opportunity to go to the opera, to recitals, to hear *Lieder* for the first time. I heard some wonderful singers: Erna Berger, Erna Schluter and Annaliese Kupper; I heard Bockelmann doing his last Kurwenal and also at the opera I first heard Theo Hermann in his most famous roles, such as Ochs in *Der Rosenkavalier* and Osmin in *Die Entführung aus dem Serail*.

It was while I was singing with the chorus one day that Theo Hermann came into the studio to do some broadcasting for us. He stopped to listen and, according to Arthur Langford, was very impressed, so much so that Arthur suggested I might go to him for singing lessons.

Theo was a Viennese living in Hamburg. He was a lovable person with a wonderful sense of humour, an absolute charmer, a real basso and, above all, a great performer.

I went to Theo on average three times a week, and week in, week out, we did nothing but breathing exercises, scales, breathing exercises, scales. He forbade me to sing anything else. If I did anything that pleased him he would put his arms around me and kiss me, which was something of a shock to me the first few times it happened, but if I did something wrong he was just as likely to slap me across the fàce.

His wife Olga, his daughter and his grandson welcomed me to their home and it was through them that I met people like the opera director Günther Rennert, and the conductor Hans Schmidt-Isserstedt.

I was getting on very well with Theo. I knew that my breath control and the flexibility and placing of the voice were improving tremendously. I was absorbing all I could from the professionalism around me and, to be honest, I was beginning to get just a bit stage-struck.

As the time for my demobilisation approached, I felt that if I could only have a few more lessons with Theo, they would give me such a sound foundation. So despite the fact that I was longing to get home after almost six years in the RAF, I arranged to get my 'demob' deferred for two months.

Even then I had to decide what to do when I got home. I had a secure job to go back to and singing was a precarious profession, but Theo and all those with whom I worked at BFN advised me that I would be foolish indeed if I didn't give it a chance. At heart I knew they were right, and I made my decision.

Cilfynydd was covered in a heavy fall of snow that January morning .in 1947 when I arrived home after six long years in uniform. I hid in the doorway for a chance to snowball the trim young schoolmistress as she made her way to school, and that was how Brenda learned that I was home.

It took me a while to get used to the feeling of being back in 'civvy street' although I was overjoyed to be at home once more, but I suffered many moments of sadness at the thought of Alun and so many boys from the town who would never come back again. I gradually settled back with the family and saw as much of Brenda as I could, then realised that the next thing I had to do was to explain to Mr Theophilus at the Pontypridd store that I would not be going back there, having decided to take up singing as a career instead.

He was very upset and repeated what so many people had already told me about the uncertainties of singing as a profession. Then he added, 'You have a good job here and we'd like to have you back. Besides, I'd made up my mind that one of the stores would one day be yours.'

This was such a shock that I couldn't think clearly. He'd always shown an interest in my progress, and would occasionally slip a ten-shilling note in my pocket to help pay my fares to night school, but this offer was something I had never expected.

I asked him if I could come back with my answer the next day, and spent a very sleepless night wondering if I were doing the right thing. Should I risk throwing away such a wonderful opportunity to venture into a career that might never be successful?

By morning, though, I had decided what I wanted to do. I thanked Mr Theophilus for his magnificently generous offer but told him I *had* to give singing a chance.

My next problem was how to finance my future. I'd heard that ex-servicemen were eligible for grants to help them get started on a new profession after demobilisation, and I thought I might take advantage. I went to the relevant office in Cardiff, only to be told that I did not qualify because singing was not considered to be a profession. I could have had a grant to become a schoolteacher, a vet, a carpenter and many other occupations, but not a singer.

I tried very hard to convince them that singing was an honourable and useful profession, and eventually it was agreed that I might be given a grant on condition that I was accepted at a music college.

So off I went to London to try for an interview at the Guildhall School of Music and Drama, which was uppermost in my thoughts as several well-known singers had been there. Fortunately I had an interview almost immediately with Arthur Reckless, who was standing in for the principal, Edric Cundell, and by whom I was now told I could not be considered for admission without a grant or scholarship.

It took a number of journeys from Cardiff to London and back to sort out this problem. Soon I had spent practically all my gratuity on travelling and was becoming quite desperate. I explained this to Arthur Reckless and he agreed to hear me sing. After the audition he said, 'It would be a good thing if you can come here because I believe you have great potential.'

I begged him to do something to try to resolve the situation and he decided he would write a letter stating that the Guildhall would accept me. This was good enough for the establishment and I finally obtained the necessary grant.

The only consolation for all these problems was the opportunity, while in London, to hear *The Rape of Lucretia* with Kathleen Ferrier, Joan Cross, Peter Pears and Otakar Kraus, and a never-to-be-forgotten performance of *Turandot* with Dame Eva

Turner and Walter Midgley. A few years later I told Dame Eva what a great thrill it had been for me to hear her sing Turandot, sitting as I was in the 'gods', the topmost (and cheapest) gallery at Covent Garden.'

I started at the Guildhall School of Music after Easter, with Arthur Reckless as my singing teacher. After two or three lessons I began to feel worried because his method of teaching was very different from Theo Hermann's, and at this stage I felt I did not want to change my technique of voice production. He was very understanding and suggested that maybe Walter Gruner's method would be nearer to the way I had been taught by Theo.

I studied with Walter for some months and I learned a great deal from him, especially about German *Lieder* singing. But I was still not happy about my technique and I began to get very confused by these different methods of teaching. I then asked to work with Walter Hyde, a very elegant man getting on in years, but one who made you feel that singing was a truly noble profession. As long as you made a beautiful sound he wasn't too worried about how you made it, and that was my salvation then.

I am sure that students of singing will appreciate the predicament I was in. I had worked very hard with Theo Hermann and begun to feel I was achieving something. I wanted to hang on to his every word and to believe all he said, but I did not have long enough with him to consolidate my technique and was reluctant to change when I studied with other teachers. I shall always be grateful to Arthur Reckless and Walter Gruner for their understanding of my problem. They did not resent it nor feel offended when I left them for another teacher.

A few years later, when I went to Geneva to study with Fernando Carpi, I *did* change my technique. I suppose by that time I had gained confidence and had a little more experience, which enabled me to realise what method was most suited to me, but it was ironic that Carpi's method was similar to that which Arthur Reckless taught.

The Guildhall was filled to capacity at that time with young people beginning their studies, with ex-servicemen and women who were returning to continue their studies, and with people like me who were just starting, but who were a little older.

And what talent there was! Many of my contemporaries became successful but it is sad that some never fulfilled their potential. However, a musical career is so often a matter of being in the right place at the right time.

For my second subject at the Guildhall School I took up the

piano again. I got on so well that Professor Gregg suggested that I might make it my first subject. I like to think he had never heard me sing!

The opera class with Aylmer Buesst was a great joy. From him we learned a traditional style of opera singing and it was a thrill to be asked to sing Don Alfonso in *Così fan tutte*, which we performed at the Guildhall at the end of term and then took to Cambridge later in July.

There was a great feeling of camaraderie between us all as students, many of whom came to hear Erich Gruenberg and me at our respective 'Prom' debuts in July 1948. I sang 'Il lacerato spirito' from Verdi's *Simon Boccanegra*, with Basil Cameron conducting. Years later, after his retirement, I went to see Basil Cameron at a musicians' home in Hereford and spent the afternoon reminiscing with him and the bass Norman Allin, who also lived there. I was proud and flattered to know that Basil Cameron still remembered that he had conducted my first Promenade concert.

In the autumn of 1947 Theo Hermann came to London to sing with Jay Pomeroy's New London Opera Company at the Cambridge Theatre. While Theo was here I took lessons with him once again. I had just finished one, early in November, when he said, 'Come, you need experience. I take you to the Cambridge. You sing for Mr Pomeroy.' Without any more ado, he called a taxi, and when I protested that I had no music with me his only answer was: 'Then we get some!'

We stopped at Novello's where I bought a selection of bass arias, including 'O Isis und Osiris', and we went on to the Cambridge Theatre where I gave an audition. To my great delight, Mr Pomeroy asked if I could start there in January to sing Colline in *La Bohème* and the Commendatore in *Don Giovanni*, and asked me to see him the following week to discuss terms.

After the initial excitement of being asked, the doubt began to creep in. Would I not be wiser to stay on at the Guildhall to study and to broaden my somewhat limited repertoire?

Three days later, while I was still debating, Theo telephoned to say he had met Karl Rankl, the conductor of the Covent Garden Opera, where they were looking for a bass. I was to go for an audition on Saturday morning. I hadn't then mentioned the Pomeroy audition to any of my friends because I was still in doubt whether to accept, but I needed a pianist for my audition at Covent Garden and I asked Dorothy Pitway, one of the piano students, if she would accompany me.

My friends at the Guildhall were all enthusiastic on my behalf:

Eldon Guller offered to take Dorothy and me in his car, and several of them came to give me moral support, waiting for me outside the stage door until it was all over.

I sang 'Il lacerato spirito', quite successfully I thought, but 'Ella giammai m'amo' didn't come off as well. I was preparing to sing 'In diesen heiligen Hallen' when Mr Webster walked down to the orchestra pit and spoke to me: 'Would you come to see me on Monday morning?' he asked.

There was noisy excitement at the stage door when I broke the news, and we became quite raucous when Theo joined us. Putting his two hands to his nose, he said in his thick accent: 'Forget the Cambridge. I think you now join Covent Garden'.

CHAPTER TWO

Enter a Nightwatchman

All weekend I wondered what would be the outcome of my interview with David Webster at the Royal Opera House. Although it was only a couple of days after my audition, it seemed one of the longest weekends of my life, and on Sunday night I hardly slept at all. The next morning, when I got off the train from Lewisham at Charing Cross, it was a dreary, dismal November day, but inside I had a feeling of warmth, excitement – and apprehension.

I was forty minutes early, so I strolled through the hustle and bustle of Covent Garden Market enjoying the humour and the wisecracks of the porters as they pulled their barrows laden with vegetables. Then I looked inside the flower market for the first time. The colours and the scents seemed beautiful to me, and I hoped they were a good omen. At ten to eleven I was at the Opera House stage door in Floral Street, asking for Mr Webster's office. I was sent up to the third floor.

Thinking it would be safer to take the lift in case I got lost, I did so, but then I couldn't find any buttons to press. I had no idea how to operate it. All I saw was a rope running down inside. Weeks later I learned it was an old water-pressure lift: you pulled on the rope and went zooming up. But for now I was taking no chances. This interview was important to me, so I clambered out and climbed four flights of worn stone steps. Sometimes, in later years, I'd dream of being stuck in a lift and not reaching the stage on cue, and I never used a lift during a performance, not even at the New York Metropolitan.

Not a little breathless I found Mr Webster's office and met his secretary, Muriel Kerr, a lady of great dignity who later became a very good friend. She took me to Mr Webster, who was friendly, immaculately dressed, and looked more like a banker than the administrator of an opera house. I suppose I was with him for little more than ten minutes, at the end of which I signed a year's contract to join the Covent Garden Opera Company – at twelve pounds a week.

Little as it may seem now, that sum represented a fortune to me then. In any case, I wanted the opportunity so badly that I would have accepted five pounds a week if that had been the wage on offer. What I didn't realise was how little my weekly wage would actually buy, especially when I found that it had to cover both my living expenses while I was on tour and the running costs of my London home.

When I left the Webster office that first time, I was so excited, longing to meet somebody I knew to impart my news. I couldn't get back to Lewisham quickly enough to tell my aunt that she now had a member of the Covent Garden Opera lodging with her. She was thrilled that I was going into a profession with which she would have loved to have been involved, having a beautiful contralto voice herself.

Two weeks went by and I heard nothing further from Covent Garden. I was just getting a little despondent when I had a telephone call from Patrick Terry, the Opera Company manager, saying I would be needed the next Monday to learn the role of the Night-watchman in *Die Meistersinger*, working with John Gardner as répétiteur.

At first I was very relieved to get the message: now I would be gainfully occupied. And then it hit me: *Meistersinger*? Wagner? *Wagner*?

Surely they were crazy to ask *me* to sing Wagner when I came from the Guildhall School and so had concentrated mainly on Mozart, and when they had many of the great Wagnerian singers at the Garden already: Hans Hotter, Set Svanholm and Kirsten Flagstad, all with big, beautiful voices.

Still, I had to find out about this Nightwatchman, of whom I knew absolutely nothing. The only scores I possessed were a few Mozart operas, some oratorios, an album of bass songs and another of baritone ballads and, of course, *The Songs of Wales*, which my Aunt Marie had given me when I was only nine years old. So I took myself off, as all the music students did, to Foyle's in Charing Cross Road, hoping to find a secondhand *Meistersinger* score. And I did. For ten shillings. A bargain, even then.

Back at home, I looked at the list of characters: Hans Sachs, Veit Pogner, Eva, his daughter, Walther von Stolzing, Sixtus Beck-messer . . . and right at the bottom: A Nightwatchman. Then I went through the score, page by page, to find what the Nightwatchman sang. I went through it twice and still I couldn't find it. Hardly surprising: the Nightwatchman's contribution consists of ten bars halfway through Act 2 and another ten bars at the end of the act. That was my lot.

I think I was quite relieved it was such a small role, but it wasn't long before I learned that there are no such things in opera as small roles. As Tyrone Guthrie insisted: 'You must make the best of the smallest role, because the smallest role can be the pearl in the crown.' For the moment, however, I learned my part, and by Sunday night I knew it thoroughly as did the rest of the household.

Monday came, and I made sure I was on time for my rehearsal, a habit I've tried to keep all the years I've been singing. I was sent up to the amphitheatre bar where I could hear a piano being played, although none was in sight. I tracked down the sound and was led into the 'Gents', of all places – there, sure enough, was the piano, John Gardner, and my rehearsal. Nor was this the last time I had to rehearse in such inauspicious surroundings: later, I learned Beckmesser there with Reggie Goodall. So many solo singers were involved in *Meistersinger*, every possible space in the opera house had to be used.

Nevertheless, it was a wonderful atmosphere of friendliness and helpfulness I encountered that day and ever afterwards from all the music staff: John Gardner, Peter Gellhorn (who was also conducting then), Leonard Hancock, Norman Feasey, Eric Mitchell, ever the gentleman, patient and encouraging. He was married to Constance Shacklock, a splendid singer who was a tower of strength to the company in those days and who, incidentally, was the first member of the company to sing abroad (she was Amneris to Joan Hammond's Aida with the Bolshoi Opera in Moscow in the 1950s). Emanuel ('Manya') Young had a real flair for Italian opera and I thought it a sad loss for the opera company when he became a ballet conductor instead.

I had several more music calls for my tiny role, some with Gardner, some with Goodall. It surprised me then that so much work went into what seemed to be such a tiny part in the opera, but they were after a certain style, a sense of line, a characterisation. When Reggie demonstrated the way in which he wanted it sung, I was terribly worried: must I really sound so old and quavery? He sounded like a lamb bleating and I mentioned this to John Gardner and Pat Terry who exploded with laughter. 'You haven't been here long enough to know that Reggie has the worst voice ever!' said one of them. 'He's the first to admit it.' It was the phrasing he was after, not an imitation of his own trembly tremolo.

Production rehearsals were at Holborn Hall, with a terrible echo that made a choral ensemble deafening and any shout from the conductor or director almost unintelligible. Karl Rankl was conducting *Meistersinger*, and in the usual way he rehearsed the chorus first so they could go if they wanted, leaving him free to devote his attention to others. The chorus has a tricky ensemble for the street riot at the end of Act 2, and they disperse quickly when they hear the Nightwatchman's horn, so the stage is empty the moment he appears.

My cue came, but Rankl called to the chorus: 'Let's do that again.' So they sang the passage again. Once more I made my entrance and again, just as I opened my mouth, Rankl called: 'Let's go back.'

A third time they sang it, and now Rankl went on, pointing to me for my cue. Instead of disappearing, some seventy chorus singers were hovering around, interested to hear what this new voice sounded like. I opened my mouth, but by then I was so tense with nerves that not a note came out. You can imagine how I felt.

By the dress rehearsal I was fine, but the first night brought droves of butterflies. I made my entrance far backstage and Rankl seemed about ten miles away – it was as though I was looking through the wrong end of binoculars. Still, I sang. I think I sang fairly well, but I was still acting the part as I tottered off into the wings and continued going strong until the stage manager finally stopped me: 'If you go on much further, mate, you'll land up in Bow Street Police Station!'

That Nightwatchman's walk! I practised it so often in my lodgings that when the family and friends came to my first night they knew every step I would take, as well as every note I would sing. Oh, it was a great night, no question about it! With Brenda came my father and stepmother, my aunts, cousins, friends from the chapel. Afterwards, we all went back to Chapel House in Lewisham to celebrate with tea and sandwiches, and the talk went on into the early hours.

At that time we didn't rehearse curtain-calls. You just went through when you were told to do so by the stage manager, and it was a thrill for me to join on to the others for my first call. I caught hold of Bill Franklin's hand (David Franklin, who'd sung Pogner), gripping it rather too tightly in my excitement and feeling somewhat deflated when he growled at me, 'Don't take my hand off, boy!'

That really spoiled my first curtain-call. I think it was Guthrie who started to rehearse our curtain-calls at Covent Garden and since then Stella Chitty, who's been stage manager for many years, has always insisted on it.

Meistersinger in performance takes more than four hours, plus intervals. Between first and last acts the lesser mastersingers have a long time to hang around backstage. Some talk, play cards, do crossword puzzles. I think it was about the second performance when Bill Franklin came into the dressing-room I shared and asked if anybody played chess. Among the assembled company was Marian

Nowakowski, who as Marian Ziegmundt had sung with the Polish Army Choir during the war. 'I play, but not for a long time,' he said in his deep bass with a marked Polish accent. 'Well let's have a game,' said Bill, 'and see how you do.'

They played, and Marian won. Bill laughed and said, 'Beginner's luck.' They played during the next performance, and the next, and each time Marian won. Eventually Bill said to him: 'I thought you hadn't played for a long time.' Replied Marian: 'I haven't. Not since I was the Polish champion!'

Just before the last performance of *Meistersinger*, I was told my next role would be the Marquis in *La traviata*. I had never seen the opera, though I loved the music, and I became more excited when I heard who else was involved: Elisabeth Schwarzkopf as Violetta, Ken Neate as Alfredo and Paolo Silveri as Germont, all singing in English then, and Guthrie to direct. As my role was confined to the first act and part of the second, I was able to spend some time watching the others and learning from them.

I noticed that Guthrie rehearsed at first with a paper in his hand. Later I discovered that this listed the name of every chorus-singer and, by the third rehearsal or so, he knew each of them by their first names. His psychology brought dedicated performances, but even so, a chorus could still sometimes get out of hand at rehearsal, whispering and talking, the volume steadily increasing.

This happened at a rehearsal of *La traviata*. Then Silveri made his entrance and Guthrie really went for him, shouting angrily. I never knew why, and I'm sure neither did Silveri, but it brought a total hush and impeccable behaviour from the chorus for the rest of the session. Some years later, when I'd come to know Guthrie and his wife very well, I remembered the incident and asked him about it. 'I went to Silveri afterwards and apologised,' Guthrie told me with a sly smile. 'I said I'd made a mistake, but I hadn't. Always go for the top! Shout at a principal and you'd be surprised at the effect on the chorus. It always works.'

Silveri I consider one of the greatest baritones I ever heard. He had a fantastic voice and a tremendous presence. It seemed to me that he would present himself as if to say, 'You're lucky to have me here'. Most of us were much less confident about the impact of our performances.

With her excellent figure and the fine bone-structure of her face, Schwarzkopf always looked beautiful on stage. As Violetta in *La traviata* she wore a period gown with a boned bodice, and when, at the end of the second act in the gambling scene, Alfredo throws money at her contemptuously and she collapses on a chair, we men were always eager to cluster round to comfort her, as we were supposed to do, so that we could catch a glimpse of that lovely bosom as she caught her breath and the bodice stood away from it.

In the same scene on the first night the role of Dr Grenvil was sung by Howell Glynne from the Sadler's Wells Opera, called in as a late replacement for Ernest Davies, who had sprained an ankle. He had had no time for rehearsal, and when we reached the big ensemble at the end of the act I heard him next to me, musically correct in every note but demanding in his powerful bass:

> 'I don't know these wretched words:
> Just sing them in my bloody ear!'

I was shattered. I didn't know singers did such things on stage. But I was still a novice in the theatre, and soon learned that there is much which the audience is never supposed to hear or see.

In those days Karl Rankl conducted almost every opera, so for some time he was the only conductor I worked with. Yet I can't say I really got to know him. He had no favourites and he kept a distance from everybody. He naturally wanted every singer to know his or her part well, but that was all. He never forgave mistakes, and sometimes he made you even more nervous by shouting out in anticipation if he thought you were likely to make one.

Now, we all make mistakes at some time or another, and you have to forgive a little. But not Rankl. There was little warmth or sympathy in him and no humour – none that was apparent to me, anyway. Once when he gave the brisk downbeat to start a rehearsal of *Carmen*, the orchestra broke into 'Happy Birthday' instead, as a greeting to him. And he shouted and raged at them furiously. It was pathetic to see him lose his temper like that, even more so when he realised what had happened and tried to make amends.

Yet I believe Rankl did much to put Covent Garden back on the musical map in the very difficult post-war years and this was a fine achievement. With so many performances required of the opera house, and only a small administrative staff, everybody had to work hard, and Rankl harder than most. He was responsible for giving that new young company its start in the world, though there were various critics of what he was doing and he received a good many public brickbats, not least from Sir Thomas Beecham, who had an eye on Covent Garden himself at one time and attacked Rankl in a letter to *The Times*.

There was so much prejudice against Rankl one way and another, and he wasn't the man to break down the barrier. I never knew whether the criticisms hurt him or not, when he was sad or when he was happy, he remained always the same. But I think it tragic that, after he resigned in 1951, he was never once asked back to conduct the company for which he'd done so much, and he died, back in his native Austria, a very poor man. It's an open secret that he was given less management support than he deserved, and I believe the Board of Directors were more responsible for this than Mr Webster.

My life underwent another big change during that first season at Covent Garden. Several times I'd asked Brenda to marry me (though she now says I never asked, I just took it for granted). Anyway, she was still teaching at home in Wales, and she kept postponing any possible date from one school holiday to another. Now that I had a Covent Garden contract I thought it gave me good reason to ask her once more.

The annual England v. Wales rugby international was played at Twickenham that year and, like half the Welsh nation, my cousins came up for the match. They were spending the weekend at my lodgings and when I opened the door to them that Friday, some remark was made about a suitcase that had been left outside. I went to get it, and found Brenda hiding round the corner. Naturally we were delighted to see each other, but more important for her that weekend was to watch her brother Glyn playing stand-off for Wales in the international match.

Even though my debut in *Meistersinger* was due the following week, Brenda insisted on going back to Wales on the Sunday as she felt even one day's absence would make a difference to the 11-plus class she was teaching. I was feeling pretty frustrated with various new feminine distractions around me, so amid the noise and bustle of Paddington Station I pressed her to make a decision. I wanted to marry her. I wanted us to marry at Easter, so I took my courage in both hands and delivered an ultimatum: 'We get married at Easter, or not at all.'

Two days later, when she came back for the first night of *Meistersinger* and my Covent Garden debut, she agreed we would be married on Easter Saturday. And so we were, to my great happiness then and ever since.

Both of us were born in the same village, actually in the same street. Brenda was a popular teacher in and around Pontypridd and everyone had followed my path to the glamour of Covent Garden, so there was quite a lot of local excitement about the wedding. We were married in Brenda's chapel and in Welsh by our Minister, Dewi Richards, a good friend.

Brenda was given away by her brother, Glyn, and she had four bridesmaids, including our two sisters. The chapel had a beautiful pipe organ and Brynmor Jones, the organist, played magnificently, so the music and the singing were very special to us both.

It was a beautiful spring day and over two hundred schoolchildren, many of them Brenda's pupils, came to the wedding and clustered round, shouting their greetings, in addition to about another hundred guests. As this was still the time of food rationing and clothes coupons, no restaurant or hotel could organise a reception at such short notice, so we held it in the chapel vestry. Family and friends sacrificed their coupons to help, and we wanted for nothing with such happiness all around us. Our only regret is that there was no official photographer and we have only family snapshots to remind us of that extremely happy day in our lives.

Our honeymoon, if you can call it that, was about four days in London, spent in a Bayswater flat loaned to us by James Gibb. Then I put Brenda on the train back to Wales. She wanted to continue teaching until the end of the summer term, and I wasn't earning enough to rent us a new home right away. Besides, I had to learn a new role for Covent Garden in a matter of days when another singer dropped out.

Ceprano in *Rigoletto* is not a big role, but he does have a lot to do with the chorus. And this was my first experience of how marvellous a chorus can be. I hadn't been to any production rehearsals, and there was no time for me to build up the character as I like to do. I had a few stage instructions, but it was really the chorus who guided me through the first time. One of them was always there to put a discreet hand behind my back and edge me in the right direction, or whisper in my ear what to do next. They were wonderfully helpful and I've always believed that the chorus, individually and together, is as important as any of the principals.

I did get caught off guard, though. When Rigoletto (Tom Williams at that time) tells the courtiers that the girl they abducted the night before is his daughter, the chorus exclaims, 'What? His daughter!' I was acting along with them when Ernest Davies, who was singing Marullo, sidled up and in a speaking voice said, 'God! His bloody daughter!' I knew I couldn't keep a straight face, and there and then I learned one of the first tricks of the trade: turn your back to the audience when you're in trouble.

Singers need to do this from time to time, and I've been no exception. You forget a word or a line but know the notes, and you can get by if you turn away from the audience until the words come back, as they usually do quite soon. Of course, you don't have to worry if you're somebody like Sir Peter Pears. He was so good at making up impromptu words that much of the time they sounded better than the originals.

On the other hand, there was a memorable occasion when Nowakowski was singing Colline in *La Bohème*. As he was about to reach his one big aria in the last act, when Colline decides to sell his topcoat ('Vecchia zimarra'), he moved to one side of the stage and whispered to somebody in the wings: 'I forget it!' A voice hissed the words at him, but there was another desperate whisper: 'I *know* the words. What's the *tune*?'

Singers today are usually taught basic principles of make-up for the stage, but when I started I had to pick up the technique from the older professionals, like another Covent Garden singer, the tenor David Tree. I laughed when I found that he would take on tour only an old tobacco tin with a few sticks of colouring in it. But Dai was fantastic. One or two sticks, and he could get exactly the effect he wanted.

Even after I'd been some years at the Opera House, Dai would go 'out front' to look at my make-up and see it was properly done. I tried to keep it pretty basic and not to exaggerate it, which is even more important now that modern stage lighting has become so skilful. I've always enjoyed the act of making up, and thereby turning myself into a different person.

Besides Dai Tree, I soon came to admire and make friends with other stalwarts of the company then: singers like Ernest Davies and Edgar Evans, with his marvellous sense of humour, and Rhydderch Davies, a big man with a big heart and a beautiful voice who, although a rival baritone, was always ready with genuine praise. They were colleagues who were ready to help or advise as the occasion demanded, and to console too.

My first season at Covent Garden was coming to an end, a full and exciting one for me with all the new experiences, getting married included. I started to think about next year. Contracts ran out at the end of June, and until you heard from Mr Webster there was no guarantee you would be asked back. Even if you were, there was still an unpaid break until the next season started, in late September or October. It was just as well that Brenda was still teaching. I was a kept man for a while.

I was duly summoned to Mr Webster, who allayed my worries and raised my spirits by telling me he wanted me to stay with the company, and to sing Schaunard in a new production of Puccini's *La*

Bohème the next season. My only experience of that opera then was a Carl Rosa company performance I had seen in Cardiff in my early teens, but it was something to look forward to. I would also have a new salary: fifteen pounds a week. That was progress!

Home I went to Wales and to Brenda for August and September. We lived in her parents' home, about twenty houses away from the one where I was born and grew up. I started to learn my new role, but for two or three weeks I was quite ill and began to worry that I wouldn't know it in time. When I was younger I never wanted other people to know I had asthma, I was too embarrassed. Then I found that the more I sang, the less I suffered from it. Whether it had to do with the breathing technique you learn as a singer I don't know, but I would sometimes get such a bad attack at home I could hardly walk. Then, by the time I reached the Opera House, made up, and started getting nervous about the performance, the adrenalin would begin to flow and the asthma would disappear. Latterly it's hardly affected me at all.

Nevertheless, the fear of not knowing a role in time has given me cause for panic throughout my career. I'm not sure why, because I actually learn very quickly, but then I like to leave it for a while, to consolidate it, and go back to the part again later, with time in hand to polish it.

Schaunard was to become an important stepping-stone for me, both at Covent Garden then and elsewhere later. That first time was one of the most exciting stage productions I can remember. It was directed by a young prodigy of the English theatre, Peter Brook, who'd been appointed Covent Garden's Director of Productions and caused much controversy in his approach to opera.

He lasted until the furore raised by the Dali-designed *Salome* in 1949, when the voluptuous Ljuba Welitsch sang and danced the lustful princess. She wanted to perform near-naked in the 'Dance of the Seven Veils', but the Lord Chamberlain's office, which still acted as the official censor for all stage productions, insisted that she wear a body stocking. Even then, she was sexy enough to rouse the usually placid bass, Norman Walker (who was singing First Soldier with myself as Second Soldier), to remark: 'Ba goom! She does something to you, doesn't she?'

At first I found it difficult to work with Peter Brook because he could never demonstrate what he wanted. His movements were awkward and he had to explain the character in words, to talk about it. Gradually I did come to feel a rapport with him, as well as to sense the tension between members of the cast, all great personalities: Schwarzkopf (Mimi), Welitsch (Musetta), Rudolf Schock, a new member of the company (Rodolfo), Silveri (Marcello), Franklin (Colline) and myself.

We were using sets that dated from the beginning of the century, and very fine they were too. To me it was a thrill to realise that I was singing where Caruso and other great opera singers had sung before. But Peter had filled the set with so many props, we could hardly move about. One by one, to my astonishment, the unnecessary props were picked up and thrown out by various members of the cast, so half of them were discarded before the performance.

Peter needed to be a real diplomat to handle this cast, particularly as tensions boiled over from the rehearsals into performance. After the second act the audience would be calling for Welitsch, but just as she was about to go out, Silveri, not to be outdone, stepped in front of her to lead her out for the curtain-call. Mad as hell, she made sure that the next time she went out first. But now Silveri caught her other hand and made it look as if she were leading *him*. Another night I saw her drop a curtsey directly in front of Schwarzkopf as they took calls. Naughty, I know, but symptomatic of their kind of performance. On the first night, and at practically every other performance, the applause erupted after the second act ensemble and we couldn't hear another note from the orchestra or even from the stage band before the end of the act. What an experience to remember!

Another night, towards the end of the opera, Schock sang Rodolfo's heart-rending 'Mimi! Mimi!', then, devil that he was, he rushed to her bedside where she supposedly lay dead. Maybe his foot slipped, but his hand disappeared under the blanket covering her . . . . She dared not move, of course, but when the curtain came down a moment later the lady leaped from her deathbed in a towering rage and chased Schock from the scene.

Everyone has an anecdote to recall from *Bohème*, even me. Doing Schaunard's bull-and-toreador act with Colline in the last act one night, displaying our student high spirits, his spear ripped through the cushion I was holding to fend him off. And it was a feather cushion, probably as old as the set. Not only were there feathers everywhere on the stage, but they also began to float down into the orchestra pit. Can you imagine the violinists bowing and blowing stray feathers from their strings as they tried to keep playing?

Perhaps the most ridiculous incident of all occurred in another performance during the first act. We students were supposed to be freezing in our Paris attic until some fuel was brought in for the empty stove. This had red crêpe paper and a light bulb inside to give the effect of a fire as soon as the match was struck. On this occasion Ken Neate didn't blow out the match properly before he dropped it into the stove. The red paper and other rubbish had probably been there for ages, was as dry as tinder and instantly caught alight. So there I was rushing for the fire-bucket to put out the fire when we were supposed to be freezing from the cold – much to the audience's amusement.

Sometimes it would be the stage-hands who organised a joke, often with the 'medicine' Marcello supposedly brings back for the dying Mimi. I've seen Jess Walters give a shake or two to the bottle, in the interests of realism, only to have the contents fizz up and blow off the cork in his face. Or when it was poured into a saucepan to heat over a candle, it suddenly frothed all over the table and down on to the floor like something from Quatermass. We certainly had a lot of fun with *La Bohème*, but we *did* take the work seriously.

There were times in later years when I thought I should never get away from Schaunard. Having sung it well over a hundred times, I asked Mr Webster if I could sing Marcello instead. He agreed and I was put down for that role. But then came Rafael Kubelik to conduct at Covent Garden and it was the first time he had conducted *La Bohème*: he wanted an experienced cast on whom he could rely, so back I had to go to Schaunard.

Something similar happened in San Francisco, and again in Vienna, as I shall tell, so whether or not Puccini was my kind of music, Schaunard was a role that came to mean much to me in my career. It was certainly because of my first Schaunard performances at Covent Garden that Peter Brook suggested to Mr Webster that he would like me for his next new production, *The Marriage of Figaro*. And he wanted me to be Figaro.

It's often been said that Figaro was my first role in a Mozart opera, but this isn't so. My debut in Mozart was in *Così fan tutte*, as Don Alfonso, at the Guildhall School of Music in the summer of 1948, at the end of the student year. Although I was by then a member of the Covent Garden Opera and had sung my first roles there, I went on having voice, piano and harmony lessons at the Guildhall School for the rest of that season and, with Opera House permission, took part in the opera class for that year's production.

I suppose I was very raw to play a role like Alfonso, who has to be wordly-wise and more than a bit cynical from his experiences, but although I was then only twenty-six I tried to give the role a sense of dignity and an air of knowing what life was about. After all, I may not have ventured far outside Wales until I was eighteen, but we grew up very quickly while we were away on war service. Coming back to the Guildhall School as ex-servicemen made many of us feel quite old by comparison with the students who hadn't been away.

Between us at that time there was no lack of talent, and *Così fan tutte* was a very successful production. I adored the opera then as I still do, believing there's a great deal more in it than we often think or portray, and right away I felt vocally 'inside' Mozart's music. Following the Guildhall School custom, we gave the opera there first, then took the production to Cambridge for more performances with a lively university audience.

After one of my performances Aylmer Buesst, a conductor of wide pre-war experience who was then teaching, came up to me and said: 'Geraint, you have something. I think you'll make it. Mozart suits you.' I was thrilled. It was the first time an experienced professional had said anything like that to me. And, of course, Mozart went on suiting me very well.

It was many years before I sang Alfonso again, but there was a curious incident at an Edinburgh Festival some years later. Brenda and I were invited to supper after one performance by Daniel Barenboim and his wife, Jacqueline du Pré. Also present were Suvi Grubb, the record producer with EMI, Luigi Alva and his wife Anita, and Alberto Rinaldi, the Italian baritone, and after we'd enjoyed Danny's spaghetti we sat talking. It arose that Rinaldi had known extra-sensory powers as a boy and had sometimes let himself act as a spirit medium. Somebody asked if he would hold a séance with us, to pass the time. Very reluctantly he agreed, the lights were dimmed, and we sat around a table holding hands.

Neither Brenda nor I were much interested, nor was Suvi, but we were quite ready to be amused. At first, things didn't work as they were supposed to and we were asked if we were all touching hands. At this Suvi, who was very dark-skinned, said sarcastically: 'You'll have to take Brenda's word that I'm touching her hand. Nobody can see *my* hands in this light.'

That started us giggling, of course, but others were taking it more seriously. Soon the séance began in earnest and the table started to tap. When Luigi asked who wanted to contact us, the tapping started to spell out: M – O – Z . . . .

Luigi then asked, very politely, if the message was in English or Italian. I really had to control my laughter, but I wanted to pay attention as questions were being asked about my Mozart performances. One question asked for my first Mozart role. The answer was spelled out: A L F O N S O.

Now this did startle me, because I'm sure nobody there besides Brenda and myself knew that I had sung Alfonso. Then there was a question about Brenda which was answered equally correctly and we were completely mystified. Again the table came down hard on

Brenda's knee, and she was very frightened. I must say that, sceptical as I was, I could not budge the table while this was happening. I wouldn't care to experience anything like that again.

Early in 1949, the post-war opera company at Covent Garden put on their first production of *The Marriage of Figaro* (there had been three performances during a guest season by the Vienna State Opera in the autumn of 1947). I discovered that my first cast would have Schwarzkopf as Susanna, Hans Braun (the Count), Sylvia Fisher (the Countess), and Eugenia Zareska (Cherubino), Edith Coates (Marcellina), Howell Glynne (Bartolo), Murray Dickie (Basilio) and, as Barbarina, a young newcomer, Adèle Leigh (she later took over Cherubino from Zareska).

I could play the piano fairly decently then and taught myself Figaro's role before we began rehearsals. Then I went to Percy Heming, as I had earlier, for some help with stage style and deportment. Heming, who died in 1956, was an outstanding baritone in English opera between the wars, and became artistic director at Covent Garden in the last two years before the Second World War broke out. He still worked there as an artistic adviser and coach, and from him I learned a great deal about movement, gesture and presence on stage.

One of his methods was to teach me basic ballet steps: as a keen rugby player not long back from the Forces, these came very strangely to me. I would practise them in the chorus room, with one door locked and the other with a chair under the handle, in case a colleague should see me and get the wrong idea. I was pretty self-conscious about it all at first, but I know now how valuable those sessions were: I've never since had to worry about what to do with my hands, where my feet should go, or how to walk down a staircase. I've often had cause to be grateful to Percy for that.

With Figaro, though, I had a problem. I would make a movement with what I thought was the kind of elegance Percy had taught me, only to be stopped on stage by Peter Brook saying, 'No, I don't want you to do that.' This happened a few times, and I told him how confused I was getting, with Percy telling me one thing and him another.

At which Peter said I was to forget what Percy had told me and just move from A to B. As rehearsals went on I realised that he wanted me to begin from nothing and find the character as I went along, to let it grow from inside me. Eventually I found this worked, and the final characterisation tied up with what Percy had been telling me.

One day Elisabeth Schwarzkopf asked me if I would mind coming to work with Walter Legge on our scenes together. I'd no idea then who he was, but I was all for trying to make improvements, so one dark evening I found my way to an old Victorian house in Abbey Road. In my naïvety I didn't realise until the next time I went there that this was the famous EMI recording studios.

Nor did I appreciate at first either Legge's position in the record business or the state of his relationship with Schwarzkopf, whom he later married. It seemed to me that the way he sometimes spoke to her in front of me was no way to talk to a lady, and one day when she was out of the room I said as much. I ventured to tell him I thought he was humiliating her, as well as embarrassing me.

So as far as making gramophone records was concerned, I think I spoilt my chances with Legge at that moment, even before I started. A few years later he recorded *Figaro* in London with Klemperer conducting. Schwarzkopf was now the Countess and Eberhard Waechter the Count, but at a very late stage in the proceedings Legge still hadn't found his Figaro. I learned in due course that Waechter told him there was 'a damn good Figaro' under his nose, at Covent Garden. Legge stayed silent then and always. I never did record Figaro with him, or indeed anything else. I wasn't the only British singer who was consistently ignored in opera recordings at that time. I still think it a tragedy that many fine singers recorded very little at the height of their careers: Edith Coates, Constance Shacklock and Amy Shuard, to name but a few.

Schwarzkopf was a perfectionist and would explore every detail of her role in a cold, calculating way which I thought affected her performances some of the time. Like all the other operas, we sang *Figaro* in English then. She, Braun and Zareska learned their English lines very thoroughly, but pronunciation on stage was inclined to be wayward. We sang Edward Dent's translation, and the Professor came to some rehearsals, cupping a hand to one ear because he was deaf. As I walked past he called to me and said: 'I can understand every word from you. But tell the others to do a little better.' Well, who was I to tell *them*?

For me, the Dent translation of *Figaro* remains the best. It may need a little modernising in places, but it has style, it has elegance, and it sings well. Several other versions I've read and sung are simply too colloquial, which doesn't suit the period at all.

My family and friends started to get excited now that I was to sing Figaro, and having a major role brought me into contact with the Press for the first time. There were requests for interviews and I had to respond, even though I was nervous, tongue-tied and embarrassed, afraid I might get too much of a build-up too soon. I was by now becoming a bit tense with the anticipation of my first night.

The performance came soon enough, and although I've tried hard to remember what it was like, I can't recall a thing about it. I don't remember how I sang; I don't remember what the reception was like. All that remains is the recollection of being sky-high for hours after it was over, and not being able to sleep at all that night.

I'd started having reviews sent by a Press-cutting agency. They arrived some days after the performance and I preferred to read them properly when I'd cooled down and could analyse how I'd performed and what they said. Brenda is different. She likes to know what they say right away and if she doesn't like what she reads, she's the first to defend me and criticise *them*.

On that occasion they weren't bad. In fact, they were all fairly reasonable. In general they said I was a young beginner, and one with a future. That was probably better than instant rave reviews: even though the comments were mostly encouraging, they made me think 'I've got to do better.'

Figaro was given several more performances that season and I began to get a grip on the role and feel more assured. Perhaps I even started to be too sure of myself because in the fifth or sixth performance, during my wedding scene with Susanna in Act 3, I started singing a beat too soon. However, I put it right very quickly and I don't think many people would have noticed. But Rankl was conducting. He noticed. And he shouted, loud enough for the audience to hear too: 'You stupid boy!'

I wanted to disappear, to have the stage open up and swallow me, but I just had to carry on. Since that time, in every one of the several hundred Figaro performances I've sung, I've always counted the beats at that particular place. It became quite a joke with various Susannas I sang with regularly, and they would count along with me. It's Figaro's line 'Un biglietto amoroso ...' after he sees in the Count's hand a note Susanna has slipped secretly to him.

Peter Brook didn't want much emotion shown between Susanna and Figaro, in the first scene no more than a light kiss on her cheek as she leaned back on a large basket. Once Schwarzkopf's arms slipped and she fell back further than intended, but too late for me to stop myself and I landed up kissing her bosom instead. For a moment I was embarrassed but not displeased. Indeed, I rather hoped it might happen again but it never did.

The season had gone well for me and as we approached the summer I had another interview with David Webster in his office. I don't remember now what roles he was suggesting for me when we began again in October, but I recall asking him if I could understudy one or two roles, something like Escamillo in *Carmen*, perhaps?

A little ritual followed the discussion of roles. Mr Webster would get up and walk to the window, then say with his back to me as he looked out: 'Now what do you really want?' This happened each year, and it was my cue to ask if there was any chance of a rise in salary. Something was usually forthcoming, and by 1950 I was on about eighteen pounds a week.

We baritones, when we start out, always aspire to sing Scarpia, or Rigoletto, or Escamillo – the big roles. In my case it happened that I took on Escamillo much sooner than I expected.

A baritone from America had already been engaged for Escamillo, and for Germont in *La traviata*. He certainly had a good voice, but his stature was against him – he was bandy-legged and when he put on the toreador's breeches and the rest of the costume the effect was simply too embarrassing. The upshot was that I was asked to take on Escamillo.

Silveri, Tom Williams, Jess Walters and Marko Rothmüller had all sung these roles in previous seasons, and I felt I was now making fast progress in the baritone league. Naturally I was determined to play the part of Escamillo as well as possible, so in learning the histrionics of the role I asked Alexander Grant, then a young soloist of the Sadler's Wells Ballet, if he would teach me to handle the toreador's cloak with the right kind of swing and flourish. This he did, and I swung and flourished away like mad. In my eagerness I didn't realise I was practising with the wrong cloak, the heavy one the toreadors wore for the grand march in the last act. The cloak I was to use in Act 2 was smaller and lighter, and when I began to swing it the way I had done the other, I nearly spun round in circles.

Came the performance, with Warwick Braithwaite conducting (he had joined Covent Garden from Sadler's Wells the previous season) and Martha Mödl having learned an English Carmen. She was a spittle-singer, so there I was having to look ardent in our duet, blinking furiously the while against the spray and, of course, not daring to move out of range. I thought I sang quite well, but that nevertheless something was wrong with my performance.

So I turned again to Percy Heming, who had been away ill when I was rehearsing, and asked if he would watch a performance and tell me what he thought about it. Percy had himself been a celebrated Escamillo (and later I was flattered that he chose to leave his own Escamillo costume to me). He duly came, and the next morning we talked about it.

'Geraint,' he said, 'You did it well, but you lacked conviction.'

I asked what he meant by that.

'When you come down those stairs for your first entrance,' he replied 'you must feel a kind of pretentiousness. The toreador is the popular idol of the time. He's a brave man, but conceited. He knows he can have any woman he likes there. So I want you to come down the stairs thinking that way.' I explained that I'd thought of all this, so he said, 'It's much cruder than that. In fact . . . how can I describe it? To put it bluntly, I want you to come down those stairs *with your cock wrapped round your neck!*'

I was aghast at what he was saying, this religious, polite and elegant man. He must have seen my reaction, because he added: 'I'm sorry. I can't explain it any other way. You see, it's the vulgarity, the show-off in Escamillo.'

At my next performance Edith Coates had taken over Carmen's role, and as I came down the stairs I had Percy's instructions very much in mind. Edie sidled up to me, but instead of saying, 'Darling, you do look lovely', as she often had done, this time it became: 'Darling, you can have me any time you like!' My God, I thought, Percy was right! Edie hadn't known what I was thinking, but her remark coming as it did, I just had to laugh. Said Percy afterwards: 'Why did you laugh? You spoiled it. You were doing marvellously up till then.' But when I told him what Edie had said, he had to laugh too.

Still I thought there was something lacking in my Escamillo. Nor was I the only one to think so. When David Webster met Brenda and me outside the Opera House towards the end of the season he mentioned that he wanted me to sing Escamillo again the following year. Brenda chipped in: 'You can't really mean that! I thought he was a terrible Escamillo.' To which Mr Webster responded: 'I know, my dear, but he's the best we've got for the moment.'

I began to realise what was wrong when I sang several performances under Erich Kleiber a couple of seasons later. The opera gives a terrific build-up to Escamillo's first entrance but then, no matter how well he sings his aria, the tension drops and there's a sense of anticlimax. Kleiber's remedy was to get more chorus involvement, having them shout 'Bravo!' and cheer at various points which he marked in the score.

This seemed to generate more excitement, both on the stage and in the orchestra. It helped to keep an uplift in Escamillo's aria and after it, and created an atmosphere which lasted throughout the scene, even when Escamillo wasn't singing. As far as I was concerned, the first time the aria really succeeded was in the Kleiber performances. After he left, I couldn't expect that other conductors should do the same, only ask if they would.

I didn't sing Escamillo a great many more times, but there was a new production of *Carmen* in 1953 by Anthony Asquith, with John Pritchard conducting and a variety of casts. I was asked to take the part the following season and found that Escamillo was required to sing two verses of his aria standing on a tavern table. I was never comfortable about this, and one night the aria seemed to fall flatter than usual. So I took it into my head to jump down from the table and sing the second verse right to the audience.

And it worked. The audience rose to it, and there was excitement again. But trouble for me. Next morning I was called to Mr Webster. The stage manager had reported that what I'd done had muddled the chorus production.

'What's this I hear?' asked Webster. 'You're not to do that again.'

'No, sir,' I agreed, 'I won't.' But halfway to the door I turned and said: 'Unless I feel it's going flat again and then I'll have to, won't I?'

Webster smiled that half-smile of his, looking over his glasses, and I knew from his expression that he would accept that.

I was never happy singing on that table. One night, after singing about fifteen bars, I had a sudden blackout of memory. I dried up. Before I could recover the prompter started singing it. So did the chorus. I think even the audience were singing it. After all, everybody knows the Song of the Toreador.

That was my first blackout on stage. It's a terrible feeling. Your heart seems to be pumping loudly in your throat. Your head feels as though it's coming off and you want to run away. Was I glad to get off that stage! When I came on for the next act I had to grit my teeth, make an effort, shrug it off somehow. But, believe me, the experience stays with you for days after.

Since the days of Queen Victoria, Covent Garden had traditionally engaged guardsmen from the Household Brigade for any marching that had to be done on stage. The Queen had been so appalled at the standard of marching she saw in one performance she went to (I think it was the triumphal scene in *Aida*), and the untidy spectacle of men of assorted heights, that she insisted her guardsmen should be brought in instead. On tour, of course, this wasn't so practicable, but the management usually went to a local college or university to pick a dozen or so students of a similar height to be presentable 'supers' in the necessary scenes.

In *Carmen* they would be dressed as toreadors and their entourages for the march to the bull-ring in the final scene, striding across the stage, then doubling round the back of the set to come in again as another group, repeating this procedure perhaps three or four times. I remember one occasion at Manchester when there just wasn't room for them to pass behind the set, and instead they had to go right outside the theatre, run round the back, and march in again on the opposite side. That afternoon they were diligently rehearsed by Ande Anderson and all went well. By the evening performance, though, the heavens had opened and the rain started pouring down. You never saw such chaos!

The first time those toreadors appeared they were spruce and smart. The second time they were obviously damp, but by their fourth entrance they were so wet and bedraggled that their make-up had begun to run, their wigs were drooping, their shoes squelched and the dye from their costumes was starting to trickle down their white stockings. It was a laughable sight, but I'm sure Queen Victoria would not have been amused.

My next role brought my first association with Freddie Ashton, now Sir Frederick, founder-choreographer of the Royal Ballet. He had directed Massenet's *Manon* for the opera company early in 1947 and I was to sing Lescaut, Manon's rakish, spendthrift cousin, in a revival. Freddie was a delight to work with, a producer I was sympathetic to. He was still dancing some of his celebrated character-roles with the ballet company at that time and used his own skill to influence operatic movements.

Schwarzkopf, and later Victoria de los Angeles sang Manon and des Grieux was sung by Walter Midgley. I'd sung with him in *La traviata*, but nothing thrilled me more than his beautiful tenor voice in the 'Dream Song' from *Manon*. He sang it in an exquisite pianissimo, a thread of sound that sent shivers down my spine, and it held the audience enraptured.

There were several other singers of that same calibre at Covent Garden then, and I have never understood why they did not get engagements abroad. Was it because we were singing in English and many of them only learned their roles in English? Possibly they thought it was a bit late for them to start singing in other languages, but there were certainly some great voices among them and it is immensely sad that they were not heard and appreciated further afield.

Lescaut was a role I enjoyed, although it lay a little high for me. I was glad of a number of cuts, in fact I doubt I could have sung it otherwise because I was then still a virtual bass, a bass with a bit of stretch in the voice. Later I settled into a bass-baritone, but I started to become careful about the roles I accepted. Instead of singing everything I was asked to do in order to get the experience, I became more discerning and checked the vocal demands of a role before making any decision.

The Opera House had scheduled a couple of performances of *Tristan und Isolde*, with Kirsten Flagstad and Set Svanholm, before the season ended in July, and I asked if I could sing Melot in them. It's not a big role, and I was confident I could do it, but my main reason for wanting the work was the extra money this would provide. Thank goodness I managed it well enough to be cast as Melot again the next year, with much the same cast, but this time with Clemens Krauss conducting instead of Rankl. After a dress rehearsal in two parts on two consecutive mornings, Krauss came on stage, paid some complimentary remarks to one or two of the other singers, then came over to me. With a twinkle in his eye and in quite a kindly way he said: 'Eee-vans. Melot does not suit you . . . .'

My heart sank. His wife, the famous singer Viorica Ursuleac, was with him and protested at the remark, but Krauss said: 'Let me finish. Melot does not suit you but you will have a fine future.'

To be honest I didn't want to hear that then. I would much rather have been told that I was a good Melot.

There were four further performances with Krauss, and for the fifth and last Rankl conducted once more. This was his farewell to the Opera House and the company he'd served so well, and it was also Flagstad's last appearance at Covent Garden. It's recorded that she took twenty-one curtain-calls, then spoke to the audience for the first and only time instead of singing: 'Please forgive me. I want to take things more easily.'

Flagstad was then in her mid-fifties and on several occasions I went to chat with her in her dressing-room while she placidly knitted the time away between one stage-call and the next, for performances that she made unforgettable. I enquired what she would do if she no longer sang. Teach, perhaps? To which she replied: 'How can I teach when I don't know myself how I sing? I just open my mouth and it's there!'

Earlier that 1950-51 season, along with almost every other British singer in the company, I had a small role (the Herald) in the premiere of *The Pilgrim's Progress* by Vaughan Williams. This was not so much an opera as a kind of festival pageant – it was the year of the Festival of Britain, and more than thirty years later we've still not seen some of the operas commissioned with special Arts Council awards for the occasion, one of them Karl Rankl's own *Deirdre of the Sorrows*.

At the same time I also had my first acquaintance with another Mozart opera, *The Magic Flute*, singing four different roles: the Second Priest, then one of the two Armed Men (or Men in Armour, as they're sometimes listed), followed by the Speaker of the Temple and, lastly but more lengthily, Papageno. The first two are small roles, but they nevertheless involved me in an opera that I found increasingly fascinating, giving me the opportunity to watch and observe the others in it.

The chorus sounded specially good just then – I'd never heard it sing so beautifully, not least in 'O Isis and Osiris' (usually known as the Ice-cream Chorus). Among the choristers were several singers who later became principals at Covent Garden and well-known in other countries, including Josephine Veasey, Charles Craig and Michael Langdon. The standard of singing was exceptionally high and sometimes amazed singers from abroad. Theo Hermann, who taught me in Germany, said about this time that it was one of the finest choruses he'd ever heard, a great compliment to Douglas Robinson, who had trained them so well as Chorus Master.

Of course, like all choruses, they had their less respectful moments. In *The Magic Flute* the men are required to signify assent to the initiation of Tamino into the Masonic order by pretending to blow horns (they were made of papier-mâché) in time with three chords from the orchestra, repeated three times.

One night one of the stage horn players broke wind in time with the music. I was standing in my priestly robes next to him and could hardly believe what I thought I heard. Next time there was no doubt; he did it again, and in tempo, to our amazed amusement. Worst of all was when the last chord sounded. We expectantly waited for a repetition – and nothing happened! Now the papier-mâché horns could be seen wobbling all over the place as the chorus tried to control their laughter. Although Edgar Evans (singing First Priest) and myself laughed a lot over this later, we were actually very embarrassed at the time and hardly knew where to look.

As I came to know *The Magic Flute* it seemed to me that, although there's a close association with Masonic ritual and sentiments, there's also a strong resemblance to traditional English pantomime. I realised then what a marvellous opera it can be for children, and it still seems an ideal introduction to opera – provided, of course, it's done well and sung in their own language.

I moved on from Second Priest and Man in Armour to sing the Speaker, who has a very beautiful scene when he questions Tamino about his motives in seeking admission to the Temple. I'd watched Paul Schoeffler and Hans Hotter playing this role and had no qualms about singing it, calling as it does for a smooth, legato line and good verbal pointing. Much as I enjoyed singing it, though, I felt it needed somebody more mature than I to make it sound right.

With Papageno, however, I was totally at home from the first time I sang it. It became one of my favourite roles and I loved to play it with the element of pantomime that I thought belonged to this child of nature, this absurd but endearing bird-catcher whom the Viennese author of the text, Emanuel Schikaneder, had first portrayed. I'd watched and learned a lot from Jess Walters in the role, but found my own approach to be more suggestive of a boy growing up, feeling strange new sensations from one scene to next and not being quite sure how to cope with them.

My difficulty here was the amount of dialogue I had to speak. My Welsh accent has always remained part of my speaking voice and here it became very evident. So much so that after one rehearsal I had a note from David Webster asking me to give more attention to my pronunciation. I sought advice from Christopher West, who'd been in the dramatic theatre (he was to direct *The Magic Flute* at Covent Garden for the Mozart bicentenary in 1956), and he generously spent some time helping to improve my accent.

About the time I was getting to know *The Magic Flute*, in 1950, Brenda and I moved from our first attic flat to one a little more spacious in an old Victorian house. The new flat was only about ten minutes away from where we were living, and the small amount of furniture and other things we'd acquired wasn't enough to fill a van. So we asked our fruiterer if we could borrow his handcart, and around midnight two figures could be seen loading it with bits and pieces, pulling it along the main road to the new address, unloading quickly and going back for more. Just as if we were doing a 'midnight flit'.

Elegant it was, the new place, and I took a pride in decorating it. I painted the dining-room pale grey and thought it very smart, but decided it wanted a touch of something to contrast. Late one night I added a delicate line of gold around the picture-rail. When Brenda saw it she became very cross, thinking I'd gone too far, and complained it would look like a palais-de-danse by the time I'd finished. She took herself to bed in a huff, and what should happen but that the bed collapsed. So it all ended in a great deal of laughter and she decided the palais-de-danse looked pretty good after all.

We were happy in that new home, and delighted still to be only a short walk from the Lewisham Welsh Chapel, where we not only attended Sunday services but met and made friends. On the first Monday of the month it was a focus of social activity for Welsh people from round about, with an evening of songs, piano music or poetry recitation in which we all took part. For several years we were regular attenders, until I started to go abroad more often and we moved further away to live.

The summer of 1951 found us back in Wales on holiday when a telegram came from Covent Garden asking if I would return there to discuss a project. It was an unusual request out-of-season, when I knew there would be very few people around at the Opera House, and I was curious why I should be asked to see Mr Webster. He mentioned the new opera by Benjamin Britten, *Billy Budd*, which I knew was announced for the autumn season, and then said: 'Mr Britten wants you to sing Billy Budd.'

Thrilled is hardly the word to describe my feelings at that moment. And although I never actually sang the role, I was proud indeed to have such a composer's confidence.

Billy Budd was Benjamin Britten's first opera to be premiered by the Covent Garden company and the first new opera with which I'd been involved, so I was naturally keen to make the most of my chance as the tragic sailor of Herman Melville's posthumously published novel, *Billy Budd, Foretopman*. David Webster suggested that I should go through the title role that Ben had asked me to sing and find out whether it suited my voice. As far as I was concerned, it was jolly well going to suit me. I was sent to Peter Gellhorn to work on it, and I couldn't have wished for a better musician.

To begin with, we made pretty good progress. I became excited by the role, though when you're learning something new you don't sing out right away: you sing it quietly, only half-strength, maybe even an octave lower than what's written, just to be going on with. After about a couple of weeks like this I thought I'd better start to sing the part properly. The first two acts I could sing, and sing well, but there was a problem in the last act. Billy has a soliloquy, as he lies 'in irons' on the ship's gundeck, shackled to a cannon under sentence of death, and I found that soliloquy vocally much more difficult than I had anticipated.

It started to worry me, and I began to think that a higher baritone was needed. Peter Gellhorn and I had a long discussion about it. He was very helpful and also very practical: 'If you're not really sure about it,' he said to me, 'if you're so worried that you don't bring it off, then don't do it.'

Deep down I knew he was right. So I told Benjamin Britten about my problem. He was very understanding and promised to look at the scene in question. Later he even wrote offering to change the notes that lay too high for me. The more I looked at it, though, the more I realised how beautifully that 'Billy in the Darbies' scene had been written. To change an occasional note wouldn't be enough for me, and if the whole passage were taken down a tone, it was going to sound much less effective in its context.

Understandably, I think, I hedged for a few days. I wanted to play the role so badly. So much so that Brenda said she woke one night to hear me babbling:

> *'Billy Budd, king of the birds,*
> *Billy Budd, king of the world,*
> *Up among the sea hawks . . .'*

She had to wake me. I was singing it in my sleep.

Neverthless, I had to be honest with myself and accept that the soliloquy really lay too high for me, and then to muster the courage to admit this and ask to withdraw, sick with disappointment. My consolation was a marvellous letter from Ben thanking me for being so honest and saying that he would still like me to be in the opera. So far they hadn't cast the Sailing Master, Mr Flint, which was my kind of voice. Perhaps I would sing that? I accepted and sang that role instead.

As we went into rehearsals, a lot of tension began to grow between the chorus and Peter Gellhorn while he was preparing them for Josef Krips, who had been engaged to conduct the opera. More and more of us began to wonder why Ben didn't conduct it himself. It was a delicate situation and I discussed it with Peter Pears, for whom Ben had written the role of Captain Vere, the ship's commander. Peter also felt that rehearsals were becoming difficult. 'Why don't *you* ask Ben?', he suggested. I demurred, but Peter pressed me.

Eventually I was cheeky enough to go to Ben and suggest that he should conduct his own opera. As Peter had said he would, he refused at first, but I argued further, urging him to do it for the sake of the work itself. Then Peter Pears joined us and I left him to continue the discussion. The next I knew about it was an announcement that Krips had asked to withdraw on account of eyesight trouble and Ben was to conduct the first performances.

Working directly with Britten was a wonderful experience, and also great fun. Sometimes he would play the piano for us himself in the foyer rehearsals, and if we'd been working very hard and needed a break, he might entertain us by playing some swing music. He had a knack of making us feel relaxed and made the rehearsals highly enjoyable, always smiling when things went wrong as they inevitably did.

Ben gave us lots of help on phrasing. He had a terrible singing voice, but he was such a fine pianist he could illustrate anything he wanted simply by playing it on the piano. What's more, he never antagonised the singers or the orchestra by talking down to us – we therefore respected him and gave of our best. I feel that the spirit of collaboration is of the utmost importance.

Ben at rehearsals was always ready to try alternative ways of achieving a desired effect, and this helped a lot in making *Billy Budd* a success at its premiere, a few weeks before Christmas in 1951. I remember it as a wonderful first night, and I thought the young American baritone, Theodore Uppman, who sang Billy instead of me, was fantastically good. He was blond and good-looking and he sang the part beautifully, as did two later British singers, Peter Glossop and Thomas Allen.

I was never conscious of the lack of female voices in *Billy Budd*. E. M. Forster and Eric Crozier wrote the libretto on the Melville story and, taking place as it does aboard a British man-o'-war under sail in 1797, it's impossible to imagine a female voice having any part in it, yet the musical balance is perfect.

During one of Ben's performances there was a very fraught moment. One singer failed to come in on cue and this had a domino effect on the rest: because one didn't utter, the next couldn't follow, and there was a total silence on stage. Maybe it was only for thirty seconds, but it seemed like half an hour.

Luckily I'd made myself familiar with much of the orchestral writing, as I always do when I learn an opera. I also have a photographic memory, so I can visualise the music as it's written on the page. I was singing Mr Flint, up on the ship's top deck in the stage setting, and therefore a bit exposed. But as the orchestra played on during the vocal blank I could 'see' the music coming to the bottom of the page. In my mind I turned the page and there was my next cue. I took it and came in; it happened to be right, and everybody else then slotted in again too.

I was scared half to death at the time, and the tension while it happened was so great I could hardly sing another note after it was over, but I was the hero of that night. Ben came to me later and said 'You caught it just in time. I was going to stop the orchestra and go back.' This is a rare occurrence, and only ever happened to me once, in a late performance of *Die Meistersinger* the year before I retired.

Billy Budd eventually became very successful in the USA. Several scenes were televised by NBC in the autumn of 1952 (the first TV showing of any Britten opera), and soon afterwards it was staged by New York's Metropolitan Opera, but then it disappeared over there and nothing was heard of it for several years. I like to think that I talked Carol Fox in Chicago and Kurt Adler in San Francisco into producing it for their respective companies in the 1970s, since when it's also been seen in several other American centres.

Another new Britten role came my way when I was asked to play Mountjoy in *Gloriana*, the opera commissioned by Covent Garden for the Coronation of Queen Elizabeth II in 1953. Brenda came to the dress rehearsal, as she usually did: she's always been helpful in commenting on the production and she would tell me if there was anything about my performance that disturbed her. This time she thought I needed to improve my diction in some places, adding: 'It's surprising, because I've never had trouble in understanding you before.'

When we were back at home, she went into another room while I sang some of the phrases she'd complained about. She wasn't any happier, so I sang them a second time. Still she couldn't get them clearly. Beginning to feel decidedly frustrated, I pushed the printed lines under her nose for her to read, stanzas such as:

> *'A garden by a river for a trysting*
> *Is perfect in the evening for a pair,*
> *Yet if one for the other long attendeth,*
> *Delay falls like frost upon the air . . .'*

Then she understood my problem in trying to convey the sense of those words through the music, the shape of the verbal and musical phrases never really helping each other.

Gloriana was no sort of success when we premiered it at a gala performance on 8 June, six days after the Coronation. John Pritchard conducted a cast led by Joan Cross as the first Queen Elizabeth, who was known as 'Gloriana', and Peter Pears as the hot-tempered Earl of Essex. The other solo roles were sung by Jennifer Vyvyan, Adèle Leigh, Monica Sinclair, Arnold Matters and Michael Langdon, but it was very much a team opera. The Queen and other members of the Royal Family were there, of course, and the rest of the audience was a very formal one, mostly invited on account of their official positions.

I dare say two-thirds of them had probably never been to an opera before, and there they were confronted by a 'modern' work, not Puccini or Verdi with which they might have been familiar. It's a matter of history that the first-night reception was very cool indeed, some of the distinguished guests finding excuses to leave during the interval, but I can tell you that it wasn't easy for us on the stage either. The production relied a good deal on distracting spotlights, but it was even worse when somebody in the auditorium moved and the light caught the diamonds and tiaras that were on display.

Yet it was apparent from the outset that *Gloriana* had splendid musical moments, as later audiences were to discover. I still think that Joan Cross gave one of her greatest performances in that title role. I had long admired her, having often been to Sadler's Wells and heard her when I was stationed in London early in the war, but as Gloriana I thought her specially wonderful.

My role as Mountjoy involved a swordfight in the opening scene with the jealous Essex. Our moves were worked out for us by a professional fencer and I rehearsed it with John Lanigan, who was 'covering' Essex for Peter Pears. When Peter came in for his rehearsal I soon discovered that he didn't have anything like such good movement co-ordination and that duel became a frightening experience for me. It lasted hardly more than thirty seconds, I think, but I was terrified every time we played it.

Later that year the Covent Garden Opera went abroad for the centenary celebrations in what was then still Rhodesia, and *Gloriana* was taken as part of the repertory. In the duel during a performance in Bulawayo my sword snapped about four inches from the handle. I didn't realise this immediately, and was already committed to a lunge at Essex, who was then John Lanigan. My broken blade pierced his hand, blood spurted in all directions and John's cry, 'You bastard!' could be heard all over the house.

What the audience made of it I don't know, but I was alarmed that I might have done John a serious injury. First aid was called in, and I was much relieved to discover that it was not as bad as it might have been.

I was fortunate to have other roles in Britten's operas at various times. One was Balstrode, the retired sea-captain in *Peter Grimes*, with his commonsense outlook on the affairs of the fishing village where the story is set. This was another role that I sang for the first time in the Coronation year, with either Peter Pears or Edgar Evans in the title role, and Joan Cross or the splendid Australian-born Sylvia Fisher, then at the peak of her career at Covent Garden, as Ellen Orford.

Peter Grimes was still conducted at that time by Reggie Goodall, who had conducted the opera at its premiere at Sadler's Wells in 1945. A few years later I sang a totally different character, the quick-witted apothecary, Ned Keene, after Britten made a direct request for me through Lord Harewood, who was then controller of opera planning at Covent Garden. I was delighted to accept, particularly as I knew there were plans to record it and I wanted to make a recording at that time. It duly took place with Britten himself conducting, his first opera on records.

On the stage I went back to singing Balstrode, not only in London but on several occasions in New York, Chicago and San Francisco, where I also had the great satisfaction of directing the opera for the first time later on in my career. I love *Billy Budd*, but to me *Peter Grimes* is a truly fantastic opera and makes a thrilling evening in the theatre. I mentioned this once to Ben, and all he said was: 'Can't stand it now!' Coming from him I was a bit taken aback, but I never had the opportunity to ask him to elaborate on this.

Another of Britten's operatic roles that I thoroughly enjoyed was that of Bottom in *A Midsummer Night's Dream*, when Georg Solti conducted it at Covent Garden in 1961, the year after it was premiered at the Aldeburgh Festival. Solti brought a sparkle, a champagne quality to the music, and the designs by John Piper were wonderfully imaginative, creating a dreamworld of fantasy and fairy magic from some very prosaic materials, such as steel wool and mop-heads.

The cast, which included Joan Carlyle as Tytania and an American counter-tenor, Russell Oberlin, as Oberon, was directed by John Gielgud. Knowing the Shakespeare comedy as intimately as he did, I think he was sometimes disconcerted by the music and its effect on the words, so that occasionally he seemed a bit lost. His real achievement, though, was to present the opera with style and good taste, and I only appreciated the extent of his skill some years later, when I had to adapt to some American productions.

At Covent Garden I wanted to incorporate a special kind of dance during the 'tongs and bones' music with the fairies and once again I enlisted the help of Alexander Grant, who not long after was to create a superb dance character as Bottom in Frederick Ashton's ballet on the same subject. He worked out some movements and steps which I could manage while wearing the ass's head, though they nearly killed me, not being any sort of balletic type myself.

There have been several other uncomfortable moments during my performances as Bottom. Usually I have to spend about twenty minutes lying with Tytania in her bower while she 'madly dotes' on me wearing the ass's head. As it happens, I have worked with three different Tytanias whose pregnancies were beginning to show, at least at close quarters. With one of them, while my ass's head was resting on her tummy (as the production required, I hasten to add), the baby kicked. It was the first time she'd felt it, and she 'ooped' with surprise. As for me, I was afraid she might be about to have the baby there and then, and there were a good many of the twenty minutes still to go!

On one occasion with Joan Carlyle I was lying so comfortably I actually fell asleep, and she had to give me a dig to wake me when the curtain eventually came down at the end of the act.

During my early years at Covent Garden I would also take concert engagements, especially in Wales. It often meant taking the 'Messiah Special', as the Paddington to Fishguard train became known, usually on Thursday mornings, because 'Celebrity Concerts' and oratorios tended to be held on nights when towns had their early closing day.

Many of the leading singers would congregate for that train. On the platform you would find Joan Cross, Isobel Baillie, Elsie Suddaby, Mary Jarred, Heddle Nash, Norman Walker and various others. The train would stop at Newport, then Cardiff, Bridgend, Swansea and so on along the line. Every time it stopped one or two singers would get off to travel on to different parts of the valleys, or to towns in west Wales, to keep their engagements.

I thought it an honour to be part of such a distinguished company. Some had many years of experience for their fifteen-guinea fee, out of which they paid their own expenses. (My fee, being a beginner, was usually five or eight guineas). More importantly, they knew how to behave as professional artists, and I gained a great deal of experience from working with them.

At Celebrity Concerts we really had to give our all, to sing our guts out in operatic arias, ballads and every sort of song, but so long as there were some good high notes everybody was delighted, not least in Wales. They expected you to sing perhaps ten or eleven times in the course of an evening, which would begin at 7 or 7.30 and often went on until 11 o'clock. It was a long session for any singer, but I soon learned how to pace myself.

One day I was up the Rhondda valley for a concert, making sure I was there about half an hour before the rehearsal at three o'clock. Along came one of the committee members and started looking through my music. I sensed a feeling of resentment, somehow. Then he pointed to my copy of the 'Toreador's Song' from *Carmen*: 'What key are you singing that in then, Mr Evans?' he asked.

'Why, the key it's written in there,' I answered, having chosen the lower key.

'Oh, that's not good enough,' said my host. 'We're paying you good money and we expect you to sing in the original key when you come to sing here.'

Piqued by this, I gathered my music together and, with a great show of bravado, walked out, saying: 'Well, you'd better get somebody else.'

Of course, it was pouring with rain. It was Sunday and the next bus out of the town was not for another hour or so. As I walked away I was saying to myself, 'Please God, let them ask me to come back.' I went into the local 'bracchi' (Italian café) shop, the only place open, to have a coffee and shelter from the rain while I waited, and happily another of the local committee members came to look for me and asked me to change my mind. I expect he thought he was being diplomatic when he said of his colleague: 'You don't want to take any notice of him. He's just being awkward because you weren't his choice, Mr Evans. We've had his nephew for a few years and we wanted a change.'

When I later mentioned this to his nephew, Roderick Jones (who was the finest Elijah I had ever heard), we both enjoyed the joke. At least I wasn't being held in comparison before I'd even started. Peter Pears once told me his greeting had been: 'I hope you're in good voice. We had Heddle Nash last year and he was marvellous.'

At one of these Celebrity Concerts in south-west Wales it was a cold, frosty day, and by three o'clock when we started the rehearsal the chapel still wasn't very warm. The Welsh tenor David Lloyd had been engaged with me, and we were told that we were expected to sing above the pulpit, standing wedged between two pews at the side of the pipe organ.

I rehearsed first. I couldn't even straighten my legs and did the whole rehearsal with my knees bent, too embarrassed to complain. Then came David's turn. He objected that he couldn't sing there. We would sing from the pulpit itself, or nowhere! I was still learning my trade so I let him battle it out. After much fuss and argument, he won his point, and beautifully he sang.

By the evening the chapel had warmed up well, and with six or seven hundred people present it was actually stiflingly hot. The concert went pretty well, neverthless, and afterwards we were given hospitality by the family with whom we were to stay the night. Hospitality was a ritual when you came for these concerts. Depending on when one arrived, it might involve lunch or high tea, and in winter there was often a fire burning in the parlour which was otherwise only used on high days and holidays. Everything was on a generous scale.

On this occasion there was a wonderful meal laid out for us after the concert, a table fit for a king, and a huge, open farmhouse fire in the hearth. Having perspired in the chapel, we perspired even more at the supper table, still wearing our tails, yet it would not have been thought seemly to take our jackets off. Underneath, we were soaking in perspiration.

The time came for us to be shown our bedroom, an attic room with three large beds, a nice room except that it was unheated and bitterly cold. We undressed as quickly as possible to get into bed, discarding our evening clothes on the spare bed.

We slept well and next morning had to be up around 5.30 to reach Swansea in time for the first train back to London. We didn't have much time, but when we came to pack our bags and fold our evening wear from the night before, do you think we could get it into our cases? It was all frozen solid. I shall never forget David cursing his boiled shirt, and trying to bend it with his foot, while I was hitting my jacket to make it fold.

Usually we sang with piano accompaniment, seldom with an orchestra, and sometimes with a church or chapel organ. I remember one church performance of Mendelssohn's *Elijah* when I felt I wasn't in good voice, the rehearsal had seemed such an effort. During the interval that evening my father came to the dressing-room with one or two singers from the choir. I said I was feeling a strain and my voice didn't seem in good form.

My father said: 'There's nothing wrong with your voice. Listen to this . . .'

And he struck the tuning-fork which, as a good chorus-master, he always carried in his pocket. The organ was a full tone sharp.

Another performance of *Elijah* in the north of England found me suffering from a touch of tonsilitis the day before. It afflicted me quite often in the early days and when I was about thirty-five, I had a tonsillectomy. Jon Vickers was another sufferer, and when he asked me about the operation and I replied, 'My God! It's the best thing that's happened to me', he decided to have it done too. Anyway, on that occasion I didn't cancel my *Elijah* engagement, because people are reluctant to believe you are ill unless you are visibly suffering from something like a broken leg. I travelled north and sang the rehearsal, still feeling it was touch-and-go whether I could make it through the performance. I spoke to the conductor and asked if he would cut 'Thou art gone up on high', which is hard enough to sing even in the best of voice. I would under normal circumstances have sung it, of course, but at the rehearsal it was as much as I could do to finish with 'It is enough'.

At first the conductor was adamant about not making any cuts, but when he heard the state I was in, I thought and, indeed, understood that he was agreeable to making the cut I suggested. Not a bit of it.

After I sang 'It is enough', he simply carried on, shouting over his shoulder as he did so: 'If anybody knows it, sing it! Or even whistle it!'

Heddle Nash and Jennifer Vyvyan were singing with me and were quite disgusted with his behaviour and I later had an embarrassed apology from the concert committee. Singers were always willing to help each other out in difficulty. Once, at a Celebrity Concert in the Rhondda Valley, I caught my finger in a swing door during the interval. Within minutes it had turned black and swollen and I was in agony. Amy Shuard and Gerald Davies were with me and instantly offered to fill in for my numbers in the second half, such was the *esprit de corps* between us.

Soon after the Royal Festival Hall in London opened for the Festival of Britain in 1951, I had my first engagement there in Mozart's *Requiem*. Other singers warned me that it wasn't an easy place for the voice, and the pianist Jimmy Gibb told me that pianists also found it difficult.

I soon found what they meant. I was singing into a void, so clear and clinical, but without any feeling of warmth and none of the vibrations and overtones I'd come to expect in other halls. Each time I sang there I tried to find a 'spot' where I could feel vocally at ease, but I never did. The orchestra might sound beautiful enough, even at fortissimo level, but I never experienced that shiver down the spine which I'd feel at great moments in the Royal Albert Hall.

At about this time David Webster asked if I would like to take up a small scholarship that was available for a young promising singer. I never knew who sponsored it, whether it was from an individual or some trust, but it was for £200 and it was to be used for the singer to study abroad.

Naturally I welcomed the chance but I had no idea how best to use the money. Joan Ingpen was my manager at the time and she made some enquiries: among those she asked was the conductor Erich Kleiber. He told her that Suzanne Danco, the French soprano who'd been singing Donna Elvira in *Don Giovanni* at Glyndebourne, had been working with Fernando Carpi in Geneva, and that the technique and quality of her voice had improved beyond recognition.

Carpi, however, was very choosy in his selection of new pupils. He was a contemporary of Caruso and specialised in the coloratura tenor roles: as there were so few individuals able to sing these roles, by the time Carpi was forty he'd made enough money to retire to Prague. Then came the war; he lost everything and only just managed to get away to Switzerland where he taught at the Conservatory in Geneva.

I turned for some help to Gwyn Morris, a friend who was working at that time for the BBC Overseas Services, and who spoke and wrote fluent Italian (he did many translations for singers, as well as helping to coach them in Italian pronunciation). Gwyn wrote to Carpi in my name and I had back a letter complimenting me on my beautiful and stylish Italian and accepting me as a pupil if I would come to Geneva.

Everything seemed set for me to go when it transpired that Sir Steuart Wilson, then David Webster's deputy general administrator at Covent Garden, had allocated the same scholarship to somebody else. There was embarrassment all round and confusion prevailed. Finally it was decided that, as I had no performances planned at Covent Garden during the summer of 1952, my salary could finance my trip to Geneva as a form of scholarship.

Brenda and I decided to go by car after Haydn Harrison, a civil servant who was a great friend from our schooldays together, suggested he would come along for a holiday and share the expenses. We set off early one morning and were well on our way to Dover before it was light.

It took us three days to get to Geneva. The car, an old 'banger', wouldn't go that fast, but it was fun. We had the address of a Madame Born who would give us lodgings and the three of us shared one large room in her small apartment with only one single bed between us. Brenda slept in a chair with a stool for her feet and Haydn made himself a bed on the sofa leaving the room whenever Brenda dressed or undressed.

She was wonderfully supportive about all this. Where some wives might well have packed up and gone home, Brenda insisted that by living in this decidedly awkward fashion I could afford to pay Carpi for three or four lessons a week, and this was the whole reason for being there. Once she mistakenly bought pastry instead of cooking fat – when she discovered this on her return she broke down and cried at the thought of the wasted money.

I had to put the equivalent of £2.50 in Swiss francs on Carpi's table before each lesson. That was quite a lot for a lesson at that time, especially as we were only allowed £35 each in foreign currency under the exchange regulations, in addition to the scholarship money. By almost starving ourselves we managed to stay abroad for about four months, moving to Salsomaggiore when Carpi went to his home there for the summer, so that I could have the maximum chance of working with him. At this point Haydn flew back to London, and Brenda and I drove on to Salsomaggiore where we found lodgings in a *pensione*. By this time our car was in need of some attention and I took it to a local garage. All I could see when I got there were the feet of the owner sticking out from under another car.

My Italian wasn't good in those days so, complete with phrase-book in one hand, I started to explain what I wanted done. The garage man slid out from under the car and said: 'Why not speak in English? I would understand you so much better.' He'd learned his excellent English as a prisoner-of-war at a town quite near our home in South Wales. His name was Lorenzo Orighi and, like the Ampollinis who owned the *pensione*, he and his family made our stay in Salsomaggiore a very happy one.

Carpi was a marvellous teacher and I learned as much from him as I had done earlier from Theo Hermann in Germany. His wife, Maria, was also a great help. She'd been a pupil of his and had a beautiful voice, but after their marriage – when she was in her thirties and Carpi was already in his seventies – he refused to let her sing though she continued to play the piano for his lessons at the Conservatory. I think she was pretty frustrated by this, so she was happy to give some extra lessons to me and to sing some duets. She too was a fine teacher and I learned no less from her than I did from Carpi. As he was very jealous, her lessons could only be given when her husband was out, usually at a game of *bòccia* (the Italian bowls), of which he was very fond. Brenda would keep watch and when she saw him coming back she would tap on the window where I'd be having a lesson with Maria. By the time he reached the farmhouse 'studio', the three of us would be walking around the corner towards him, as if we'd just arrived ourselves.

Carpi's other pupils had included Otakar Kraus (in the 1930s) and Jennifer Vyvyan, who was the only British entrant to take part in the international concours at Geneva while we were there. Brenda and I went along to the competition and almost damaged our voices, we shouted so much when she was awarded the *premier prix*!

We found ourselves warmly welcomed in Salsomaggiore, with a friendliness from the local people which we had never thought to expect. As soon as it was known that I was an operatic singer they took us to their hearts. Old men would gather round to listen to me exercising my voice in the basement of our *pensione*, no doubt making shrewd remarks about my future. The shopkeepers soon came to know us and everybody made us feel very much at home. When the time came for us to leave, our new friends wept quite openly and Brenda summed up our feelings when she said, 'If I had to live anywhere else, Salsomaggiore is where I'd like to be.'

CHAPTER THREE

The Glyndebourne Years

By 1950 the Glyndebourne Festival in Sussex, which had been started privately in 1934 by John Christie and his wife, the singer Audrey Mildmay, was beginning to settle again into a regular summer pattern after the uncertainties of the post-war period, and it was at this time that I had my first contact with it. A letter arrived from Moran Caplat, the general manager, asking if I would audition. I'd read about Glyndebourne, of course, to me the name had a magic ring to it, so I was excited at the possibility that I might be asked to sing there.

An audition was arranged for me at the Wigmore Hall in London, and I'd just decided what I should sing for it when, with a couple of days to go, I had a message from Mrs Christie. Would I sing some of the Harlequin role in the Richard Strauss opera *Ariadne auf Naxos*? Apparently there were plans for Sir Thomas Beecham to conduct it, and he would be coming to my audition because he'd not yet cast the various roles.

This took me aback. I was rather in awe of Sir Thomas, and I certainly wanted to sing well in front of him. *Ariadne* was an opera I'd never sung nor even seen and the Harlequin role was quite tricky to learn. Much of it is conversational, broken up into short phrases with little in the way of a continuous line except for one short melody, so I thought I'd better make the most of that. To learn even some of the part in two days meant a good deal of very hard work, but I did it.

I took care to be in good time for my audition at two-thirty, but by three o'clock there was still no sign of Sir Thomas. About ten minutes later, much to my relief, Moran Caplat suggested we should start anyway. I went to the platform to begin with 'Il lacerato spirito' from Verdi's *Simon Boccanegra*. I'd learned it to sing at the Proms and thought I'd been quite successful, and I felt it gave me an opportunity to show my range of voice.

At the end of the aria I would sing the alternative top note and then go down to a bottom G, but after I'd done so in the audition performance the unmistakable voice of Sir Thomas shouted from the back of the hall, 'What the hell does he think he is? A tenor or a bass?'

Such was my first encounter with Sir Thomas Beecham, who had arrived halfway through the aria and stood at the back until I finished. He was on form that day with sharp-tongued comments: 'Another Welshman. We'll have to take Glyndebourne down to Cardiff before long.' And after my efforts at the Harlequin part, which I read from the score and sang in German, all I heard was Sir Thomas loudly demanding to know what I was singing: '*Messiah* in Welsh?'

In spite of these and other rude remarks I carried on singing, but by the time I had finished I was totally shattered. I wasn't introduced to Sir Thomas then, and perhaps it was just as well. Mrs Christie apologised for him while John Christie helped me on with my coat, and she promised that I would be hearing from them.

Audrey Christie was as good as her word, and although I didn't sing with Sir Thomas until *Die Meistersinger* some time later, I did get a letter from Glyndebourne within a few days asking if I would take over from Erich Kunz as Guglielmo for the last three performances of Mozart's *Cosi fan tutte*. Would I? You bet I would!

The festival at Glyndebourne itself that year lasted less than three weeks (there were more performances at Edinburgh, where the *Ariadne* took place, than in Sussex), and I arrived there in the middle of it. My instructions were to rehearse in the Organ Room with John Pritchard, who was at that time assistant conductor and choir master. I don't suppose either of us realised what the future held for us, but John has become one of the finest conductors I've ever worked with, respected by orchestras and singers alike and now deservedly knighted.

We were rehearsing for some time and I was in the midst of Guglielmo's aria 'Donne mie' when a tall, white-haired man came in. 'I'm sure that's Fritz Busch,' I thought, and kept on singing as he went to the piano stool and edged John away. Gradually, without the slightest break in the music, his fingers took over from John's at the keyboard and he played to the end of my aria. Then he stood up, walked to the door and half opened it before he turned and said, 'Very good, Eee-vans.'

He had obviously come to hear the new boy, and for all I knew he might have been listening outside the door – it was a clever approach because he made it seem so casual that I was completely at ease. I discovered this was characteristic of Fritz Busch in performance too. He was known as the outstanding Mozart conductor of that time and most singers considered it a privilege to work with him. There was no fuss, no waving about of arms. He put across all he wanted in a simple and understated yet always precise way.

On one occasion he was rehearsing Fiordiligi's great rondo aria 'Per pietà, ben mio' with its prominent obbligato horn parts, and with the celebrated Dennis Brain playing first horn. It went well, but Busch asked the orchestra to play it again. Somewhat reluctantly, they did so, at which Busch said: 'Thank you, gentlemen', and with a glance at Dennis Brain he added, 'It was so good I just could not believe my ears the first time!'

To me, he offered some early advice: 'Mozart suits you. Concentrate on Mozart for a few years, because when you know how to sing Mozart you can sing most other composers.'

Just before my first performance at Glyndebourne he told me to enjoy it: 'What I want is a performance from there to there,' and he made a broad sweep with his arm to indicate a rounded performance, a long phrase from start to finish. Erich Kleiber said much the same to me when he conducted *The Marriage of Figaro* at Covent Garden: 'Forget the eighths and sixteenths, Eee-vans. I want an enjoyable performance from beginning to end.'

Così was already in performance when I first went to Glyndebourne and Mrs Christie arranged for me to see it from their box. The production was by Carl Ebert, and it had an elegance and a kind of balletic grace to it, as well as a splendid cast. Of course I concentrated on Kunz, because I had to fit into the role he had created then and I felt pretty apprehensive about taking over from such a fine and experienced artist (he'd sung in the Glyndebourne chorus before the war).

It worried me that at the start of his duet with Dorabella ('Il core vi dono') he sang slightly under the note. If this was happening to him, I thought, what price me? So I kept practising it to myself over and over again until my room-mate, the tenor Murray Dickie, who was singing Pedrillo in *Die Entführung aus dem Serail*, eventually screamed at me: 'If you sing that damned thing once more you'll drive me mad.' And for years afterwards he would greet me with that phrase whenever we met, while I in my turn would call out to him: 'Ding-dong! Time for tea.' This stemmed from an incident at his London home when friends were visiting for a performance of *The Marriage of Figaro* at Covent Garden in which Murray and I were singing. Going to call her husband from his bath, Anne Dickie saw him stooping over, as she thought, to retrieve something from the floor, still naked. Reaching one hand between his legs she called gaily, 'Ding-dong! Time for tea!' and went into their bedroom. There she was confronted by her husband dressing and realised what an embarrassing surprise their visitor must have had.

Così was a wonderful introduction to Glyndebourne for me. It brought my first meeting with Sena Jurinac, who was singing Fiordiligi and who became a treasured colleague over the years. I grew to love her, admiring her enthusiasm and dedication to all that she did as well as the beauty of her voice. Her sister in the opera, Dorabella, was Blanche Thebom from the Metropolitan, New York, another delightful singer to work with in the ensemble that was so important to this opera. Alda Noni sang Despina, the perky servant girl (as she also did Blonde in *Die Entführung*). She was a charmer in the role, but I'm also grateful to her and to her mother for helping me so much with my Italian diction. Her mother and I could often be seen sitting by the lake in the garden with the score between us, as if we were in deep conversation. The truth was that I, a Welshman, knew very little Italian then, and she knew no English, let alone Welsh, but her coaching in the Italian inflexions was very valuable to me.

My male colleagues were Mario Borriello, who made Don Alfonso the life and soul of the operatic comedy, and the tenor Richard Lewis as Ferrando. I first knew of Richard when I worked for the British Forces Network in Hamburg. I was presenting a programme of recordings which included Britten's 'Serenade for tenor, horn and strings' and had to choose between two available recordings, one with Peter Pears, the other with Richard Lewis. I preferred the latter, not knowing either singer at the time, and so became an admirer of Richard's vocal qualities even before I met him.

It seemed to me that singing at Glyndebourne with such a cast as this, and with Fritz Busch and Carl Ebert, was a major step forward in my career, and I was greatly encouraged to be asked to return the next year (1951) to sing Masetto in *Don Giovanni*. It was an opera that I'd wanted to perform in ever since I first saw the Vienna State Opera production which they brought to Covent Garden in 1947. Paul Schoeffler sang the title role then with Erich Kunz as Leporello, Josef Krips conducted, and I caught the last performance of the legendary Richard Tauber as Don Ottavio.

Now here I was with a role in the opera for myself, and whereas in *Così* I'd simply taken over a role in an existing production, this time I was creating a role from scratch. To build up a character in this way is something I've always enjoyed doing as much as performing it, and I count it a great experience to have worked in conjunction with two such artists as Ebert and Busch. They complemented each other to such an extent that they could produce the best musical and histrionic results from each of the operas they staged and performed.

My second year at Glyndebourne saw the development of my love and respect for the festival and all it represented, and this continued to grow for the next ten years. By this time Audrey Christie had become ill and would never recover before her death two years later, but although the artists no longer lodged in the house she still made it her responsibility to see that we were well-housed and looked after. We came from many different countries (always carefully specified in the programme-book cast lists), but Mrs Christie made us feel that we all belonged to a Glyndebourne 'family', writing us friendly letters even from her sickbed.

We not only worked and dined together, we also played tennis and table tennis or went shopping. Over the weeks we came to know each other so well that we were moulded into a responsive team, and this was nearly always reflected in our stage performances: throughout all the preparations for this opera or the next, we never counted the time we gave to such concentrated rehearsal. I count Carl Ebert as one of the greatest opera directors I ever worked with, while musically I learned just as much from Jani Strasser.

Jani was Hungarian-born, a singing teacher in Vienna with whom Audrey Mildmay had studied in 1932, and at the Christies' invitation he came to help the Glyndebourne project from the outset, remaining connected with it until his death in 1978. At the time I met him he was Glyndebourne's chief coach, later being named Head of Music Staff and, finally, Consultant on Interpretation. This last was what he'd really been all along, and he possessed a great talent for it.

I'm sure that anybody who worked with Jani Strasser at Glyndebourne would agree that to remember just one-third of what he taught you would still be of benefit for the rest of your career. He was the best possible person with whom to go through the score, and no detail was ignored. I fancy we sometimes thought this painstaking approach was a bit of a nuisance when we were trying to get a grip on a role and its music, but I knew full well that Jani was right to draw our attention to it.

I think I've worked with most of the famous Dons of our time in Mozart's opera except Ezio Pinza, but Mario Petri at Glyndebourne that year was exceptional. He was ideally suited for the role, both vocally and physically; he moved like a panther and he was a Don Giovanni both on and off stage. Never have I seen so many people, especially the chorus ladies, clustering in the wings to hear someone sing. They hung on his words even in the recitatives, and when he sang his serenade they almost swooned, such was his magnetic personality. It's sad that his career was so short.

The production was designed by John Piper, who was not only a great artist but a skilled technician in relation to the theatre. Other designers have seemed to me to take much less account of the demands of the singers, particularly the women who are frequently expected to climb steps up scaffolded structures in heavy period costumes, and then to phrase beautifully when they start to sing, always supposing they have reached the relevant place at the right time.

The Piper sets involved no such problems, although the performances that year were not without unfortunate incidents. The first was when Fritz Busch suddenly became ill during a performance and a call was put out for John Pritchard, as assistant conductor, for the second act. He was in Eastbourne and managed to arrive just in time towards the end of the hour-long dinner interval. For Busch, alas, it was a warning signal and he died in London a few weeks later. I count myself fortunate indeed that I had the chance of working with him even for so short a time.

The second incident occurred when the Glyndebourne production was taken to the Edinburgh Festival in August. This involved Genevieve Warner, the American soprano who sang Zerlina. She was 'mugged' one night (many years before that word became so sickeningly familiar) on her way back to her hotel. Her attacker tried to strangle her in order to steal her handbag, and she had to spend some time in hospital. Although the injuries healed and she returned to Glyndebourne four years later to sing Zerlina again, her beautiful silvery voice was never quite the same.

By then I was cast for Leporello at Glyndebourne instead of Masetto. It was a role I'd sung only about half a dozen times, in English at Sadler's Wells a couple of years previously. I was able to learn a role very quickly, but unless I went on to rehearse it right away, I was apt to forget it again just as quickly. This happened originally with Leporello at Sadler's Wells. After about four weeks of other work before rehearsals began, I found I couldn't remember a note of what I'd previously learned and had to spend another three or four days relearning it. Then it was fine.

This was the only time my commitments allowed me to sing at Sadler's Wells, and I chiefly remember being impressed by the sound of the male chorus there. That was not so surprising in retrospect as it then included such voices as David Ward, Peter Glossop and Harold Blackburn, all of whom were to become outstanding principals.

The producer at Glyndebourne when I sang my first Leporello there was Peter Ebert, who no doubt felt overshadowed by the reputation of his famous father, the redoubtable Carl (whom we called 'the Prof'). Peter's task was not made easier by Giuseppe Valdengo, who was singing the Don. Valdengo knew the role backwards and was by no means inclined to spend much time rehearsing it, making repeated excuses for not turning up. Indeed, there were some aspects of the production, including the moment off stage when he and I had to exchange our cloaks in about 30 seconds, which were never rehearsed at all before the actual performance. Fortunately we just made it without tangling them up.

Glyndebourne's stage director was Douglas Craig, a former singer who later became administrator of the Welsh National Opera and then director of Sadler's Wells Theatre. Having been a performer he knew what Valdengo was up to and reprimanded him in no uncertain manner. Annoyed at this, Valdengo haughtily demanded of Douglas: 'You are Commendatore, eh?' An equally irate Douglas replied: 'Si! I am Commendatore.' He was surprised at the effect this had on Valdengo, and it was not until he was told how impressed the Italian had been at his 'title' that we in turn appreciated the results of this little misunderstanding. Not long after this Douglas was apointed CBE and so became a genuine Commendatore after all.

All of us were glad that Peter Ebert had a success with this production (he even managed to reduce the number of scene changes). I also thought I achieved some measure of success as Leporello, judging from the audience's response and the greeting I had from Ebert senior after the performance. He came backstage and put his arms round me, kissing me in a very Germanic way. I think I felt then that he'd really accepted me because, after all, I'd been engaged in the first place by Audrey Christie and not by him.

Brenda and I were staying at the time at the White Hart Hotel in Lewes, and I felt so elated I couldn't sleep. All I had to read was the hotel Bible, so the morning seemed a long time coming. As soon as it seemed discreetly possible I slipped out to buy some papers to see what they said about my performance. I looked at one after the other, but there was hardly a mention of my name. It didn't help my ego, but it taught me never to read critics the morning after, whether or not I thought I'd been successful.

Peter Ebert's Glyndebourne debut had been the year before, in the first-ever double-bill at Glyndebourne, when the *Ariadne auf Naxos* of Richard Strauss was preceded by the first stage production in Britain of Busoni's one-act *Arlecchino*: the latter was, indeed, the first Glyndebourne opera *not* staged by Peter Ebert's father. It's a *commedia dell'arte* story of Harlequin, Columbine and others, but there's so much dialogue that I'm sure only a small proportion of the audience could properly follow our German-language production, and had it been given in English I believe it would have been more popular.

The outstanding success in it was Ian Wallace in his sympathetically comic characterisation of the central role, Ser Matteo. My role was that of Abbate Cospicuo, which I much enjoyed except for the annoying headdress I was supposed to wear. This was a large, round felt hat over a white cloth wrapped closely round my head which enclosed both ears. The designer evidently had no idea that this would inhibit a singer's sense of his own vocal resonance and I had to cut holes in the cloth around my ears before I felt able to sing properly.

There were no such problems in *Ariadne*, which had a different designer in Oliver Messel. Although I had only a minor role as the Music Master in the Prologue, it was important and Carl Ebert directed me with his usual thoroughness. So much so, indeed, that after the dress rehearsal he said to me: 'Very good, Geraint. But now be Geraint Evans, not Carl Ebert.' The deepest impression left with me of this performance was of Sena Jurinac's eloquent and moving portrayal of the unnamed Composer whose teacher I was supposed to be.

With the first post-war production of *The Magic Flute* at Glyndebourne in 1956, the Mozart bicentenary year, I was able to add Papageno to my other Mozart roles there and found myself having to save a potential disaster on the first night. The serpent which threatens Tamino in the first scene became entangled in the scenery and did not fall to the ground when it was killed. Carl Ebert and the designer, Oliver Messel, rushed backstage, the former stamping his feet in rage, the latter almost in tears. Waiting in the wings for my entry, I had an idea. I went on and stood with one arm draped around the creature as if it were a branch. At the point where Tamino asks if it was I who killed the serpent, I gave it a sharp jerk, praying it wouldn't bring down the whole tree as well. Luck was with me. The serpent fell to the stage and I was able to leap back as if in fright at seeing it. From then on the performance went so smoothly that the beautiful new Pamina, Pilar Lorengar, could even be forgiven her atrocious German for the loveliness of her singing and her smile.

At around this time I felt that things had come pretty much to a standstill for me at Covent Garden, so I was more than delighted to have a message from Moran Caplat asking if I would sing the role of Ford in Verdi's *Falstaff*, which Glyndebourne was planning to produce for the first time in 1955 with Carlo Maria Giulini conducting. Naturally I accepted and looked forward to the prospect of working with Giulini.

To prepare myself I asked Emanuel Young if he would work with me on the part. Manya had been involved with the New London Opera Company at the Cambridge Theatre in the years just after the war and had worked with Carl Ebert, the conductor Alberto Erede and the great Falstaff of the day, Mario Stabile, when they produced Verdi's opera there. I thought Manya an ideal person for me to work with because he knew the opera and all the traditions connected with it so well. So we began on the Ford role.

I'd already learned Ford's great 'Jealousy monologue' from the second act to sing at concerts and found it marvellously well suited to me, but after a while I realised there was something wrong in relation to the part as a whole. In some parts of the music I was nervous of the high tessitura for my voice, and I couldn't be convinced that it was right for me, something I needed to feel with any new part. As with Billy Budd at Covent Garden a few years earlier I knew I'd be letting a major opportunity go by, but at the same time I didn't want to spoil my progress at Glyndebourne. It takes courage to say 'No', but eventually I rang Moran and said I thought I shouldn't take on the Ford role because I wasn't yet ready for it.

It was a difficult decision to make and I hoped I wouldn't regret it. As it turned out, I did the right thing, because a year or so later I was offered the Falstaff role for 1957, when the opera was to be revived. This was beyond all my expectations. I'd got to know some of Falstaff's music when I was studying Ford and had sensed a taste for it then, but to be asked to sing it was something else again.

So back I went to Manya Young and we went through the part together. This time we were both confident that it was right for me. When I started to learn any role I didn't think too much about the character at first. I concentrated on the music, and as I began to memorise that I'd try to let it tell me something about the part, to explain what the composer wanted. Then I'd start to build the character. In this case I read through anything to do with Falstaff in Shakespeare's plays and anything else I could find about him; I studied prints, discussed the part with one or two Shakespearean actors, and absorbed all the information I could, letting it fill out the music. By the time I started the Glyndebourne rehearsals I already had a good foundation for the role.

It was still Carl Ebert's production, but this time Vittorio Gui was the conductor, and what a splendid theatre craftsman he was. I could feel him breathing the part with me and phrasing it accordingly.

With his expertise and encouragement, and 'the Prof' to direct me, I cannot imagine a better chance to make a success of a first Falstaff, but little did I realise what it would come to mean for me in the following years.

As the rehearsals continued and I was steadily developing the character, the enthusiasm around me was tremendous. Not only did Jani Strasser give me all the help he could in his thorough way, but singers in the chorus who'd been students with me at the Guildhall School would show their encouragement, and friends in the orchestra like Frederick Riddle, the first viola, Jack Brymer and Gwydion Brooke, the clarinet and bassoon principals, seemed as thrilled as I was, willing me to make it a success. It would have been a disaster if I hadn't, with all that I had going for me.

That period was one of the greatest times of my life, and I shall certainly never again experience anything like the excitement of my Falstaff first night. It was an unusually hot June evening, so warm that side doors were opened in the theatre, the orchestra players shed their jackets and John Christie went on stage to give permission for the men in the audience to do the same. In my Falstaff costume, with its superb Osbert Lancaster design, I was wearing kapok padding, and this got so wet with perspiration that it twisted round and became a kind of tourniquet on one leg, which went quite numb by the end of the opera. The tension of the performance was such that I was unaware of what was happening, but it was just as well the opera did not go on any longer as by the time I was back in the dressing room and peeling off the layers, my leg was beginning to turn a very nasty colour.

I was immersed in the performance, of course, but I did become aware of the audience starting to applaud before the end of the first scene, when Falstaff rounds on Bardolph and Pistol after his monologue on honour among rascals. Later on, when I sang Falstaff elsewhere in Europe and America, it became a kind of barometer for me whether or not I heard applause at this point, and whenever I did I took it as a good omen for the rest of the performance.

My reception at Glyndebourne after that first Falstaff was something I shall never forget, the sort of thing every performer dreams of getting perhaps once in a career. At the curtain-calls even the other principals were applauding: Orietta Moscussi, Oralia Dominguez and Fernanda Cadoni among the ladies; and Juan Oncina, Antonio Boyer, John Lewis and Hervey Alan, whose Bardolph and Pistol were excellent foils for me. The chorus members were applauding too, and even the orchestra stood to join in, the string players tapping their music stands with their bows in the traditional way.

Gui was extremely complimentary to me. 'Eee-vans, you're a great Falstaff,' he declared after the performance. That worried me somewhat. At that stage I only wanted to be thought a good, reliable artist. Now I realised I not only had to live up to what was being said about me, but that I also had to improve on it as well. To work at that was the next challenge.

Falstaff was included in the next summer's festival repertory, but before that the Glyndebourne company came together for a Maytime visit to Paris as part of the Théâtre des Nations festival there, the first time the Glyndebourne name had been taken abroad. *Falstaff* and *Le Comte Ory* were each to have four performances at the delightful Théâtre Sarah Bernhardt, whose one-time dressing-room became mine for the *Falstaff* evenings. I don't think I've ever been surrounded by quite so many mirrors as I was there, but I did feel impressed by the tradition they represented.

Rossini's opera, an engaging comedy with a French libretto, first performed in Paris but virtually unknown there, launched our visit. I thought it a splendid production, but the preview audience and the French reviews were unenthusiastic. Moran Caplat seemed disappointed and when it was the turn of *Falstaff* he came round asking us to pull out all the stops. And indeed we did. The result was another ecstatic reception, beginning after the first scene, only in Paris some people even climbed on to their seats to stand and applaud. Even the French critics enthused about it, principally the teamwork and the sense of ensemble which was then Glyndebourne's hallmark. The Paris performances brought Ilva Ligabue into the cast to sing Alice Ford, and a great Alice she was. She came on Jurinac's recommendation, with Graziella Sciutti as Nanetta and Mario Borriello as Ford.

Right after the performance I telephoned home to Brenda. She asked how things had gone and I answered, 'Not bad at all.'

'Not bad?' she almost shouted. 'It was terrific! I thought they would never stop applauding.'

'How do you know?,' I asked, astonished.

'I heard it on the radio,' she said. 'Gwyn Morris picked up a broadcast from Paris and called me after the first scene, thrilled by the performance and the audience's response. He told me the wavelength and said they were still applauding. He was right. They were still doing so even when I found the station, so of course I listened to the rest of it.'

In Paris we were all amazed to hear this. None of the company, including the management, knew that the performance was being broadcast as well and I still don't know if that made any difference to the contractual arrangements. I remember the occasion as second only to the Glyndebourne first night, and was stimulated by the fact that we had a wonderful cast already together when we returned home for the regular festival a week or two later.

With Glyndebourne's great Mozart tradition I was eager to sing Figaro there, but when I broached this to Moran Caplat he explained that as I was singing it so often at Covent Garden, there wasn't much point in getting me to sing it at Glyndebourne. If I had a break in my Covent Garden performances, he promised to think about it again, and it transpired that I was asked to sing Figaro in the 1958 revival at Glyndebourne. That was the first time I sang it in Italian, with Graziella Sciutti as Susanna, Teresa Berganza and Josephine Veasey sharing Cherubino, and Michel Roux as Count Almaviva.

Roux had begun his career in the French music-hall before turning to opera, and under his elegant surface the tradition still lingered. When, in the second act of *Figaro*, the Count hands me the letter I am supposed to have written to fix his assignation with Susanna, I never knew from one performance to the next what message, often rude or suggestive, he would have written on the paper, though these were always mild by comparison with some of the messages that appear today. Of course, you learn to expect this whenever a sheet of paper is handed about on stage, but it's often difficult to control one's reaction in full view of the audience.

Berganza was a newcomer to British audiences that year and she became a favourite with them as well as a marvellous colleague. At the interval she felt disappointed by the reception from the audience. Behind the curtain, Roux pointed out to the auditorium, pinched his nose with two fingers and with the other hand made the gesture of pulling a chain. Teresa hadn't encountered this before and had to have it explained to her. She was hugely amused and, full of mischief as she was, it wasn't long before she was using it herself.

Came the last act when she and other members of the cast stood with their backs to the audience looking to the Count as he begs his wife's forgiveness with the beautiful phrase, 'Contessa, perdono...'. At this moment Teresa caught his eye and jokingly made the gesture she'd learned, discreetly hidden from public view, of course, as if she didn't think much of Roux's singing. Poor man, he was so taken aback that what should be a lovely legato phrase came spluttering out like 'per–her–do–ho–ho–no'.

The joke was made still richer when Hans Schmidt-Isserstedt, who was conducting, came up to Roux after the performance and anxiously enquired: 'Were you running out of breath there? Shall I take it a little quicker for you?'

Another time I was singing Figaro's last-act aria, 'Aprite un po' quegl'occhi', when I happened to turn to the wings and caught sight of Teresa standing there sucking a lemon. The saliva pumped into my mouth and it was all I could do not to choke.

I also recall a Covent Garden rehearsal at which she wore breeches to get used to being Cherubino again while the rest of us were in rehearsal clothes. The breeches were a snug fit on a trim figure and she realised that the eyes of the men around her, including those of Georg Solti and myself, were following her about the stage. After some whispered plotting with colleagues, Teresa made her next entry with apples strategically placed in the breeches, causing Solti to collapse helplessly and the rehearsal to disintegrate, while the orchestra stood up the better to see what on earth had happened.

I hope I don't give the impression that we were always fooling around on the stage. Nothing we did interfered with the standard of performance as a whole, but it did reflect our own enjoyment of our work and this in turn can be communicated across the footlights to the audience. Especially when, at Glyndebourne, by the time they come back for the second part of the opera, they have spent the long interval wining and dining and are seemingly far more receptive and appreciative of what takes place on the stage.

It was a special joy to work with Graziella Sciutti in *Figaro*. Her singing was captivating and she moved beautifully; with her marvellous stage sense she seemed always to be in the right place at the right time, and she was a naturally easy person to work with. Our partnership as Susanna and Figaro was repeated in several famous opera houses after we first performed it at Glyndebourne, and it was one of the smoothest and most enjoyable associations in my stage career.

I'm not sure that Alun, my elder son, was so fond of her then. He was about three and a half and watching a rehearsal of *Figaro* one day when we reached the part where Susanna slaps Figaro's face. At this Alun, I learned after, became most indignant, and when he later saw Jani Strasser, who always made a fuss of him, he forthwith demanded: 'Why did you let that lady smack my Daddy's face?'

Jani tried to explain that it was all part of the opera and that I really wasn't hurt, but Alun wasn't to be consoled. 'Why don't you smack her bottom and send her home?' he asked angrily, and it took Moran's assistant, Janet Moores, a while to console him; he was very fond of 'that pretty lady', as he called her.

The following year Graziella was only able to sing Despina in *Cosi fan tutte*, for which I was again engaged as Guglielmo, and when we came to *Figaro* late in the season, Susanna's role was taken by Elisabeth Söderström from Sweden. She had the unusual distinction of doubling this decidedly soprano part with the mezzo role of Oktavian in *Der Rosenkavalier*, which Glyndebourne had staged for the first time: a silver rose for the festival's silver jubilee. There was still more rejoicing when it was known that she had been decorated by the King of Sweden at much the same time as I was appointed CBE in the Queen's birthday honours.

All the hundreds of letters and telegrams I'd had about the CBE award were in the flat I'd rented in Hove. One day, when Brenda was away, in London but on the point of returning, I thought I'd surprise her by tidying the flat, so I put the messages on one side and decided to burn the envelopes. I started a small fire in the grate without knowing that some previous occupant had wadded paper in the chimney, to stop draughts, I suppose.

The fire started to draw and I turned away, only to hear something fall behind me. I swung back to the fireplace and saw two smouldering lumps of crumpled, browned newspaper on the carpet. Grabbing one of these I threw it on the fire, but as I picked up the second ball of newspaper it exploded in my hands.

My first reaction was shock and then a searing pain in my hands, and when I looked at them and saw patches of flesh like raw meat I realised they were badly burned. I knew I should get emergency treatent and somehow I managed to telephone Glyndebourne, dialling with a pencil held between my teeth. The secretary, Helen O'Neill, and Martin Isepp, the répétiteur, promised to come right away.

This they did, but by the time they arrived I could no longer use my hands because of the pain and I had to turn the lock on the door of the flat with my teeth to let them in. They were kindness itself in helping me to dress and then taking me to the West Sussex Hospital, where I had to remain for about three weeks before the burns healed sufficiently for me to leave hospital.

It meant, of course, that I had to miss the first half-dozen or so Figaro performances and, as soon as this was known, two of my fellow-baritones that year, Sesto Bruscantini and the Argentinian, Carlos Feller, offered to sing my performances in my place provided that the fee was still paid to *me*. When I heard of this I was deeply touched by such generosity, though I couldn't accept it. I mention it here only to show the feelings of comradeship which were paramount among the artists at Glyndebourne at that time, and which made the Glyndebourne Company such a special ensemble on and off stage.

There were other tokens of friendship which also moved me very much. Harry Secombe and Harry Worth, who were appearing in a theatre show at Brighton, came to visit me in hospital and cheered up everybody else no end, nurses as well as patients. When they happened to coincide with Glyndebourne friends, especially the exuberant Italians, pandemonium broke loose in the hospital, and I do believe this helped the patients more than any medicine.

Eventually I was well enough to sing the last few performances of *Figaro* that season, and after the first of these another surprise awaited me. Having missed the customary first-night party when all the cast and music staff have supper together in the Glyndebourne dining-hall, often singing impromptu folksongs from the countries they represent, I little knew that a special celebration had been arranged to welcome me back.

It was Harry Secombe's doing. He organised a dinner at the White Hart in Lewes, contacted the Glyndebourne management and arranged that there were an equal number of guests from the festival and from his own show in Brighton. Of course we sang. We sang far into the night, I seem to remember, and I think the other guests at the hotel must have realised how lucky they were, because next morning we were told there hadn't been a single complaint.

That was a truly joyful occasion. Everybody contributed something. Harry agreed to sing as well if I would join with him. We sang a duet from *La Bohème* and, having been told that he was a variety artist, the Glyndebourne guests were quite astounded at the quality of his voice. Michel Roux thought he should sing opera seriously, but Harry demurred. 'I love singing arias,' he said, 'but I'm known as a comedian and, even if I did try to sing straight, people would still interpret what I did as being funny. It just wouldn't work.'

Roux disagreed heartily and told him and the rest of us about his own beginnings in music-hall. The repartee that went on between them after that was another sort of entertainment. Some years later, when I produced *Falstaff* for the Welsh National Opera at Cardiff, I tried hard to persuade Harry to sing Bardolph. I'm sure it would have suited him well, but he still either couldn't or wouldn't bring himself to attempt it. A pity.

We always looked forward to the orchestra's end-of-season party at Glyndebourne, which gave us a chance to relax after the hard work we had put in during the festival. All the staff took part as well, and it was a regular occasion for good cheer and plenty of party turns, such as Ryland Davies wonderfully mimicking John Pritchard, and Harry Kellard, the best property-master in the business, readily dressing for the occasion in full drag, which he did most beautifully.

Another sequel to what might have been a very serious accident to my hands concerned a gold ring of my mother's which my grandmother had given to me when I was fourteen. At first I was embarrassed to be seen wearing it, and took it off when my grandmother wasn't around. Gradually I became more used to it, however, and in time I even felt I couldn't sing unless I was wearing it. When my hands were burned, the ring had to be cut off.

Just at this time the people of Cilfynydd were planning a celebration to mark the fact that a boy from the village had received the CBE. After hearing the news of my accident on the radio, word also reached them about the loss of my ring. I knew nothing of this at the time, of course, but it was decided they would give me a new ring. They collected from house to house to pay for it, and then organised a splendid concert at the chapel to present it to me.

I was told later that even with tickets limited to two per household there was no room to spare that night. Joan Carlyle, Edgar Evans and Michael Langdon all took the trouble to come from Covent Garden, for which I was deeply grateful. I was also grateful to Norman Kay who was accompanist, and not least to my Aunt Avarina, who sang as well as any of us. They still talk about it at home as a night to remember, and the diamond-set ring they gave me I have to this day.

After this I spent two more happy seasons at Glyndebourne, as Falstaff, Leporello and Papageno, and I was under contract to them for the 1962 festival when an invitation came for me to sing Figaro at the Salzburg Festival, an event that was a peak of achievement for any Mozart singer. This created a terrible dilemma for me because I regarded it as a point of honour never to break contracts, even though this meant I sometimes had to refuse engagements which I'd have loved to have taken up.

Over the past few years Glyndebourne had shown more confidence in me and had given me more chances than Covent Garden had done, and I shall always appreciate those opportunities and the experience they represented. It had been a tremendously valuable period for me as well as enjoyable in every respect, but after ten years I felt it was time for me to expand a little when the opportunity occurred. And what better opportunity than Salzburg?

Accordingly, I went to talk it over with Moran Caplat, who was delighted that a singer Glyndebourne had nurtured should now be invited to Salzburg. It was a wonderful chance for a British singer, he told me, and without any hesitation he released me from my contract. I've had cause to be grateful to him many times over this, and I sometimes wonder how my career might have developed if Moran had not been so understanding about the Salzburg invitation, and pretty well as excited about it as I was.

He was one of the best administrators that I've ever worked for, not least because he understood singers and their problems and was sympathetic to their temperament. In moments of tension he was a calming influence, and he encouraged me greatly in those times of depression that every singer suffers. I owe him much, as I also do John and Audrey Christie themselves.

Having been a singer, Mrs Christie also understood everything that affected us, and I thought her a wonderful person. She wasn't at all demonstrative, but she liked to look upon us as an operatic family and she always made a point of welcoming newcomers. Her usual method was to invite us to sherry in the house before lunch, or before dinner according to how the rehearsals were going, and the first time I was asked to one of these gatherings she made me feel welcome at once, slipping her arm under mine and saying, 'It's nice to have you here. Enjoy yourself.'

As for John Christie, he was one of the great English eccentrics. How could he be otherwise when he built an opera house in the Sussex downs, fifty miles from London, assembled the finest international talent to perform in it, and expected the public not only to respond at higher than metropolitan ticket prices, but to put on evening dress in the middle of the afternoon to do so? Yet he made Glyndebourne a name respected throughout the operatic world and laid the foundation of an opera festival in Britain which has greatly helped the development of the art and its wider enjoyment.

Mr Christie often suggested that I took a walk around the gardens with him, those gardens which were a particular source of pride and joy to the extent that the head gardener was named with the other festival staff in the programme-book. Like the Walrus and the Carpenter, we talked of many things, Mr Christie and I, not cabbages and kings particularly, but plenty of other topics, from miners to the Arts Council. I recall a miners' strike on one occasion provoking a heated argument, with my background in a mining area naturally putting my sympathies on their side. Another time it would be the iniquities of the Arts Council, as he saw them, in giving a large grant to Covent Garden and nothing at all to Glyndebourne. Although I felt he had a valid argument, I staunchly defended Covent Garden as the national opera house. Since then, although the summer festival at Glyndebourne is still financed by private subscription and support from commerce, not public money, some Arts

Council support now goes to the Glyndebourne touring company. This takes the festival productions to other parts of the country, giving understudies from the festival and younger singers, many of whom have excellent voices, the chance to sing leading roles. George Christie, John's son, put this idea to the Arts Council, who were at first reluctant to respond. I then spoke strongly in support, believing it was a good policy, and I should like to think that the case I made helped to ensure that the Council gave its support.

Having spent his own personal wealth on Glyndebourne in the first place, and now being dependent on private and business subscribers, Mr Christie was always very conscious of the need to monitor expenses carefully, provided it didn't affect the standard of performances. He could often be seen making the rounds of the theatre and other buildings when the performance was over and everybody had left, checking the lights and switching off any he thought were unnecessary.

I caught up with him once as he was doing this in the organ-room, and walked along with him as he snapped off the lights in the gents' toilet, and then did the same in the ladies' without thinking twice. One occupant, however, still remained. Furiously she emerged into the corridor and accosted me: 'Who was that man? How dare he come into the ladies' room!'

By this time John Christie, oblivious of the fuss, was already on his way into the courtyard, and I had to pacify the aggrieved woman. 'I'm sure he'd no idea you were there, Madam,' I said. 'I know he didn't see you because he only has one eye and he doesn't see awfully well with that. Anyway, Madam, *that* was Mr Christie!'

For all these and other eccentricities, I admired him. More than that, I was very fond of him, and in the early 1960s I was sad to hear a number of comments from a variety of people that standards at Glyndebourne weren't as high as they had been. Some business sponsors were seriously considering whether they would continue to support the festival although, as I pointed out, some fluctuation was as inevitable as it is in a commercial organisation.

Still, it depressed me to hear these reports and I talked about them in Salzburg and elsewhere to friends and colleagues who'd enjoyed appearing at Glyndebourne as much as I had, and who'd had their own personal successes there: artists like Sena Jurinac and Mirella Freni, Luigi Alva and Sesto Bruscantini. I even had their agreement that we'd take a reduced fee to sing at Glyndebourne again, provided the engagements weren't too protracted. Over the years we'd all developed our reputations through appearances at Glyndebourne, and built up a following among members of the public. We felt that, if we could now give something back, it would be a privilege and a pleasure to do so. I put this offer to Glyndebourne myself, and also proposed Donizetti's *Don Pasquale*, which I knew hadn't been staged there since 1938 when Audrey Christie sang Norina. I never heard a word from Glyndebourne about any of this, nor about any further engagement there when I delayed accepting another Salzburg invitation because I felt I owed Glyndebourne a prior allegiance if they wanted me. Hearing nothing, I signed a Salzburg contract and continued to appear there for the next ten years.

During this time I realised that something had gone wrong in my relationship with Glyndebourne, but there was nothing I could attribute this to until, one day, a letter reached me from one of the trustees there concerning an award I'd received. The writer thought it would be churlish not to congratulate me, but at the same time called me 'a very naughty boy' for not having acknowledged publicly the debt I owed to Glyndebourne for the chances the festival had given me.

I felt sad to read this, because not only was it true that I owed much of my international career to Glyndebourne, but I had in fact acknowledged this many, many times in interviews with the Press, and on radio and television. Alas, an interviewee has no control over the way the results are edited, and it is a simple fact that practically every time I spoke about Glyndebourne, the reference had disappeared by the time my remarks were printed or broadcast. People often say they were 'misquoted'. Not me, I'm just sorry that I wasn't quoted more.

This state of affairs even soured my friendship with Carl Ebert when we were both guests at a music society lunch in Los Angeles, when I was performing there with the San Francisco Opera. Delighted to see 'the Prof' and his wife, I went to greet them. He ignored me completely; she was obviously embarrassed, and I was terribly upset.

Back at my table was a good friend, the Swedish mezzo Kerstin Meyer. She realised I was puzzled and concerned, and I told her what had transpired. She promised to ask Mrs Ebert discreetly the reason for her husband's behaviour, and later told me that the Prof had read an interview with me in *The Times* which had included his name with those of other opera directors I'd worked with and admired, such as Peter Brook, Tyrone Guthrie, Günther Rennert and Franco Zeffirelli, but without mentioning in particular all that he'd done for me at Glyndebourne.

I not only remember lines, I also remember interviews, and I knew without doubt that I'd once more gone out of my way in this interview to say what I owed to Carl Ebert, and to acknowledge his hard work with me, especially on the role of Falstaff. Yet here again my remarks had been truncated, and a distinguished artist was hurt not by what was said, but by what was *not* said. I sometimes wonder why this isn't taken into consideration more seriously by those responsible, who can cause more mischief in this way than they ever know.

On this occasion I was at least able to explain what had happened to Mrs Ebert, who assured me that her husband would understand, and I was glad indeed to have a kindly letter from him sometime later. It helped to make up for the sadness I felt that my name had apparently been under a shadow at Glyndebourne, where I'd enjoyed some of my greatest successes.

CHAPTER FOUR

Stresses and Strains

For a few years during the mid-1950s, although I began to spread my wings at Glyndebourne, I felt I wasn't making much forward progress at Covent Garden. I was given some new roles, but they were either in existing productions being revived, or else not of any great consequence. The latter included Rimsky-Korsakov's pantomime fantasy, *Le Coq d'or*, which Igor Markevitch conducted and Robert Helpmann directed. I enjoyed working with Helpmann because, like Frederick Ashton, he was an experienced ballet dancer and understood the histrionics of style and the technique of presentation on the stage.

Mattiwilda Dobbs was the seductive Queen of Shemakhan and Howell Glynne the doddering King Dodon. John Lanigan and I played the stupid sons of Dodon who squabbled like children and ended up killing each other by mistake. Only one very painful occasion lingers in my memory. During a scene with the King and his councillors, John and I sat on pedestals on either side of him. I plonked myself down, and nearly shouted aloud in pain. Sliding a hand cautiously under my posterior, my fingers found carpet tacks and blood, and I realised that there were more tacks still sticking into me.

They had apparently been left there after the painted stagecloth was tacked down and nobody, including me, saw them in time. The pain soon worsened, and as I was playing the part of a not very intelligent Prince, I thought it wouldn't be too much out of character if I got up and wandered offstage in the middle of the scene. So I did, and as soon as I was out of the audience's sight I took myself at some speed to the props room. The rest of the tacks were removed amid laughs and rude remarks in plenty at my expense from the props men, but the relief at being rid of them was great.

Another new role I created at Covent Garden was Antenor in Sir William Walton's *Troilus and Cressida* in 1954. Richard Lewis and Magda Laszlo took the title roles, with Peter Pears and Otakar Kraus in support. There was always an element of excitement attached to anything new, but my own role was quite short, five or ten minutes on stage, so I didn't feel greatly involved with the production. Sir Malcolm Sargent conducted: it was his only appearance at Covent Garden in the post-war years and I can't honestly say I thought he made the most of it. He had a reputation for skilful sight-reading, but he still had problems with the opera (including giving me a cue a bar too soon on one occasion), and the composer was often called on to help in rehearsals.

Sir John Barbirolli was a more frequent guest at this time, and after I sang Schaunard when he conducted *La Bohème*, he encouraged me to work on some of the more important Verdi and Puccini baritone roles, those in the medium range of voice. The first I sang under him was Amonasro in *Aida*. Paolo Silveri and Jess Walters had both sung the role the same season, and although I knew their voices were bigger than mine, I felt I could make myself equal to them.

Amy Shuard, a much-admired colleague at many concerts we gave together, as well as in opera, was the Aida then, and one passage I found thrilling to sing was our scene in Act 3, when Amonasro exhorts his daughter to discover Radames' military intentions. There was a phrase that I felt could and should be sung in one breath, at the line 'Pensa che un popolo vinto, strazziato', and Barbirolli encouraged me to try: 'It would be wonderful if you can,' he said. I had a go, and it worked. Of course, it was only a small detail in the whole, but achieving it made me feel good and perhaps helped the rest of my performance. For a time I also used it during the course of my warming-up exercises, as a yardstick to gauge what shape my voice and breath control were in that day.

Sharpless, the American Consul in Puccini's *Madam Butterfly*, was also a test for me, but a test of emotional involvement rather than vocal technique. I never cared much for the opera when I listened to it as a member of the audience. I thought it sickly and sentimental, but taking part was another matter. Then the opera became one of the most moving experiences I've had on the stage, and especially when Victoria de los Angeles sang the title role.

The test for me came in the scene in Act 2 where Sharpless tries to read, to Butterfly, Pinkerton's letter telling of his marriage to an American wife who is now coming with him on his return to Japan. Butterfly is so overjoyed at the thought of seeing Pinkerton again that she simply doesn't hear anything else. Sharpless, I believe, should read the letter in a cold, detached way, without showing any emotion. Victoria achieved such heart-rending pathos and sensitivity in this scene that I could hardly read the letter for fear of breaking down.

John Lanigan was a handsome Pinkerton with a voice to match, and I think he never sang better than he did then, as good as any guest tenor. Rudolf Kempe conducted those performances most eloquently, and I remember when Victoria questioned his tempo at one point, saying it was a little faster than the last time they had done it together, six months before, Kempe replied: 'I'm six months older – and now six months wiser.'

One night, as the music moved into the love duet that ends the first act and the chorus and I were slowly making our exits, I heard a gasp from the audience. Glancing over my shoulder I saw one of the blossom-covered trellis panels, twenty feet high, a lovely design by Sophie Fedorovich, start to sway and fall. Darting back across the stage, not at all in character with my staid consular role, I caught the panel in time to stop it crashing down. But then there was no way I could leave it, and I spent the rest of the scene holding it in place, doing my best impersonation of an ostrich: keeping my head turned away while the rest of me was in full view. The newlyweds on stage sang their love duet as if oblivious of me and everything else – but the twenty minutes it took them felt more like an hour to me.

Brenda and I had been married for seven years and were still childless when we moved into a new home in 1954, a charming converted coach house in Beckenham. Ken and Pam Taylor, from whom we bought it, became very good friends, and their daughter, Gail, is our godchild. She is a very remarkable young lady, a wonderfully happy person in spite of being spastic and blind. When she was little she always wanted me to sing for her, 'Mammy's little baby loves shortnin' bread'. Incredible as it may seem, she even passed her A-level in French when she was only fourteen, and she has a wonderful ear for music. Often she will telephone me to talk about some television programme I've been involved in, and I get very emotional when I hear her discussing the programme as if she had actually seen it.

Once we were settled in our new home, we thought we should make enquiries about adoption. No sooner did we do so than, to our great delight, Brenda became pregnant. I've heard it said that women sometimes become pregnant after adopting a baby. Maybe in our case the thought of adoption was enough, or was it perhaps the old adage, 'New house, new baby'?

All went smoothly with Brenda until the day the baby was due. She telephoned the hospital where she had made a reservation, only to find that the maternity unit had been closed following an outbreak of scarlet fever and expectant mothers were being sent to other hospitals in the area.

When the ambulance came for Brenda it was scheduled to take her to a maternity hospital at Erith, which was some way from where we lived. There was no point in arguing, that was the nearest available hospital, and we set off, me following in my car. I started to panic when I found that the ambulance men, taken out of their regular area, didn't know their way to the hospital. We stopped to ask a milkman. We stopped again at a little grocery shop. Eventually a man working in a field told us where to find the hospital, which had been converted from an old mansion.

Alun was born early the next morning, and when I went back to the hospital that afternoon the nurse said: 'Well, I know who you've come to see!' And she took me to see the baby first. Then I went to visit Brenda, who naturally asked if I wanted to see our son.

'I'm ahead of you,' I said, 'I've seen him. He's an ugly little thing, isn't he?'

Brenda was more than a bit put out by my comment. Back came her retort: 'The likeness was strong enough for the nurse to know you were the father, anyway!'

A few months later, one of the most wonderful experiences I've ever had was when Brenda put the tiny naked body of my son into bed with me while she answered the telephone, and I cradled him tenderly against my bare chest.

My career didn't begin to take me far from London until Alun was five or six years old, so I was with him like any other father, playing with him and watching him grow during those early years. When Huw was born it was a different matter: I didn't even know he had arrived until I read it in a newspaper, but that's a later story.

Meanwhile, the Covent Garden Opera was preparing a new production of *The Magic Flute* for the Mozart bicentenary in 1956. It was designed by John Piper and directed by Christopher West, and after the enjoyment of singing Papageno in the old production, I was delighted to be cast for the role again and looked forward to working on it afresh. I met John Piper when he designed the Glyndebourne *Don Giovanni*, and found him totally charming and easy to talk to about his ideas.

He showed me a painting of what he had in mind for me as Papageno. It was beautifully coloured (and he later made me a present of it), with a kind of tailcoat that swept back, and a cap with a peak to it suggesting a birdlike beak. It was as if Papageno dressed himself to resemble the birds he was supposed to catch, and that set me thinking. I wondered if the tailcoat could be wired at the back to shape a more birdlike tail, and eventually I plucked up the courage to put my idea to John. Encouraged by his response, I then mentioned that the peak of the cap seemed rather long and would mask Papageno's face from seats high in the amphitheatre and the 'gods'. He took the point instantly – he was one of the practical designers, concerned that the performing artist should be comfortable in whatever was designed for him to wear.

I also had a number of discussions with Christopher West about his ideas on the characterisation of Papageno, but then a week before we started production rehearsals I received a 'yellow peril', a typewritten note from the management, telling me I would not be singing Papageno after all.

I was shattered. I'd sung it in the previous production and I'd been discussing the new one with both the producer and designer.

Something snapped inside me. I had to sort this out. I grabbed the memo and ran up the steps to David Webster's office. They were the same stone steps I'd climbed for my first appointment there, only this time I took them two at a time. I burst into Miss Kerr's office and would have gone right through to Mr Webster's had he not come out at that very moment.

I glared at him, banged the memo on Miss Kerr's desk, and shouted at them both: 'I don't know what this bloody opera house is coming to.' They were totally taken aback. I don't remember what else I said then, only that I stormed out of the office, slammed the door behind me and went straight home. I don't often lose my temper, but when I do it upsets me terribly.

Brenda was waiting for me at home with a telephone message from Miss Kerr, who was very concerned at what had happened. They had never known me to lose my temper or to behave like that before, and when I calmed down I realised that Mr Webster was not responsible: he didn't even know that I had been dropped from the role.

The next day he sent for me, and I seriously thought that my days at the Opera House had come to an end. But, diplomatic as ever, he had spoken to Rafael Kubelik, who had come in as music director the previous year, and he now suggested that I should talk to him. I went to Kubelik and told him that I felt extremely humiliated to be notified at this stage that I would not be playing Papageno when it had already been announced.

'But Mr Walters is the number one baritone here,' he replied.

Much as I admired Jess Walters, who was a fine Papageno and with whom I was on excellent terms, I didn't think this was the way the casting should be decided. 'I really wasn't aware that we had number one and number two baritones in this company,' I told Kubelik. 'I thought each of us was chosen for whatever role he was best suited.'

And I couldn't resist adding: 'It doesn't matter anyway, I'm doing the new production at Glyndebourne.'

The upshot was that I did do the Covent Garden Papageno, in a production which opened in mid-January and was given on Mozart's birthday, 27 January. Richard Lewis sang Tamino and Elsie Morison, who later became Kubelik's wife, was Pamina. John Piper had tried to overcome the problem of frequent scene changes by relying on gauze curtains which were simple and beautifully designed, but which made the rest of the production look rather uninteresting.

A month later the company was on tour in Cardiff, where I sang my one hundredth performance of Figaro at the old Gaumont Theatre. It's a tragedy that this theatre was demolished – in my opinion it would have been ideal for the Welsh National Opera, which still has no proper home base. Time had gone so quickly for me, it was difficult to realise I'd sung Figaro a hundred times since 1949, and it was a happy coincidence that the occasion found me almost at home. I had a number of congratulatory messages and telegrams, including one from Brenda: 'Congratulations on your first hundred. Not another hundred please.'

She wasn't to know then that I would be 'Figaro here, Figaro there' on several hundred more occasions. More than five hundred in all, I reckon, and I always loved playing it and continued to have a great sentimental feeling for it. But even having sung that hundredth performance in Cardiff, I still felt I could improve upon it.

Perhaps I did, because shortly after this, when the company was doing a performance of *Figaro* in Coventry, a note was brought round to my dressing-room from Dame Peggy Ashcroft and Donald Sinden, who were then appearing in the Shakespeare season at Stratford-upon-Avon and were spending a free evening visiting us instead. Their note asked if I would join them for supper after the performance and I sent them a reply saying I'd be delighted. When we reached the restaurant I discovered not just Dame Peggy and Donald, but a group of about ten from the Stratford company, who sat me down at the head of a long table and treated me like a guest of honour. This warm and generous tribute from fellow artists on the other side of the profession thrilled and moved me very much.

It was a condition of Arts Council support for the Covent Garden Opera that some of the repertory should be taken on tour outside London most years and, in spite of all their disadvantages, these tours were great fun, because we were touring as a company: we were, if you like, playing as a team, which to my mind is always the best possible basis for good performances.

My salary at this time had risen to about fifteen pounds a week from the twelve at which I had started, but only those earning below fifteen pounds were given an extra subsistence allowance for touring. The consequence was that although I was graded as a principal singing principal roles, I was actually no better off than the chorus singers.

We had to live as cheaply as we could, and it was still possible then to find theatrical 'digs' where two pounds ten, or two pounds fifteen shillings a week, would cover bed, breakfast and sometimes an evening meal as well. We often shared rooms and that would save us five shillings each on the charge. Once I remember five of us sharing a large attic, which not only saved us ten shillings a week each but also gave us plenty of laughs and good comradeship.

We usually went back to the same places each year, like Mrs McKay's in Manchester, a lovely place to stay, with everything clean and spotless. She also had her 'principles', though, and was very firm about them. Once Brenda had been in Scotland with me and decided to stay in Manchester overnight before going on to London. Mrs McKay absolutely refused to accept that Brenda and I were married, and nothing we or the other singers could say would make her change her mind. There was no question that Brenda could share my room. She was welcome to stay there, but she was put into a little box-room as far from mine as possible, and we didn't even have the courage to meet on the landing!

At around this time there were backstage rumours at Covent Garden that a new production of *Die Meistersinger* was in prospect for 1957, and I made up my mind that if I was asked to sing the Nightwatchman again I'd refuse. I'd served my apprenticeship in that role. However, Otakar Kraus and I were having a cup of tea together in the canteen one day when he mentioned that Kubelik had asked him to sing Beckmesser in the new production and he really felt his voice wasn't suitable for the role. 'It would suit your voice better than mine, Geraint,' he said. 'I think I'll tell Kubelik that.'

He was as good as his word, and a few days later came a message asking if I would sing Beckmesser, just as if I'd been the first choice. I didn't care, though, and I was overjoyed at the chance of a new role that I felt I could get my teeth into. I'll always be grateful to Otakar for recommending me for what, as it turned out, was to become one of my special roles.

Beckmesser is a difficult role to play, and a dangerous part to sing unless one is very careful with the voice in such a long opera as *Die Meistersinger*. I felt it would be a great help if I could hear some experienced Beckmessers like Benno Kusche, who had sung in the previous Covent Garden production when I was the Nightwatchman, and who I knew was singing it at Munich, and also Karl Schmitt-Walter, the Bayreuth Beckmesser at that time. I summoned the courage to put this to David Webster and asked if he could use his influence to get me the necessary tickets for Bayreuth. He did, and off I went.

I went first to Munich, where I stayed with a friend and colleague, the soprano Elisabeth Lindermeier, who became Rudolf Kempe's second wife. I watched and absorbed a fine performance there by Kusche, who had a marvellous command of the role, with Kempe conducting superbly. I then went to Bayreuth and collected my ticket from Wieland Wagner, who knew exactly why I was so keen to see the performance. André Cluytens conducted, though not as well as Kempe.

Schmitt-Walter was as stylised a Beckmesser as Kusche, but in quite a different way, so I had two very skilful portraits of the character to think about. I remember that Schmitt-Walter characterised the first verse of Beckmesser's serenade to Eva in an almost improvisatory manner, as if a little unsure of himself, but in the later verses he naturally sang in strict tempo. In Munich, Kempe conducted this in such a lilting way that you could imagine the audience almost swaying in time to it, a fantastic effect.

The famed acoustics in the Bayreuth Festspielhaus certainly impressed me. I could feel the music all around me, as if it were coming from some three-dimensional source, yet the voices were never obliterated by the sound of the orchestra. However loudly the orchestra played, the voices were still clearly heard, and I was conscious that the singers never had to push their voices to reach the audience. It was an exciting new sensation for me then.

But the whole of Wieland Wagner's production made a terrific impact on me, and I felt I could even smell the beautiful summer evening at the start of the second act, when the apprentices are looking forward to the next day's midsummer festivities. My only disappointment was the scene of the midsummer song contest at the end of the opera. Instead of suggesting a meadow by the River Pegnitz, outside Nuremberg, it was so stylised into an enclosed arena that to me it looked more like a bull-ring.

Came the first night at Covent Garden, and I was both nervous and apprehensive at singing such a major role, although I had had great help from the producer, Erich Witte, himself a fine character tenor who was already known in London for his Loge in *Das*

Rheingold. As an experienced singer he could understand the singer's point of view in the staging, but he was also just as much involved in the dramatic character.

We worked hard together on the scene in Hans Sachs's workshop near the start of the last act, when Beckmesser is alone on stage with a long passage of silent mime which has to be phrased exactly to the music. Every glance, every movement of the hand, every step of the feet, even every pause of stillness, has a meaning, a purpose. It must tell the audience what Beckmesser is doing in Sachs's workshop, describe his relationship with Sachs, his inward feelings and the turmoil in his mind.

Over the years I came to appreciate the significance of this scene and the scope it offered the singer, but I remained grateful to Witte for helping me to shape it on this first occasion. It wasn't as though the staging was his only concern, either. Richard Lewis had to drop out through illness and Witte took his place in the tenor role of Walther von Stolzing. He'd sung it before in Germany, but he relearned it in English for Covent Garden.

Witte was physically rather short, but he managed to convey the impression of height because of his innate dignity of presence and his bearing on the stage. He had great taste in all he did, whether as a singer or as a director, and I thought he made a splendid Walther. Kubelik conducted, and it was immensely satisfying to work with him and with the other singers, who included James Pease as Sachs, Peter Pears as the apprentice David, Marjorie Thomas as Magdalene, and Joan Sutherland singing her first Eva.

About this time David Webster suggested I might consider singing the title role in *Don Giovanni* instead of Leporello. This intrigued and attracted me, but before giving an answer I thought I should find somewhere to perform it as a try-out. Joan Ingpen made enquiries and discovered the Dublin Grand Opera was planning to produce it. They were happy to have me sing the role.

I had permission to borrow a costume from Covent Garden and I chose one from the *Rigoletto* wardrobe. When I tried it on in Dublin, I wasn't too happy about the way it looked. I wanted to open the neck of the doublet and turn it back, but it wouldn't stay put. Joan Hammond was performing in Dublin at the same time and, coming to wish me well, she found me wrestling with my costume. When I explained what was wrong she told me to take off the doublet and give it to her, and she sat down there and then and sewed it the way I wanted.

Joan Ingpen came to the performance with Lord Harewood, who was then in charge of opera planning at Covent Garden, so I presumed he was reporting back to Mr Webster about my performance. I felt quite comfortable in the role and thought I'd given a pretty good performance, although at the back of my mind I still had some doubts about whether I was entirely suitable.

Bruce Dargavel sang the Commendatore, and a wonderful voice he had. In the third or fourth performance he somehow missed a cue in the last scene when, as the stone statue, he confronts Don Giovanni. I grasp his hand; he sings 'Kneel and pray!', I then have to refuse and sing 'No!' several times in response to his repeated commands. This time, however, he missed the first 'Kneel and pray!' so I added an extra 'No!' to cover him. The same thing happened again; I sang another 'No!' to fill in his music and yet another 'No!' as my answer to him. Not a sound had come from his lips.

I'd sung that 'No!' goodness knows how many times when a voice was clearly heard shouting from the gods in a broad Irish accent: 'For God's sake sing "Yes" and get off the bloody stage!' The audience fell about with laughter, and I must admit I couldn't help joining them myself.

When I returned to London, David Webster was still waiting for my answer about singing the Don at Covent Garden. From this I gathered he must have had a favourable report about my performance, but I asked for a little longer to make up my mind. I wanted to discuss it with Rudolf Kempe, who was to conduct the new production (although this in fact never came about); I just didn't feel I had the height and the presence for a Don Giovanni, compared with Pinza and John Brownlee in the past, and Siepi and Hotter who were singing the role at the time. I said jokingly to Kempe:

'I think I have duck's disease.'

'What is that?' he asked anxiously.

'My bottom is too near the ground,' I answered.

By this time Kempe knew that I was a very successful Leporello at Glyndebourne, and he said: 'I know you could sing the Don, and a good Don. But why not be the best Leporello?'

So I went back to David Webster. I told him I would rather sing Leporello in the new production because, as I had remarked to Kempe, 'my bottom's too near the ground' to be the Don.

'But it's such a nice bottom,' he said, looking over his glasses with a wicked smile on his face.

All the same I stuck to my decision and I never sang the title role at Covent Garden. Once or twice in later years, finding myself singing Leporello to a Don Giovanni no taller than I was, I wondered again if I'd been wise to opt out, but on reflection I think the success I've had as Leporello has justified that decision.

My other Irish excursion was to the Wexford Festival in 1957, where Peter Ebert was producing Donizetti's *La figlia del reggimento* with Graziella Sciutti in the title role. When we were at Glyndebourne he asked me if I would sing Sergeant Sulpizio. I knew that Wexford had begun to acquire quite a reputation for offbeat opera since the first festival in 1951, thanks to the enthusiasm of one man, Dr Tom Walsh, a local doctor whose love and knowledge of opera was matched by a good ear for voices. Even so, it was a festival of several surprises for me.

The first was the stage itself. I think it was the smallest on which I've ever performed. Looking out at the auditorium, which was also tiny, I had the feeling that I could have shaken hands with the people in the dress circle. But what an audience they were, overflowing with enthusiasm. After the trio with Graziella, myself, and Patricia Kern as the Contessa, it seemed they would never stop applauding. Whereupon Bryan Balkwill, who was conducting and was close enough to have a conversation with us from the pit, decided to give an encore.

This I'd never done before during an opera, but we sang it again. The same thing happened: more applause and cheers; it was still impossible to continue. We stood there waiting, but still they applauded. So we sang the trio for the third time.

Another surprise was the fantastic hospitality at Wexford's two main hotels, situated at opposite ends of the town and rivalling each other to see which could attract the most leading artists to stay. After every performance both hotels would be packed with opera-goers and artists alike: we were expected to become part of the community spirit which continued into the small hours. Three or four o'clock in the morning was considered early for bed.

Then there were the priests. They were all over the place. It seemed they took their holidays at the festival, where they had a rare dispensation to attend the theatre and, I think, to drink wine. There were never enough seats for them in the auditorium so they swarmed backstage, crowding the small space in the wings or even sitting the performance through on the steps to the dressing-rooms. Back at the hotel afterwards, I always knew where to find Graziella. She would be surrounded by priests and, being a very petite person, almost totally hidden by them. I told her I was never sure whether they were complimenting her on her voice or admiring the low-cut dresses she wore!

One gathering at the hotel was still going strong at six the next morning, when I suddenly became aware that everybody was leaving, saying they'd be back shortly for breakfast. Soon I was quite alone and there was no sign of anybody except the hotel owner. He must have felt a wreck during the festival because the only time he could possibly have gone to bed was perhaps for a couple of hours in the afternoon.

'Where is everybody?,' I asked him.

'They've gone to Mass. They'll be back in an hour.'

'I hope they all make it to the church,' I replied.

I went to freshen up and, sure enough, they were all back in time for us to sit down to a hearty breakfast together.

I was persuaded to go to Mass myself once, with one of the friends I'd met there, although I'm a Methodist, not a Catholic. It was the first time I'd been to a Catholic service and I was quite surprised to find that we had to queue outside waiting for an earlier Mass to end, and then found another queue waiting when we came out.

The Mass itself I found deeply impressive. And having gone that first time I had no compunction in later years about going into Catholic churches when I was in other countries. To me it was the same God, and I often found spiritual comfort and peace of mind just sitting alone in one of those churches for a while, thinking of home, perhaps, and meditating in silence. A religious upbringing such as I had remains with you, and although I am by no means a regular worshipper, my faith continues to mean a lot to me.

The year after Wexford I was asked to take part in a very different festival nearer home, when Leeds celebrated the centenary of the first music festival held there in 1858, which became a regular triennial festival from 1880. Lord Harewood, whose family home is nearby, was the artistic director for the centenary festival, and he planned it on a larger and more ambitious scale than usual, involving the whole Covent Garden Opera company with Handel's *Samson*, conducted by John Pritchard, and concerts by Benjamin Britten and Peter Pears, Otto Klemperer and Yehudi Menuhin, among many others.

I was to sing the baritone solo in Walton's *Belshazzar's Feast*, with the special festival chorus assembled for the occasion and the BBC Symphony Orchestra conducted by Rudolf Schwarz. In the same programme were Teresa Berganza, singing Mahler's 'Wayfarer' songs, and the pianist Annie Fischer in a Mozart concerto. The three of us waited together while the orchestra played the *Oberon* overture, and Annie became so nervous she started to lose her voice, her speech being reduced to little more than a croak.

The effect of that on two singers who had not yet performed was almost contagious. Teresa was on first, and although she knew the Mahler songs backwards, Annie's croaking voice affected her psychologically. She was no sooner on stage than she started to panic, demanding a music stand and her music. Everything was held up while this was brought, but then she gave a wonderful performance. So also did Annie in her turn, and by the time she left the platform her voice was back to normal, although I still remember her agonised remark to me: 'Thank God – till next time.'

After the interval, it was my turn. I'd rehearsed the night before without a score, knowing the work well and not having any problems. But I liked to have the score with me in performance, remembering Heddle Nash's advice: 'You never know when you might want it. Even if you only sit on it.'

I started to go up the steps to the platform with the score under my arm when George Harewood, who'd been backstage to congratulate the other two, took the score from me, saying: 'Come on, Geraint. You don't need that. You know it backwards,' and wished me luck.

At that moment I was head and shoulders in view of the audience, who started to applaud. If I turned back, they might think I had stagefright or whatever, so I went on, cursing George. Not having the score, even to sit on, started me worrying, especially before my first entry, when the baritone sings, 'If I forget thee, O Jerusalem . . .' As we approached this, it was my turn to panic: 'My God, what are the words? What are the words?' But I opened my mouth and they just came!

Even then I wasn't home and dry. The concert was in Leeds Town Hall, with one of those bathroom echoes that reverberates back at you. With a full orchestra it smudged itself around the hall, but when I began my unaccompanied recitative, 'Babylon was a great city', I could hear my own voice coming back at me, slightly off-pitch from the notes I was actually singing. And that terrified me in case I couldn't accurately pitch the note on which the orchestra would then join in, but, thank God, I was right in tune.

Afterwards there was a reception to meet the Queen and the Duke of Edinburgh, who had attended the concert. We lined up to meet Her Majesty, who spoke French to Teresa and had a long chat with the orchestra leader, Paul Beard. George Harewood (a cousin of the Queen) edged her discreetly away because the photographers weren't much concerned with us, they were waiting for Her Majesty to meet the other Duke, Duke Ellington, who was also performing at the festival with his band. I suppose this had been arranged by Lord Harewood's younger brother, the Hon. Gerald Lascelles, who was a keen jazz buff and himself played in a jazz band.

Duke Ellington was a wonderful person. I had a long talk with him on that occasion, and it took me back to my time with the British

Forces Network in Germany when we used to exchange records with the American Forces Network, and I would listen with them until well into the night to Duke Ellington and other jazz musicians. Later, in Los Angeles, Paul Schoeffler and I would sometimes find ourselves the only white people in a jazz club where one of the best bands was performing. I also recall a meeting with Louis Armstrong, whom I admired and instantly liked as a person. Who wouldn't? His laughter and his high spirits were always infectious.

George Harewood recognised that the best of jazz which Ellington certainly represented, could have its own place even in a traditional festival like Leeds, with its emphasis on the choral tradition. He had catholic tastes in music, but I soon recognised his encyclopedic knowledge of opera. When he first became controller of opera planning at Covent Garden in 1953, there were many who thought that he owed the job more to his Royal connections than to his own ability, but they soon changed their minds as his vast knowledge of operatic detail, and of singers past and present, became ever more apparent.

We had a friendly association over the years, which on one occasion brought him to Pontypridd, where my father was still conducting the male voice choir. I had taken part in previous concerts of operatic excerpts introduced and linked by David Webster at Rosehill in Cumberland, in the charming little theatre built there by the textile magnate, Miki Sekers, who was a generous donor to Glyndebourne, and I wondered if we could do something similar at Pontypridd. George readily assented to be the operatic compère on the Webster model, and we had a tremendously successful evening with Victoria Elliott, Constance Shacklock and Rowland Jones as the other soloists, and Edward Downes as accompanist.

Years later, for my sixtieth birthday, Colin Davis gave me George Harewood's autobiography, *The Tongs and the Bones*. I started to read it one night after a performance, when I usually can't sleep, and I was even more disturbed, not to say hurt, to come across his slighting reference to me. He often complimented me on my performances at Covent Garden, but his book dismissed me completely in comparison with other singers from abroad who are not even named. I still wonder why he wrote as he did, especially as he has since backed so many fine British singers at the English National Opera.

George Harewood was responsible for much of the planning and casting that went into the splendid production of Verdi's *Don Carlos* that marked the centenary of the Royal Opera House in 1958. Giulini conducted, and Luchino Visconti directed for the first time at

Covent Garden, with a cast that included Gré Brouwenstijn, Jon Vickers, Boris Christoff, and Tito Gobbi as Rodrigo. When the production was revived the following spring, Gobbi was unwell and had to cancel, and I was asked if I would replace him.

I had seen Tito's performance and been very impressed by it, but while I thought it was a role I could manage, I wanted to be quite sure before I took it on. There were about three weeks to go before the opera was to be performed again, so I asked David Webster if I could have a couple of days to see how the part suited me. I worked with James Gibson, who was then a répétiteur, first on Rodrigo's main aria, 'O Carlo, ascolta', then on the quartet in which he also takes a leading part. When I knew I could sing these, I told Mr Webster I'd do it.

Jimmy Gibson was wonderfully patient and sympathetic, and although we then had only three weeks for me to learn the role, the pressure helped me to absorb it more quickly and I thoroughly enjoyed doing so. It was worth learning, even in a hurry, because it's such a satisfying role to perform, so sympathetic in expression and including some of the opera's most beautiful music. The rest of the cast already knew their roles, of course, but they were so good to work with, I knew I was in safe hands.

I don't think I realised at the time just how safe some of the hands were. We had only one orchestral rehearsal on the stage, and we weren't even in costume for it. At one point Jon Vickers saw that I was in the wrong place, and that I needed to be on the opposite side of the stage. Being exceptionally strong physically as well as vocally, Jon put his two hands around my waist and lifted me bodily while I was still singing, then set me down where I was supposed to be. What I don't think he knew was the strength of his grip when we came to my aria, after Rodrigo has been shot and is cradled in Carlo's arms: Jon was so emotionally involved and clasped me so tightly that I could hardly get enough breath to sing the phrases. I was sorry that the repertory schedules prevented me from singing that role again in later years.

There were other strong hands around, as I discovered while rehearsing *The Marriage of Figaro* one day with Joan Sutherland. We were sitting on chairs side by side when she made some remark that I didn't catch above the sound of the orchestra. So I leaned forward the better to hear her, putting my arm round her waist as I did so. Her jumper and skirt had parted company, and my hand touched the bare skin between. Instantly she swung round, and slapped me across the face with all her strength.

Everybody saw it and was astonished because it was so unlike her.

After all, she and I had 'grown up' together at Covent Garden, where Joan joined the company in 1952. I know that Mr Webster was once told by one of the music staff that neither she nor I would ever be much good and ought to be allowed to go. He refused, saying: 'Just let's bide our time.' I think we can both claim to have proved his trust was well-founded.

Joan's overnight success in *Lucia di Lammermoor*, in which I sang Enrico, Lucia's brother, came in 1959, after a lot of hard work all round, with all of us willing her to succeed. I thought the potential in her voice had begun to show a few years before this, when she sang Jenifer in the premiere of Michael Tippett's *The Midsummer Marriage*. The quality and agility of her voice fascinated me as it developed, although I recall one strange mannerism she had. Being very much the artless newcomer, instead of covering any mistake she made by moving on quickly, she would draw everybody's attention to it by pulling faces and grimacing about it.

Her movements on stage weren't very fluid at that time, but in Franco Zeffirelli she had a wonderfully sympathetic director who was prepared to take great trouble with her, and she herself was ready to work until she dropped in order to do well. One afternoon we went over and over the Lucia–Enrico duet, during which Franco wanted me to throw her to the floor as the anger and tension between us mounted. I lost count of the number of times I threw Joan down that afternoon. It must have meant plenty of bruises for her, but she was determined to do it properly.

For my part, I can say that working with somebody as pleasant as Joan meant that I didn't mind how many times we went over the same passage to get it right. We had a great team to work with, of course, not least Tullio Serafin, a singer's conductor if ever there was one, and a fine artist in all he did. In performance he phrased with the singer. He knew exactly when one would want to take a breath, and somehow he allowed time for this without changing his basic tempo.

Zeffirelli was the designer as well as producer for *Lucia di Lammermoor*, and he made stage pictures that perfectly conveyed time and place and can still be remembered in every detail. I was involved in the opening scene, set on the steps of Ravenswood Castle, where he made extraordinary use of perspective. He put tall men on the lower steps, middling men above them, and on the higher steps he had boys, in identical costume and wearing moustaches and beards, giving a marvellous effect of distance and making the Covent Garden stage seem three or four times deeper than it was.

We all knew from the dress rehearsal that this could be something tremendous for Joan, and we kept our fingers crossed for the first night. Not only the principals but the whole of the chorus and orchestra were behind her, committed to making it a success. What she did achieve is now history, in spite of the nerve-wracking knowledge that Maria Callas was in the first-night audience, which I think was not very kind of her. But Joan won through, and I felt for her the same exhilarating excitement that I'd enjoyed when I sang Falstaff at Glyndebourne.

Before that year was out Zeffirelli was back at Covent Garden to design and direct those celebrated operatic 'twins', known the world over as 'Cav and Pag': Mascagni's *Cavalleria rusticana* and Leoncavallo's *I pagliacci*. I was in the second of these as Tonio, with Joan Carlyle and Jon Vickers, and with Bryan Balkwill conducting. Ted Downes was conducting *Cavalleria*, which had Amy Shuard, Charles Craig and Otakar Kraus, so both operas were strongly cast and showed what could be achieved with the home team.

After the superb stage effects which Zeffirelli had managed with his designs and lighting in *Lucia di Lammermoor*, he excelled himself particularly, I thought, at the start of *Cavalleria*. The dawn of Easter Day broke over shadowy figures in the village street beside the church, the scene gradually becoming brilliantly sunlit in the hard, Mediterranean contrast of light and shade. It was a fantastic stage picture which has stayed with me, and *Pagliacci* brought the other end of the day, sunlight fading into night.

Tonio in *Pagliacci* sings the Prologue in front of the curtain, telling the audience that what they see is taken from life. Then he precipitates the tragedy on stage. I played him not as a conventional clown or buffoon, but as a man of some intelligence with a chip on his shoulder or, rather, a hump on his back, which made him feel inferior, disadvantaged, among the other strolling players. They looked on him merely as a cripple, whereas his outward deformity had nothing to do with his normal human feeling and emotions. When people touched the hump on a man's back for luck, as they did in those days, it must have deepened his embarrassment.

It was a role I found satisfying to play and agreeable to sing, except in Vienna not long afterwards where I was typically expected to go on without any rehearsal and suddenly found in the Prologue that everything seemed much more of an effort. I could feel the blood pressure increasing, my head began to throb as if it might burst and, to put it crudely, I felt I needed two jock-straps to stay with it. I had forgotten completely that the pitch in Vienna was almost half a tone up on Covent Garden, where Leoncavallo's Prologue took me to my upper vocal limit. The higher Viennese pitch made me totally giddy, and when I disappeared through the curtains on my last note I didn't know which way I was facing. Sent out for a curtain-call, I came out with my back to the audience when I thought I was facing them. The effort had entirely disorientated me.

Back at Covent Garden, I had little more than a month after the first Tonio before I was given a new challenge: the four baritone roles in *The Tales of Hoffmann*. It wasn't a new production, having previously been staged in 1954 by Günther Rennert with a nice sense of the macabre, when I had sung the role of Spalanzani. I startled some of the others and the stage staff then by playing him as a 'camp' character, tight-kneed and limp-wristed, though this seemed to be generally approved in relation to the rest of the production.

Now, for the quadruple role – Councillor Lindorf, Coppelius, Doctor Miracle and Dapertutto – I had already had the advantage of seeing two fine artists perform them, Hermann Uhde and Otakar Kraus. I wasn't ashamed to borrow from them what I thought were the most effective elements in their portrayals of the different characters, then adding some touches of my own. There were so many quick changes of costume and make-up during the performance that there was hardly time to think, so it was vital to spend time polishing the different characters beforehand, to ensure that I had no difficulty in switching from one to the next.

Rehearsals were with Ande Anderson, who was staging the Rennert production for this revival. We had grown up at Covent Garden together and were great friends, sharing the frustrations as well as the joys of operatic life. I put to him a suggestion that we could achieve a more sinister effect for Doctor Miracle by using an identically dressed double and having each of us appear in totally unexpected places with only a count of four in between. Ande thought it was worth a try, so we worked it out and put it into the performance. And it succeeded, with the help of Ignatius (Iggy) McFadyen, a stalwart of the chorus and their longest-serving member. I heard there were all kinds of questions from the audience afterwards, asking how I'd managed to be in so many different places so quickly.

Not everything worked quite so smoothly. In my quick-to-disappear sequence I was supposed at one point to crawl off the stage with a black veil over my head, so that my face wouldn't show. Around the stage there were three or four electric fans, blowing the curtains and giving a ghostly feeling to the scene, and on one occasion my veil caught on one of those fans. To me, crouched on hands and knees, it seemed that somebody was tugging me in a direction I knew I shouldn't be going, and I started to argue from under the veil: 'I don't go that way; I go this way . . . . For God's sake leave me alone.' And so on, until the veil was actually torn to pieces in the fan blades and I could see what had happened.

This, of course, was out of sight of the audience. But I wasn't so fortunate another time when I made ready for Doctor Miracle's surprise entrance up through a trapdoor in the stage, to be seen through a skeletal piano which was one of the props in the design. First our intrepid stage manager, Stella Chitty, would cue the stage staff involved, one to release the spring opening the trapdoor, and two to wind the wheel that pushed me up through it. On this occasion the trapdoor hadn't opened and my head was against it, forcing me to crouch lower and lower and shout to them to stop. They stopped, very briefly; the spring was released and the trap opened, and up I went into the full view of the audience. No sooner was I there than Stella, not realising my delay, called them to take me down again without time for me to utter a sound. No sooner was I up than I was down, like a puppet on a string, and there was a gale of laughter from the audience.

Having worked with Zeffirelli in *Lucia* and 'Pag', and with Giulini in *Don Carlos*, I was delighted to learn they would have charge of the new production of *Falstaff*, a role I'd now sung with the Glyndebourne company in Sussex, and in Paris and Edinburgh, but had yet to sing at Covent Garden. I think Franco knew the success I'd had with it already, and the foundation of character which Carl Ebert had helped me to build, and we knew from previous experience that we approached roles in a similar way, so we had a very harmonious relationship.

Of course, it was a very different production at Covent Garden, and Franco wanted some changed nuances of character which I readily incorporated, but I'm happy to think he trusted me as I did him. He was again the designer as well as director, and trying to keep up with everything sometimes made him late for meetings. One such occasion was a costume fitting when I was trying the fancy costume Falstaff puts on in the second act to go a-wooing. I'd gone half an hour early to the Wardrobe where they were making it, so as to put on all my padding first, and then I sat around waiting for over an hour. There was no sign of Franco.

Came a point where I thought I'd waited quite long enough. I tried the costume, and with the help of the costume-maker we tidied up the fitting details, take a little in here, give a little more there, and so on. I felt I'd be happy with that, so I took off the costume, removed the padding, and who should arrive but Franco, eager to see the costume.

'You're too late,' I told him.

'But I had such a late lunch,' he protested.

'Well go and think about what a nice lunch you had,' I said, 'We've had the fitting. We've made the alterations, and I think you'll be happy enough with the result.'

He let it go, and didn't see the costume until we had the first costume rehearsal, and how relieved I was that he approved, having trusted me over it. My earlier fashion-design training had come into its own.

There were a couple of awkward moments in his production. In the last scene, in Windsor forest, Franco wanted Herne's Oak, visible in the centre of the stage, to disappear before the final ensemble, and the net supporting it on either side to be lifted with it. But he also wanted me to chase Alice Ford around the oak during our duet. First we couldn't do this because of the net, so eventually we persuaded Franco to cut into the net so we could pass through it. Even that wasn't really successful, because the oak was so wide that by the time we had found the gaps in the net, been round the back and come out again, we'd lost contact with Giulini and the orchestra.

Then there were the stairs in the first scene, the Garter Inn, two flights of them, one on either side, supposedly leading down from the entrance door on one side, and up to an upper gallery which led to bedrooms on the other. Each flight had about sixteen steps. They terrified Regina Resnik, a wonderful Mistress Quickly, because she had to make her first entry down one flight to sing her 'Reverenza!' to me, and she was always afraid her heavy costume might make her trip before she reached the stage.

For my own part, they proved a killer in the second act. To make my costume-change while Ford sang his monologue, I had to go up the stairs to the top, as if going to my room, down at the back out of sight, make the change quickly, back up again into view, and down once more to rejoin Master Ford. Believe me, that was some sweat.

Still, that same flight of stairs inadvertently provided one of the most successful comedy effects, which came about by pure accident at the dress rehearsal. Having chased Bardolph and Pistol around the stage with a broomstick at the end of the first scene, I went halfway up the stairs to throw the broomstick after them. As I threw it I lost my balance, flopped down on the steps and bounced down each one to the floor, much to everybody's amusement.

'Keep that in! Keep it in!' called Franco. So I did, and it worked marvellously on the first night, producing much laughter from the audience. After that I'd let it happen if it wanted to, so to speak. If I felt myself falling I'd go with it, but I wouldn't force it to happen, because then it wouldn't look convincing. I always felt that production incidents like this shouldn't be too contrived, but if one happens and it works, and suits the character and situation, by all means let it become part of the performance.

I was sometimes asked if I didn't hurt myself falling down the stairs like that, but under the padding I wore I didn't feel it at all. I went on falling most of the time, yet when the opera was revived for perhaps the third time some years later, there was one newspaper critic who pounced on this as something 'new' I'd put in deliberately for the sake of comic effect. Apart from the fact that he must have seen me do it before, and presumably forgotten it, I insist that there's a big difference between what is deliberately contrived and 'doing what comes naturally' in the context of an opera production.

Giulini was so sensitive and yet vivacious in the performances he conducted, and he had a responsive cast for the new production. It was my first meeting with Mariella Angioletti, who sang Alice, and with the delightful Mirella Freni as Nanetta (in later years, when I often sang with her and with Teresa Berganza in *Figaro*, I never knew what mischief the two of them might get up to next). Mirella with Luigi Alva made an ideal pair of lovers, while Josephine Veasey, who had come from the chorus but was now equal to any international guest, suited the ensemble excellently as Meg Page, both in tonal timbre and personality.

I've said Regina Resnik was a wonderful Quickly, and in truth I believe she was one of the great operatic artists of her time. She had such intelligence about the way she sang and acted, matching the vocal ensemble, timing her movements to fit perfectly with the other performers, creating a full character with everything she did. In Falstaff's scenes with Quickly, I used to have in mind the thought from Shakespeare that this was the woman who crept into Falstaff's bed to keep him warm as he lay dying. It always came across that Regina's Quickly would indeed be capable of caring that way.

John Shaw was a fine, forthright Ford, inclined to bluster at times, perhaps, but singing exceptionally well in our exchanges. To back all these up I couldn't have wished for better support than from John Lanigan as Dr Caius, and especially Robert Bowman and Michael Langdon as those splendid ruffians, Bardolph and Pistol, with Frank Egerton as Bardolph in later performances. I shall ever be grateful to Bob Bowman for singing Falstaff's falsetto phrase for me one night when I had a touch of cold. It's when I pretend to quote Alice saying she's in love with me, a single sentence only, but I would always practise it during my warm-up beforehand.

On this occasion I knew my voice would crack or dry up, so I said to Bob, 'Will you do me a favour and sing that for me?' He said he'd have a go, so when we reached that line, he turned his back to the audience and sang the line while I mouthed the words. And nobody realised it, nobody commented: it was another example of the comradeship that existed between fellow singers.

That *Falstaff* production had a popular success at Covent Garden for more than fifteen years, and after performing in it on so many occasions, the last in 1978, my only regret was that I didn't have the chance of another new *Falstaff* production there. Other operas, like *The Magic Flute* or *Don Giovanni*, seemed to have more than their share of new productions.

Verdi, of course, can make or break a singer, partly because his operas have continued to be a mainstay of the classic repertory, and also because of the rich diversity of roles they offer to every kind of voice. In my own case, having taken me to the top with *Falstaff*, he also brought me one of the unhappiest nights of my career in *Rigoletto*, the title role of which I sang once and once only. It even caused Covent Garden to take the almost unprecedented step of postponing a first night just a day or so before; it put my future in jeopardy for a while, and it came about like this.

I was busily preparing for a new Covent Garden production of *The Marriage of Figaro* in the spring of 1963 when I was asked if I would consider singing Rigoletto, which Zeffirelli was to produce the following year with Georg Solti conducting. Now Rigoletto is one of the roles that all baritones aspire to sing at some point in their career, if they can manage it at all, and my first reaction was to jump at the chance.

Then I remembered that the part does lie quite high for the baritone voice, and it had become traditional for the singer to take certain high notes in performance instead of those written, like the G usually heard at the end of Rigoletto's soliloquy, 'Pari siamo', instead of the E in the score. So first I asked for a day or two to think it over, and when I looked at the music I realised that I wouldn't be able to take the high notes that had become customary.

With this doubt in mind I went to Georg Solti and explained my problem. But he was immediately reassuring. 'I'm doing it as it's written,' he declared, meaning that I shouldn't sing those higher alternatives. The role now became more practicable, but I still wanted to work on it for a week or two before I decided whether to accept, and David Webster agreed that I could do this. He arranged that Eric Mitchell should coach me, and once the first night of *Figaro* was over we began to work on it.

I knew Rigoletto's two main arias, and had sung 'Pari siamo' at concerts, but never a note of 'Cortigiani!' in public. These are items no singer can claim to know unless he's sung them publicly and successfully. Eric was marvellous, painstaking and patient, while also understanding that the management needed to know as soon as possible if I would sing the role or not. A couple of weeks later I was much happier about it. I'd sung it through from start to finish at least twice, to be sure I could manage it all, and Eric told me he thought it would suit me very well.

His opinion was confirmed by Ted Downes, with whom I also worked. He said to me: 'If Solti really doesn't want you to sing the optional notes, you can do it fine.' Coming from Ted, I felt I was on the right track. He was always forthright when he was advising singers. If he thought a role didn't suit, he'd say so without any hesitation. So I went back to the management and agreed to sing it, and during the next few months I started to look forward to it, and to working again with Zeffirelli.

From time to time I had an occasional call on it with Eric or Ted, to make sure that it was growing into the voice, as it were, and in due course we began full rehearsals about three or four weeks before the first night. At the end of the first week I began to feel more vocally tired than I should be. I mentioned this to Solti at a musical rehearsal. Thinking as I did that it was just a passing condition, he simply said, 'Take it easy. Take it easy.'

During the second week, still feeling there was something wrong, I went to my doctor, Maurice Woods, an old friend whom I'd consulted over many years. He simply thought I was getting tensed-up: 'I know you, Geraint. You always want perfection. It's nerves, working up to the first night.'

Maurice knew me very well, and he knew more about the human body than I did, so I accepted what he said, although I still felt that my problems weren't entirely due to my nerves. I'd sing for about ten or fifteen minutes and feel exhausted. The voice was still there but there was no support for it, no power to make it work for me. Even working with Franco on the histrionics alone, without singing, I'd begin to feel languid, tired, no energy.

Both he and Georg Solti continued to say 'Take it easy'. With Georg I knew he meant that when he said it, but when it came to actually rehearsing the adrenalin would start to work in him and he'd expect you to give all you could as well. I tried to put my worries to one side, to force mind over matter, and during the next week I thought I'd succeeded: I could sing more without getting quite so tired.

Now came the dress rehearsal, and halfway through it all the previous trouble attacked me again. I felt a pressure on my chest, as if it held me tight and didn't breathe with me, so that I had to fight an inside battle to force any voice through.

By this time I'd also been to the specialist, Ifor Griffiths, whom many singers consulted over voice problems, and who pulled no punches if he thought somebody shouldn't sing. He'd say 'You don't go on', and tell you why. This time he examined my throat, then noticed my wrists and ankles were swollen. 'Touch your toes,' he said. I did so and couldn't immediately straighten up, as if my back had locked. Ifor wondered if my problem was psychological, if I was playing the hunchback before I was ready for it, but there was nothing he could recommend so far as my voice was concerned.

Before the dress rehearsal was over I knew I had to take the terrible step of telling those in charge that I couldn't do it, I couldn't sing the opening night. It put them in a dreadful situation, because there was no way they could work anybody else into the role at that notice. David Webster was marvellous: 'We won't open until you're better,' he told me. 'When you're ready let me know.'

The first night was put back for a week. I rested a few days, then tried vocalising a little and decided I was over the worst. So I called Mr Webster, a lot of announcements and stories appeared in the Press about the new opening night, and the excitement built up again.

That morning I felt quite good as I did some warming-up exercises, and still felt confident when I went to the dressing-room to put on costume and make-up. Rigoletto doesn't have a lot to sing in the opening scene, but what there was I sang well enough, and the scene as a whole went splendidly in Franco's lavish setting for the ducal ball.

Back in the dressing-room I did a fairly quick costume change for the garden scene with Gilda, checked my appearance in the mirror, tried the voice a bit . . . the tightness was coming back.

Mind over matter again, I thought to myself. It'll be all right. Probably just some phlegm. I went on stage, sang the conversation with Sparafucile, then Rigoletto's soliloquy, 'Pari siamo', then into the duet with Anna Moffo's Gilda. And as this went on I could feel the voice getting worse and worse, and having to fight harder and harder to keep it going at all. By then it was obvious to the audience as well as backstage that I was in trouble.

During the interval Ifor Griffiths came back to see me, and checked my throat again. 'I don't care what they say,' I remember him declaring, 'there's nothing wrong there' – pointing to my throat – 'but from there down I can't say.'

I determined to go through with it, come what may. My next testing moment was 'Cortigiani!', where Rigoletto rounds angrily on the assembled courtiers. All I remember is half singing it, half speaking it, just to get through. It was John Dobson who afterwards told my wife that he, Ronald Lewis and some of the others were actually in tears as they saw the effort it was costing me. 'I never want to see anyone on stage like that again,' John said to Brenda. 'His eyes were like a hunted animal.'

From this point my own memory is pretty hazy, because I started to lose mental as well as physical control. I know I went on for the last act. I sang a bit, croaked a bit, spoke a lot, but I've no clear recollection of finishing the performance. Perhaps my grief over the dying Gilda was all the more realistic because of the state I was in. I don't know. I don't remember finishing the opera. I don't remember the curtain-calls. I certainly don't remember, as it was later told to me, being brought on for a call, holding up my hand to stop the audience applauding, and saying: 'Ladies and gentlemen. This has not been the management's fault. This is all my fault.'

To which they shouted back, 'No!'

They were, I'm told, sympathetic. They could have booed me off the stage. They could have ended my career there and then. I do remember finding myself back in the dressing-room and would have been ready to jump out of the window if people hadn't been there to calm me down. But the audience had, by and large, understood that I was in trouble physically. Afterwards I thought maybe they'd called to mind the other performances I'd given, the good perform-ances. And I was sad that I'd let them down now, over one of the biggest chances of my career, and in a role I knew I could have performed successfully if all had been well.

Happily, Peter Glossop was available to replace me, stepping in without rehearsal to take over from the next performance, and a fine job he made of it. The jinx hadn't stopped with me, though. Anna Moffo was herself a replacement for Mirella Freni; then Anna went ill and Elizabeth Vaughan took the Gilda role.

Meanwhile, I was taken home after this débâcle. Brenda had been in agony during the performance, not knowing what was happening to me, and she then had to look after me while I slumped in a chair for about two weeks, still not knowing what was causing the trouble. My body began to fold over, and I was starting to do Rigoletto's lop-sided walk. When I took a bath, I found I couldn't lift myself out of it. From my waist up I felt my body was seizing up; I couldn't contract or expand any of the muscles.

The symptoms began to suggest disturbingly that I'd contracted polio. Family, friends and doctors were worried, and still puzzled. I took tablets which calmed me down and made me drowsy, but which did nothing for whatever was afflicting me. Swabs were taken, but they were negative. I had one examination after another, but without result. I stayed at home for about five weeks, my condition not changing very much, until the time came when I was due in New York for my debut at the Metropolitan opera. And it was there, as I shall tell, that a Viennese-born doctor diagnosed the virus or whatever it was, which he'd come across only two or three times in his career, and was able to treat me successfully.

The question then arose as to whether I should sing Rigoletto again. On one side I was told, 'You must sing it to get your nerve back', but I thought that word of my fiasco would have spread quickly round the profession, and perhaps no other management would want to take the inevitable risk. Even if I was asked, as happened in San Francisco, I couldn't be sure that whoever was to conduct would be satisfied with the 'as written' notes, like Solti, instead of the higher ones, which I knew I simply couldn't tackle.

So I made my decision. I'd been fortunate to have a great deal of success in other roles, and it wouldn't be the end of the road for me if I let one role like this go by. I came to terms with my own disappointment, and made up my mind never to sing Rigoletto again.

CHAPTER FIVE

American Adventures

My first of many visits to America, North, Central and South, came about through an outstanding operatic personality on the West Coast who developed a keen appreciation of British singers and their qualities. He was Kurt Herbert Adler, a Viennese by birth who spent nearly thirty years (1956–81) as general director of the San Francisco Opera Association. He had worked with Max Reinhardt in Vienna and as assistant conductor to Toscanini at Salzburg between the wars, had emigrated to America and gone to San Francisco as chorus-master in the 1940s. During his time as general director he steadily lengthened the season and varied the repertory, making San Francisco one of the most opera-conscious of American cities, with standards to match.

I met him outside one of the dressing-rooms in Covent Garden after singing Beckmesser in *Die Meistersinger*. He made some complimentary remarks and then broached the idea of my going to sing at the San Francisco Opera the next year. So far I had only been abroad to Paris with the Glyndebourne company and was eager to accept, but I knew that I couldn't manage this in 1958. He promised to keep in touch and was as good as his word. Some months later a letter came asking if I would sing Beckmesser at San Francisco in the autumn of 1959, and also the Music Master in *Ariadne auf Naxos*. This time, happily, I was able to say I would go.

One big difference for me would be to sing Beckmesser in the original German for the first time which meant, of course, relearning the role right through. My plans for this went awry when I burned my hands and had to spend time in hospital, and I thought I wouldn't be able to prepare my part in time. The possibility of having to cancel San Francisco so that they could get another Beckmesser began to nag at me, but when I raised this with Joan Ingpen, she wouldn't hear of it. She bullied me to get cracking on it, confident that I could, and this provided the necessary incentive.

Richard Lewis travelled on the same flight with me. He had been there before, having sung the first American production of Walton's

Troilus and Cressida there a few years previously. I was glad to be in the company of somebody who was already familiar with the proceedings. The flight then was several hours longer than it is now, and many of the people around me were sleeping. I was envious of them being so relaxed. For my part, I was too excited to sleep a wink, and tried to pass the time by going over and over my German lines for Beckmesser. Even so, it still seemed a long flight.

We were met at the airport by two of the Opera Association's Ladies' Committee with a car, and I was to discover that, no matter how many times you had been before, you were always met at the airport and welcomed in this way. It was one of the friendly touches that made San Francisco so enjoyable for a singer at the opera, and I always appreciated it. Richard and I were driven to one of San Francisco's old hotels, the Whitcombe on Market Street, where he'd stayed on his previous visits.

My mind was filled with all the images of the city I'd seen in films since boyhood, from Jeanette Macdonald and Nelson Eddy, the earthquake and the fire, through many others. Now I was seeing a dream in its reality, and very beautiful it looked to me. Much as I was looking forward to performing, I think at that moment I wanted to see the Golden Gate Bridge even more, and I wasn't disappointed. With each later visit, San Francisco became even more attractive, and when I went across the bridge to Sausalito, the view over the bay made the city on its steeply rising hill look like a wonderful, tiered wedding cake.

Another friend and colleague I met again there was Sena Jurinac, who was singing Eva in *Die Meistersinger* and the Composer in *Ariadne*, as she had done when we were both at Glyndebourne. And among the new friends I made was Paul Schoeffler, the baritone who sang Sachs. I had admired him from the time he sang with the Vienna State Opera at Covent Garden in 1947, and the fact that we had two and a half weeks of rehearsal meant that Schoeffler, who had sung Sachs with many a Beckmesser, was able to give me a great deal of help. His advice made me rethink the role, to give it more dignity and polish, and I was eager to absorb every little suggestion he made. I was also fortunate that Paul Hager, who directed the San Francisco production, knew his *Meistersinger* very well.

Paul directed most of the operas there for some years, and this was the beginning of a very sound working relationship between us, as I later sang in a number of his productions. Except for the San Francisco seasons he was based in Vienna, from where he was able to keep Adler constantly advised and in touch with all that was going on in European opera. They worked marvellously together as a team, and between them gave the opera season a solid foundation, while the conductor, Leopold Ludwig, who was the music director at Hamburg until he died in 1979, contributed significantly to the performance of much of the German repertory there.

We worked hard at rehearsal, often until about ten o'clock at night or even later, but I always enjoyed what I had to do. Rehearsals were certainly preferable to hanging around in the hotel. Now and again there were invitations to parties given by members of the Opera Association for the cast of each opera, and I came across the excellent American custom of having namecards pinned to your lapel, which helps a lot when you're with people you don't know.

One aspect of this soon became apparent to me, though: the snob value of a non-English name. I remember attending one of these parties on my first visit with another newcomer, an Italian *comprimario* who had one or two small character roles. He was no more known to the other party-goers than I was, but because his lapel-card had an Italian name, I found that 'Evans' was quickly bypassed in favour of that. Even after I had had some success with *Die Meistersinger*, I was still more often introduced as 'Mr Beckmesser' than by my own name, almost as if an opera singer could never have such an ordinary name as Evans.

Another evening during my first visit, after we'd been rehearsing *Ariadne* for about eight or nine days, we finished unexpectedly early, at about 5.30 pm. Richard Lewis and I decided to take the opportunity of a free evening and have a dinner out together. So we dressed accordingly and then thought we might give ourselves a cocktail at the top of the Mark Hopkirs Hotel, with its fantastic view over the Bay. What I didn't realise was the lethal effect of American cocktail measures when they kicked back afterwards, especially when I'd had nothing all day but a ham roll and a Coke for lunch.

We sipped and drank our way through two cocktails and admired the view without feeling a thing. But when we moved on to find somewhere for dinner we took the express lift to ground level. Lifts to me were smooth, steady things, but this was a power dive. Only Richard and I were in it, and when it reached street level those two cocktails had blown our senses back up into the sky and left us reeling. The lift doors opened; people were waiting to go up, and what they found were the two of us lurching about inside like total drunkards, practically unable to find the way out. And all on two cocktails!

Came the first night of *Die Meistersinger*. The orchestra was locally engaged for the season, but included many San Francisco Symphony players who hadn't gone on holiday, and a number of experienced musicians who also held teaching appointments in various academies. Everything went well in the performance until, at about 11.30 pm, I noticed Adler pacing anxiously up and down backstage. Soon afterwards a note was discreetly passed to Ludwig as he conducted. Then I saw the orchestra librarian crawling through the orchestra pit to give Ludwig another note. And another.

I discovered later that they were imploring Ludwig to speed up the performance of this long opera because at some point after midnight the Union agreements meant that overtime payments to the orchestra, chorus and stage staff escalated to a rate that would practically have paid for a whole new production. That night we finished well over the time limit, and the next day frantic decisions were being made to cut various passages before the second performance so as not to bankrupt the company.

My Beckmesser role suffered along with the others, and while I coped with this as best I could, I shall always be grateful to Schoeffler for his timely assistance on one occasion. Schoeffler not only knew his own part backwards, but Beckmesser's as well, and during our colloquy in Sachs's workshop, in the first scene of the last act, I forgot one of the cuts in my part and went on singing instead of breaking off. The next thing I realised was that Sachs was singing over the top of me. It threw me enough for me to stop singing, then I understood that Schoeffler had taken up his cue for just this reason. He saved that situation: one of the advantages of working with an experienced artist.

Just before joining the procession of Mastersingers for the final scene, I realised I had no badge and chain like the other Masters were wearing to represent their Guilds. I told Alex, my dresser, to find me something in a hurry, anything that would look suitable. He rummaged among the props and found something which I hurriedly put on. As I went to take my place I lifted the badge to look at it, and what should I see but a Welsh dragon with the motto '*Cymru am Byth*' ('Wales for ever'). I smiled secretly to myself, stepped out a mite more proudly, enjoyed a great success in my debut, and for the next twenty-one years treasured it for luck, taking it with me every time I went to the USA, whether to sing Beckmesser or not.

Part of the San Francisco engagement was a regular two-week visit to Los Angeles, where the company performed at the vast Shrine Auditorium, which held about five or six thousand people. From the main front curtain there was a stage apron of about ten feet or more to the orchestra pit, and because of the limits of lighting we couldn't come forward more than three feet beyond the curtain-line anyway.

This meant the conductor was quite a distance away from where we were singing, and keeping in contact with him was difficult enough, not to mention projecting across that vast stage apron and orchestra pit before your voice could reach the audience.

Another shock was the volume of sound an enthusiastic audience of that size makes in such a resonant auditorium. I was taken aback by it when I had such a warm reception for Beckmesser, but when Jurinac encountered it after her Composer in *Ariadne*, the applause by the thousandfold echoing round and round the house so frightened her that she backed away several feet, as if she were being attacked instead of applauded.

It was Kurt Adler who first asked me if I'd be interested in singing the title role in *Wozzeck*, which had never been performed on the West Coast. I didn't answer right away because I realised this was a challenge, and no ordinary challenge at that. Alban Berg's opera about the downtrodden soldier, from whom everything is stripped away until there is only his life left to lose, had been a *cause célèbre* in several European opera houses including Covent Garden, where Erich Kleiber, who had conducted its original premiere at Berlin in 1925, also conducted its first British performance in 1952.

I had sat in on some of those rehearsals, read the play and thought it wonderful. The music didn't exactly appeal at first, and I was certainly impressed at one of Kleiber's orchestral rehearsals when he stopped to correct one of the horns for playing a wrong note in the midst of all that was going on. By the standards of classical opera, most of the notes in *Wozzeck* sound 'wrong', but I found the effect overwhelming. I had admired both Marko Rothmüller and Jess Walters in the Covent Garden production, and I decided to take up the challenge Adler's offer presented.

To learn the role I sought out John Matheson, who'd worked with Kleiber at Covent Garden and knew the work backwards. I couldn't have had a better coach: he could pick out on the piano just the essential notes and harmonies so that I could fix them in my mind through sheer repetition. I was very grateful to him for helping me to learn the role in a relatively short time.

Wozzeck calls for a method of *Sprechgesang*, a kind of musically pitched speech which was quite foreign to me. The Covent Garden performances had given me some idea of how it should sound, and as I worked on it I found ways and means of acquiring the technique. The secret is to deliver it with a singer's technique, always keeping the vocal support you need for a singing line. I would pay attention to musical values, and mix a falsetto voice with my ordinary tones.

By the time I went back to San Francisco I knew my role really well, something I've tried to do throughout my career. On a later occasion, when Richard Lewis and Michael Langdon also had roles in *Wozzeck* there, Leopold Ludwig told the three of us that it was a special pleasure to work with British singers because we were always thoroughly prepared for our parts and could therefore be the more responsive to the style of production and performance.

The part of Wozzeck was a challenge to which I responded with everything I could summon up within me. The subject may be depressing but to bring it off well affords immense inner rewards. I became totally committed to it emotionally, and at first I delved into the character so deeply that it affected me psychologically.

Looking back now, I never thought of *Wozzeck* as an opera. To me it was a tragic play to which the music brought a gut feeling of emotion that spread within you as the character came to life. Had I approached it as an opera in the usual sense I doubt I would have brought it off. For one thing, the musical idiom is so special. Had I tried to sing it as I would Verdi or Puccini, I would never have finished a performance. It took many performances to come to grips with it. Gradually I began to appreciate the phrasing of the orchestral writing, and the more performances I did, the better I was able to pace the role and become more detached from it. And the more detached I became, the better I performed, I'm quite sure.

We sang it in English, and I'm convinced that it should always be sung in the language of its audience, whether in Germany, Italy or anywhere else. You need to be aware of all that happens and the feelings that are expressed exactly as they're uttered. Otherwise the impact is quite lost.

Trying to build up the character during rehearsal I needed a pair of jackboots to get the effect of a soldier's plodding, trudging walk. The wardrobe master had no boots in my size, only in a couple of sizes bigger, and he thought they would be too uncomfortable for me to use. But I said I would try them anyway, and after I'd worn them for a few minutes I realised that the bigness gave me just the effect I wanted, the monotonous trudge, trudge, trudge from one place to another. After that, I always asked for boots two sizes too big for me in *Wozzeck*, just as I demanded very tight shoes for Beckmesser making me feel the more irritable because the shoes were pinching. All my characters have been built from the feet up.

Marie was sung at these first San Francisco performances by Marilyn Horne. She had understudied the role in Germany and relearned it in English. Even now I think that she sang it better than anybody else I've heard, not only musically correct and vocally true, but wonderfully convincing in the character. Ludwig conducted, and I think everybody was worried about the public reaction to something which had none of the glamour of classical opera, but which was grim and hard and uncompromising.

In the event, we had a marvellous success. Afterwards Robert Watt Miller, who was president of the Opera Association, came up to me with the remark: 'I can't say I like this opera at all, but I suffered to the end. But one thing I will say: you moved me.' I took that as a great compliment, and I admired him for giving the opera a chance and trying to accept it. There are always beginnings.

The critics gave it wonderful reviews, and eventually Kurt Adler actually had to put on an extra performance. Can you imagine? An extra performance of *Wozzeck* by public demand. We felt we had really achieved something, and it was also a thrilling sense of fulfilment for me in a new kind of role that I'd attempted for the first time.

The stage-hands no less played their part. They hated it musically, couldn't grasp the idiom at all, but they soon came to realise how much depended on quick scene-changes: Berg's music only allows a very limited time to get from, say, a street scene to an interior. So they set up bets to see how quickly they could do this, always trying to improve on their previous time.

There could have been a nasty hiatus during one of the rehearsals, on account of a trick played on me by the electricians. They had a metal stool at one side of the stage where they could sit for a bit of a rest, and because the artists and others also found it convenient during rehearsals, the electrical crew often couldn't use it. So they wired it in to the system to give interlopers a gentle shock with the flick of a switch. I found out about this when I sat there myself during the first dress rehearsal for *Wozzeck*, three nights before it opened. What they hadn't realised was that I was soaked with perspiration which dripped through to cover the metal seat. The result when they flicked their switch was that I had a shock which threw me about six feet away. Out cold.

I must have come round fairly quickly. Less than a minute, probably. There was a great commotion all around, and the first thing I heard was Kurt Adler with his German inflexion saying: 'Mein Gott! Find out about our insurance!' Then I heard a woman's voice calling for a doctor. Dr Gropper came, and for a while I'd lost some of the reflexes on one side of the body. Everybody expected me to sue, and couldn't understand why I didn't. But I'd worked so hard for that first night, just three nights away, and it was more important to me to get fit to see that through than to withdraw at that point and start legal proceedings.

Two other new roles came my way that season. One was the villainous Paolo in Verdi's *Simon Boccanegra*, with Tito Gobbi in the title role and Giorgio Tozzi as Fiesco. I enjoyed the performances, as I also did my first acquaintance with the comedy character of the title role in Puccini's *Gianni Schicchi*. This medieval Florentine rogue, who impersonates a dead man in order to make a new will, thus ensuring his own advantage and that of his marriageable daughter, is quite a different kind of operatic comedy. It ends in farce, but it seemed to me that it should be taken very seriously at the start.

Paul Hager was once again the director, and we worked out that at the beginning, when the bereaved family first calls on Schicchi to help them, I should make him seem a fairly devious character, a real schemer out for his own ends. The other members of the family also take the situation very seriously, having found themselves apparently disinherited, and then when Schicchi is brought in and does his impersonation on the supposed deathbed, the comedy becomes more effective for being both farcical and sarcastic, something I kept in mind when I later sang the role at Covent Garden.

We played *Gianni Schicchi* in English, partly because we gave some school performances. They were very successful in a way that they would never have been had we sung in Italian. I've always thought school performances extremely valuable in building future audiences. We'd given some in the early post-war years at Covent Garden, but unfortunately they'd been allowed to disappear. American opera houses take their responsibilities much more seriously in this respect, and there are school performances built into each season.

I've always found school audiences intensely responsive and rewarding and they must be given fully committed performances every time. The only time I've every been booed on stage was after playing the brutal Claggart in Britten's *Billy Budd* before an audience of Chicago schoolchildren. I'm glad it was for the right reason! They identified totally with Billy, one or two of them shouting remarks like 'That's got the bastard' when he laid me out with the fatal blow, and making such a demonstration at my curtain-call that Richard Lewis, who was singing Captain Vere, jokingly called out: 'Hey! He's not as bad as all that!'

I would like to think that every schoolchild had the opportunity to attend opera, ballet, concerts and drama as part of the school curriculum. In latter years I've spent some time lobbying Government ministers and politicians about this. I believe that singers and musicians alike would agree to accept slightly lower fees to perform for school audiences, for the sake of securing their future public. And with the establishment of our regional opera companies (Welsh, Scottish, Opera North, Kent Opera, Glyndebourne Touring Opera) and their touring engagements, schoolchildren could be brought to see them where they were appearing, as occasionally happens now.

I had an encouraging response from Margaret Thatcher when she was Minister for Education, and from Edward Heath when he was Prime Minister. Before I had got very far, though, the Government changed, so I started all over again with Richard Crossman when he became Education Minister. I made my case at a reception attended by several European diplomats, but before I'd finished Crossman interrupted: 'And what operas would you show to children of that age?' (I'd mentioned the ages of ten to twelve or so.)

'From my experience the safest bet would be the Mozart operas,' I said.

He disagreed: 'I think Verdi and Puccini would be best.'

One of the Italian Embassy staff now joined us and we put the question to him. I thought he would also plump for Verdi and Puccini, but without any hesitation he declared:

'Mozart, naturally.'

At this, Richard Crossman walked away, and I wasn't able to carry the matter any further. Since then, the economic problems have made it more and more difficult. Yet I'm convinced this ought to be as much an educational priority as anything else we can offer the children.

Another operatic milestone in San Francisco at this time was the first American production of Britten's *A Midsummer Night's Dream* in 1961, some months after it was staged at Covent Garden. Having played Bottom in this production, as I've told, with Gielgud directing, Solti conducting, and those magical sets of John Piper, I suppose I had been spoiled, but I didn't find the San Francisco staging, which had come there from Canada, very satisfactory. It became known to us as the 'sewer production', because the central feature of the set was a mound with a central opening like a sewer-pipe, into or out of which most of us had to go at one time or another.

I thought the general effect of the San Francisco production unduly coarse and lacking in taste, especially when it came to the play-acting of the rustics in their Pyramus and Thisbe affair. My fellow-singer, who was doubling Flute and Thisbe, really upset me and some of the other rustics with the vulgarity of his caricature. It was the first time I felt I must take a stand on principle, and I warned him I'd play him at his own game.

The situation is that Thisbe, lamenting over the dead body of Pyramus, decides to kill 'herself' with his sword which is normally in view. So I, Pyramus, lay with the sword hidden under me and Thisbe began to panic more and more as 'she' failed to find it. Eventually, just before the comedy would have fallen apart, I produced the sword as if it had materialised out of the air. The audience roared. Thisbe 'died' only just in time, without the usual opportunity to overplay the death throes – and never tried to overdo it again! As a whole, though, the opera was only moderately well received.

I made many good friends in San Francisco through the Opera Association, though in the case of Robert Watt Miller, the Association's president, our relationship began somewhat inauspiciously. He never went anywhere without wearing a hat, usually a brown fedora unless he was in evening dress, when it would be black. I don't remember seeing him without it, except maybe at meals. He always wore it to the theatre, and when he came round to the dressing-room.

I'd only been there a few days on my first visit when this figure, whom I hadn't then met, marched across the stage with his hat on. In British theatres a man always doffs his hat when he steps on to the stage. I'm not sure if it's a symbolic tribute to the art, or just a superstition, but I wanted to respect this. So without knowing who he was I went up to Mr Miller and politely asked him to take off his hat when he crossed the stage.

'I always wear my hat,' he retorted, and walked away. I don't know what went through his mind, but after a few steps he did take off his hat. And whenever he met me later, or came to my dressing-room, he would always make a point of taking off his hat, making sure that I knew it. The same when he came on stage, looking first to see where I was before taking off his hat to walk across.

Dr Gropper was the theatre doctor, and a very good friend to many of the singers. He'd come to America from Berlin and had a love of opera dating back to his earliest years, so apart from treating us when we needed him, he and Mrs Gropper would often have six or seven of us round to their apartment after a performance, where there would be food and drinks while we discussed the evening. There might be Schwarzkopf, Jurinac, Sciutti and Paul Hager, talking about *Figaro*, perhaps; analysing the performance and discussing how we might improve it. Dr Gropper would be fascinated to listen on the inside, as it were, and I found it greatly useful to remember what we'd all talked about when it came to the next performance.

A number of people I met in those early days have remained very firm and dear friends throughout the years, like the Schwabachers, an old San Francisco family who had a ranch not far away. Jimmy Schwabacher, his sister Marie Louise, and her husband, Alan Rosenberg, an eye surgeon, were immensely hospitable. Our two boys were thrilled to visit their ranch and discover a collection of genuine treasures of the old Wild West in a converted barn. One of the antique covered wagons was there, and when I sat in that my own imagination took off and carried me back to the time I played Cowboys-and-Indians in my childhood.

Then there were the Garlands, whose eldest daughter, Peggy, was my introduction to San Francisco when she met me at the airport on my first arrival. Dr Garland had been a specialist in miners' diseases, and many were the discussions we had about the dangers of working in the mines. His dear wife, Edith, made me one of their large family, and I still look on her home as a place where I might pop in at any time and be sure of a warm welcome.

Nor shall I forget the wonderful parties given in my honour by Otto and Susan Meyer, and their daughter Ursula. These and many others were the great supporters of the Opera Association, the enthusiasts who helped to raise the money on which it all depended. There was no public subsidy such as we were beginning to develop and accept in Britain. San Francisco, like other cities in the United States, relied on the generosity and subscription of private individuals, and on commercial institutions, without whom there would have been no opera company there at all.

The chorus for these opera seasons was recruited from people in other professions who gave up their holiday time to rehearse, then came from their places of work to sing at the evening performances as required. They were paid a regular contract fee for the performances, so they were a professional chorus who thought of themselves as such, and I found them as good as any European chorus under full-time contract. There were doctors, nurses, schoolteachers, and many other professions represented, and it was after I went to a popular restaurant on Fisherman's Wharf called Allioto's that I discovered the owner of that was another chorus member.

Once I recall Tito Gobbi, always a gentleman, trying to protect the chorus against the conductor's rantings while we were rehearsing *Simon Boccanegra*. He called out to him: 'Please, Maestro! Please remember they are amateurs.' Amateurs, forsooth! The chorus were most indignant at this, and we nearly had a strike on our hands. Poor Tito! This chorus put me in mind of the Welsh National Opera chorus, who were first formed on a purely amateur basis and only later became professional. There's much to be said for the chorus system of keen part-time professionals, and I'm sorry it couldn't continue under the later union agreements.

Kurt Adler, as I said, first went to San Francisco to train the chorus, but deep down his ambition was to conduct. He's been able to do so in more recent years, and very well too, but at the time I met him all his efforts as General Director had to be concentrated on running the company on a limited budget, which he did with strict authority. His judgment in music and singing couldn't be faulted, but he also knew exactly what could be achieved in staging, and if he was the least bit unhappy with any detail, he would get it corrected. Do it well, and do it now, seemed to be his motto.

His know how and his sometimes overbearing manner could frighten people on occasion, and upset them too. I once heard him go to a conductor in rehearsal and declare: 'It's all too slow. It's so slow we'll never finish the opera.' I felt embarrassed for the conductor, but Adler didn't care. He had to make his point. It happened to me, some years later, when I was directing *Falstaff*. Adler interfered so much in what I was trying to do that I could take no more of it. So I turned and shouted at him: 'For God's sake, Boss, sit down!' And he sat down. I wondered if that might be my last contract but Kurt's wife, Nancy, who always had such a calming effect on him, said to me: 'I'm glad you told him that. If he kept on much longer, I'm afraid he'd have a heart attack.' And whether he got on with people or not, I have to say that Kurt was almost always right in what he said. He did a wonderful job there.

I think that Adler had a respect for Richard Lewis and myself, as British singers whose work was always well-prepared and of a good standard, even before Leopold Ludwig said how much he enjoyed working with us because of this. So I called to mind other singers in Britain who were no less qualified, and when future repertory was being talked about I started to mention one or two names who I thought would be suitable for particular roles.

The first to suggest itself was Michael Langdon, who'd just had a success at Covent Garden as Baron Ochs in *Der Rosenkavalier*. When I knew that Adler was looking for an Ochs, I told him about Mike and Hertha Töpper, who'd been the Covent Garden Oktavian with Mike, backed me up. The result was that Adler took our word; Mike had another success in San Francisco and, as a result of that and Paul Hager's support, found himself invited to sing Ochs at the Vienna State Opera.

A similar thing happened with other British singers. I told Adler that Stuart Burrows was one of the finest Mozart singers I'd heard, and he proved me right when Adler invited him to San Francisco for Tamino in *The Magic Flute*. I like to think that Adler came to trust my judgment over the years. He certainly gave an opportunity to many British singers, whose success in San Francisco was an increasingly valuable stepping-stone to their international careers, often taking them to the New York Metropolitan and to European opera houses.

One year Adler went out of his way to support a British Week in San Francisco. It was mainly a trade occasion, but we both thought we should try to make a British contribution in the opera house. I suggested the Royal Ballet, who I thought were going to be on the East Coast, but when Adler made enquiries it didn't work out. Then I heard that the English Opera Group would be touring in Canada and the USA, so I suggested he tried to fix a visit by them. And he succeeded. He worked tremendously hard to raise the extra backing that was needed, and he did both Britain and Britten proud. They brought their production of *A Midsummer Night's Dream*: Princess Alexandra attended a gala performance of it and Britain's prestige in the arts was enhanced as much as it was in trade.

Two years after I made my debut in San Francisco, I began another long and enjoyable association with the Lyric Opera of Chicago, although my first visit there wasn't as auspicious as it had been in San Francisco. Marilyn Horne and I were invited to take part in the world premiere of *The Harvest*, an opera by the American composer, Vittorio Giannini. It was a tale of steaming passions on a farm in the American southwest at the turn of the century, with William Wildermann as the blind father, and myself as the eldest son whose city-born wife, played by Marilyn, raised lustful thoughts in father and younger brothers, leading to inevitable tragedy.

The first (and, I think, only) performances were given in October 1961 with the composer conducting. I thought the story worked quite well, and some of the music was vocally very attractive with good, strong melodies. But the whole seemed to me to be overblown in a Wagnerian style which I didn't think very well suited to the subject, and the orchestra was as big as it would be for any Wagner or Strauss opera.

Marilyn and I imagined we had been invited on the strength of our

Wozzeck performances in San Francisco, but even after the first night we realised that *The Harvest* couldn't be called a success and, as we went back to our hotel, feeling depressed, we asked ourselves if this might be our last as well as our first visit to Chicago. Not knowing anybody else there then, and not wanting just to sit around the hotel in that frame of mind, we took ourselves to an all-night cinema across the road where there was a film we quite wanted to see.

Inside, as our eyes became accustomed to the darkness, we realised we weren't in very salubrious company. I noticed one man tottering up the aisle, shaking very badly, who came back some minutes later apparently quite normal. 'He's been for a fix,' Marilyn commented, and I started to feel more than a little uneasy. We sat on for a while until I had the fright of my life when, as I watched the screen, I became aware of a long 10-foot pole right in front of my eyes with what looked like a boxing-glove fixed on the end of it. It went straight across our line of vision as we shrank back in our seats, and jabbed somebody three seats away who was fast asleep. Cinemas weren't for sleeping in, and it was the job of the attendant, I learned afterwards, to keep customers awake during the night performances. But that finished it for us that night, and we left without more ado.

We need not have worried about the Lyric Opera, though. Both Marilyn and I were asked back many times after that. I went there to sing all the main roles in my repertory, and, later, to direct as well.

Chicago's General Director was Carol Fox. She was, I think, the only woman then to hold a top position in international opera management, and she was one of the most capable administrators I've known. She was a big woman in every sense: big in stature, big in spirit, big in everything she did, and she didn't suffer fools gladly. When Carol entered a room she commanded attention. Nobody could ignore her.

Her ambition had been to become a singer herself, and her parents had sent her to study in Italy. The hoped-for career never developed, unfortunately, because of ill-health. For many of the years that I knew her, she suffered badly from asthma, and having been afflicted myself at one time, I can appreciate what this meant. Her great love of music nevertheless involved her with the opera company in Chicago, and with her drive and personality she could not fail to be successful. Over more than twenty-five years she built the Lyric Opera into one of the most distinguished and well-respected companies in the world.

To Carol, Italy was the operatic Mecca, and her feeling for Italian opera and the Italian style of singing made Chicago's opera predominantly Italianate. Pino Donati, who was married to the singer Maria

Caniglia, was her Artistic Adviser, and in 1964 Bruno Bartoletti joined her as Music Director after spending some years with the Maggio Musicale orchestra in Florence.

Carol could proudly boast that she was the first to bring Maria Callas to the USA, and she dominated every aspect of the opera house she controlled. Like Adler in San Francisco, she sat in on every rehearsal, quick to notice anything that went wrong histrionically or vocally, and no less quick to let you know about it in no mean terms. Yet I felt that underneath the tough exterior she was a little insecure.

Her strength was that she was always a woman of her word. Once she had given it, she would stick to it; once she had faith in somebody, she would support that person against any odds. I admired her and became very fond of her. Our families became great friends, and we miss her very much since she died in 1981.

A few years earlier, she had suffered a terrible injury in Florence when, walking one block from the opera house to the hotel where she was staying, a motor-cyclist mounted the pavement and tried to snatch her handbag. The strap over her wrist didn't break and, with her hand caught in her pocket, she was dragged bodily along the street. After this her health deteriorated very quickly and she was in great pain. She struggled valiantly to cope with this and tried to continue running the Lyric Opera, but the strain eventually became too much.

Her life was so tied up with the opera house that she didn't live long after she retired from it. By then her stalwart assistant, Ardis Krainik, had for some time been her second-in-command. Just as John Tooley kept things going at the Royal Opera House during Sir David Webster's last couple of years there, so Ardis, without making it obvious, ran the Lyric Opera when Carol became ill. And just as John Tooley was the evident successor to Sir David, so Ardis was the obvious choice to continue the smooth running at Chicago.

Nothing moved me so much as the dedication and enthusiasm of the chorus, in Chicago no less than in San Francisco, when we gave *Peter Grimes*. Britten gives the chorus a starring part in this if ever there was one and they really made the most of it. In both cities the chorus was thrilled and excited by it, and of course this communicated itself to the audience. Many of the chorus singers were in tears the first time they sang it, and often in later years I was asked when we would perform it again. Such reactions aren't usual with modern opera, and I believe we should be grateful to Britten and to *Peter Grimes* for all that it continues to achieve in the theatre.

Thinking to follow up the success of one British opera I began to urge *Billy Budd* on both Chicago and San Francisco, and because we were constantly being nagged in Britain about the export drive and the need to earn dollars, I thought I would do my share and suggest that the sets and costumes for *Budd* should be hired from Covent Garden, where there was an excellent production. Adler and Carol Fox came to London within a few weeks of each other, so I made my sales pitch to each of them in turn, believing it would be better still if the production could go from one opera house to the other.

Billy Budd duly went to Chicago in 1970 where they gave the first American performance of Britten's revised version in two acts, with Ande Anderson and myself jointly directing it. Theodore Uppman sang the title role, as he had done at the Covent Garden premiere, and I strongly recommended Richard Lewis as Captain Vere, with myself as Claggart.

I had begun suggesting various British singers to Carol Fox, just as I had at San Francisco, and I'm happy that several went there after we discussed possibilities for particular roles. As I've said, Carol was very Italian-minded, and there was a regular supply of the best Italian singers appearing with the Lyric Opera. Soon the most promising American singers were also engaged for Chicago, and gradually more British singers came to be engaged as well. Taking part in *Così* in 1972 there were four Welsh principals: Margaret Price, Anne Howells, Ryland Davies and myself as Don Alfonso.

With conductors it was sometimes more difficult. Georg Solti took the musical directorship of the Chicago Symphony Orchestra in 1969 (overlapping with his last couple of years at Covent Garden), and we would often be in Chicago at the same time during the autumn season. I tried hard to persuade him to conduct the opera, and I know Carol did as well, but he never did. Some conductors make demands on rehearsal time that simply can't be contained in opera budgets, especially the American ones which are dependent on private funds. However, Solti came to my performances occasionally, and I in turn went to some of his concerts, as well as enjoying the occasional steak and kidney pie which Valerie Solti cooked in their apartment.

Donizetti's *Don Pasquale* was one of the roles I sang several times at Chicago, on one occasion nearly causing my own downfall. The tenor Alfredo Kraus was Ernesto, and during our duet in the first act, when old Pasquale is being very boorish to his lovelorn nephew, I thumped a table with my hand to emphasise my words. The next moment Alfredo was grabbing my arm and pushing me to one side of the stage. I thought he'd gone crazy. Definitely not rehearsed. But then I looked back and saw the scenery flats toppling down all around. My blow to the table had apparently dislodged one of them, which then brought all the others down in a domino effect, until they'd all collapsed. There were gasps of concern from the audience, mixed with some laughter.

Happily we were alone on stage for the duet so nobody was hurt. The curtain was brought down while the stage was re-set and then we began the duet again. Once more I brought my hand down to the table, but this time I stopped short of striking it, with a glance to the audience ('doing a Jack Benny' one newspaper called it), and this time they laughed louder than ever. The episode was front-page news in Chicago the next day. I sometimes think the public is more entertained when opera goes wrong than when it goes right.

There was a night at Covent Garden when the safety curtain stuck during *Figaro*. There were thoughts of abandoning the performance when I said to John Tooley: 'Let's go on and do it as a costume-concert in front, while you see what can be done with the curtain.' He agreed. The audience was told. Ladders were brought into the orchestra pit, up which the ladies in their long dresses and the rest of us clambered to get in front of the safety curtain. Loud applause from the audience. We started the scene, but we'd hardly sung two or three notes when that curtain went up behind us. Much amusement. Even more relief.

My travels took me to South America as well as North, and in 1963 I went for the first time to Buenos Aires. The Teatro Colón there has long been the leading opera house on that continent: it reckons to have international seasons comparable to those elsewhere, and over the years most of the leading opera singers from Europe and the USA have appeared there. My first invitation was for *Falstaff*, which would be newly produced for me, but owing to other commitments I just couldn't get there until three or four days after the rest of the cast.

When I did arrive there were long faces all around. Plainly not much had been done in the way of rehearsal, and when I saw the stage I was appalled. There was such a mixture of bits and pieces I couldn't believe it: an early twentieth-century rocking chair for Alice Ford; louvre windows at the back of the set; an oak chest instead of a laundry basket. Nothing matched anything else, and nowhere was there a semblance of period or style relating to Verdi, nor to Shakespeare.

But that wasn't all. The director for the production was from Europe, but the cast was depressed because he didn't seem to know what he wanted. He was trying to work from bar to bar, as it were, and after three days of this some of the singers went to the theatre director and said they couldn't work like that. When I turned up they told the opera house director that they wanted me to direct the production and they wouldn't perform unless I did something with it.

At this time I'd never done any directing and I was decidedly apprehensive. But the feelings of the others were clear enough, so I realised something had to be done quickly to resolve the situation. The production director proved extremely approachable and even admitted that he knew very little about the opera – he was perfectly happy that we should carry on as if he were still directing us, accepting that those of us who knew the opera well would ask him from time to time if we could do things in a certain style. In this way we all felt we could work effectively without embarrassing him.

I then discovered there was a vast quantity of scenery and props in the basement of the Colón, a veritable Aladdin's cave. So my first suggestion was to investigate this and see if we could come up with a more convincing stage design. We did so, and I think we improved it. And because the director was fundamentally very capable, even if he didn't know *Falstaff*, the situation soon improved and we managed a reasonably successful first night. Fernando Previtali conducted, and the audience was enthusiastic. We knew backstage that it wasn't that good, but after a few more performances it started to come together and turned out to be a very successful production.

That same season I also sang Leporello in *Don Giovanni* under Hans Schmidt-Isserstedt, with whom I'd previously worked at Glyndebourne. He was a fine conductor, not least in Mozart, and I thought him generally under-rated on the international scene. The standard of orchestral playing at the Colón had declined since the days of Erich Kleiber, who worked there regularly from 1937 to 1949. Now it seemed they were no longer used to playing Mozart, and I knew what Schmidt-Isserstedt meant when he said to me at one rehearsal, in an aside: 'Mozart must be turning in his grave.'

I also sang my first performance of *Don Pasquale* in Buenos Aires, rather more suddenly than I had bargained for. The schedule I'd agreed allowed me at least ten days before the first night to prepare and rehearse the title role. During the *Falstaff* performances, however, the dates were suddenly changed, leaving me with no more than four days before the dress rehearsal to polish Don Pasquale. My nervous apprehension over this can be imagined, but fortunately I could rely on two experienced friends and colleagues to guide me: Luigi Alva and Sesto Bruscantini.

Even after the scheduled rehearsals we would still go on working together, and our efforts were so concentrated that by the first night I felt I'd been working on the role for a month. Happily the performance went fantastically well, and we had to respond to demands for an encore, after the Pasquale–Malatesta duet with Sesto.

The Colón itself is a splendid theatre, with wonderful acoustics for the musical balance. With a few hundred more seats than Covent Garden, it was the last great opera house to be built in the lavishly ornate 19th-century style. It opened in 1908, having been built mainly for the large numbers of Italian emigrants who went to South America at the end of the last century.

On both sides of the auditorium, on a level with the orchestra stalls, I was intrigued to see openings with drawn curtains behind wrought iron grilles. During one performance I noticed an occasional movement of these curtains and asked what these places were for. I was told they were boxes where bereaved persons who were keeping their period of mourning could come to hear the opera, but not see or be seen.

The Colón was a majestic theatre but, I regret to say, not one of the cleanest. Brenda and Luigi Alva's wife, Anita, were sitting together during a performance of *Falstaff* when they both began to feel distinctly uncomfortable. Soon they realised they were badly bitten by fleas from the upholstered seats. Anita in particular was in agony, having a broken leg covered in plaster at the time. Nor did we escape on the stage, but we had a friend working in Buenos Aires, Barney Miller, a director of the Johnson's Wax firm, and when I told him about the fleas he brought us some de-lousing spray which, from then on, I put on the inside of my Falstaff costume.

I'd been warned by Hans Hotter that the Colón management sometimes forgot to pay its artists. 'Make sure you're paid for one performance before you do the next,' was his advice. I let it go for the first couple of Falstaff performances, but when there was still no sign of any fee I had to take some action as I was running out of cash. I'd asked for it, but nothing had happened, so at the third performance I sat in my dressing-room wearing just the under-padding for my costume and said to my dresser: 'I'm not going on until I've been paid for my two performances so far. Would you please tell the management?'

Of course there was a great commotion. But I sat tight. Twenty minutes after the time for curtain-up the performance still hadn't begun. A couple of minutes later I was on stage – in the meantime I'd had my fee in four or five paper bags stuffed with dollars. They'd had to raise the money wherever they could, all in small notes, 1, 5, 10 or 20-dollar bills. I handed the bags to my dresser, and asked him to count it while I went on. It was exactly one dollar short, but I decided not to push for that!

Singing in Buenos Aires was great for the ego. The opera public were wildly enthusiastic and loved everything they saw and heard. They would mill round outside after the performance and demand autographs by the hundred as soon as they spotted one of the singers. I'll never forget spending about two hours signing my name with the rest of the cast until the Intendant (Director) came to rescue us.

The first time I was in Buenos Aires, Brenda joined me. In those days we never travelled together, and she would usually join me after the rehearsal period. But on my second visit she brought our two sons with her. Alun was then nine and Huw almost three, and coping with them both became quite a nightmare when she found they had to change planes in Paris. Huw, the little devil that he was, always pressed buttons to see what might happen, and he found one in Paris that put all the airport escalators out of action. Brenda hurried him away praying that nobody had seen him do it.

Huw was very blond-haired and caused quite a sensation in the streets of Buenos Aires. Passers-by couldn't resist touching his curly hair in an indulgent sort of way, but he became hugely annoyed when this happened. Somewhere he'd acquired one disturbing extension to his vocabulary: 'Bugger off!' he would say to them, and they'd pass on, smiling and not understanding his English. Much to my relief.

This was the year, 1965, when I was due to sing in Mexico City for the first time after finishing at Buenos Aires, so for once the two boys, Brenda and I travelled as a family on the flight. With us were Anita and Luigi Alva, who were going home to Peru. At the stopover in Lima, I thought I'd stretch my legs and go with them to the airport building, but Luigi was no sooner inside the Customs room than he was recognised, having become practically a national idol since his international success as an opera singer.

So there was Luigi trying to clear the washing-machine he'd brought with him, and a television set for his mother, and all the rest of his luggage, while the Customs officials and a crowd of other people were milling round to greet him. He told them I was his English friend and another singer, and I found myself not only swept up in the warmth of their welcome, but physically swept through into the airport foyer.

Meanwhile, the plane containing Brenda and the boys was preparing to leave. She started to make a fuss because I hadn't returned, and it was only when some of the airport staff came to look for me and forced a way through the crowd of Luigi's fans that I was able to get back to the plane, just in time.

Mexico City to me had a folk feeling about it. Whether this was created by the murals on the walls of the university and other large buildings, some ceramic and some painted, or the general appearance of the people and furnishings, we felt there was a strong peasant element. And this was intensified after we'd been told about the craft markets just outside the city, where we found all manner of wares being sold.

During our time there, we weren't without incident where the boys were concerned. While I was rehearsing (for *Falstaff* and *Don Pasquale*) Brenda would take them around and then arrange to meet me when I finished in the late afternoon. One day it was teeming with rain, and as I was a little early in finishing I decided to take a taxi to the hotel before they came to meet me. Of course, I missed them, but I thought the rain would make them return pretty quickly, and I waited for them there.

Sure enough, Brenda returned. So did Huw with her. But there was no sign of Alun. She said he'd run on ahead of them, but I hadn't seen him. By this time darkness had fallen and the rainstorms had caused a power cut. All the lights went out and candles were produced. I went to see if Alun had somehow missed me and gone to our room. The lift was out of order, so I had to go by the stairs. Still no sign of him. By this time we were both worried. Brenda began to panic and went outside to search the nearby streets, calling his name and seeing only the reflection of candles in shops and windows.

Back at the hotel about half an hour later, still without him, the lights were restored. And who should appear but Alun, now able to emerge from the lift where he'd been trapped when the power failed as he was going up to our room. But what really upset us then was his story of two men who were also in the lift when it stopped, and who talked him into clambering up through the little trap door in the roof, with their help, to see if there was a way out. We felt quite sick when we thought what might have happened if the power had come back while he was standing on the roof of the lift.

Anybody approaching the Opera House in Mexico City for the first time could be forgiven for wondering if he or she was seeing straight. The building is, in fact, sinking to one side, just a fraction a year. It's not as bad as the Leaning Tower of Pisa, and once inside it's not particularly noticeable, but it does make you doubt your eyes.

Here I met Tito Capobianco, the Argentinian producer and artistic director who worked for some time with the New York City

Opera, and then took charge of the San Diego Opera in California from 1977. He took his work very seriously indeed, but he was also one of the most elegant and handsome men I'd encountered. As we came to know each other better, I'd pull his leg and say that I couldn't understand why he spent his time organising temperamental opera singers when he might well have been a cinema hearthrob himself.

Tito was the kind of director I most appreciated, because he was always ready to try something a different way if you or he felt it wasn't working. He never minded a singer changing something if it was better suited to that person's personality or frame of mind. And, believe me, there was plenty of reason for making changes when we found what the Mexican opera house had to offer in the way of props and staging.

It was rather like Buenos Aires all over again, only here the worst problem concerned the laundry basket in which Falstaff has to hide before being tipped out of the window. Usually this has a false back so that I rolled away out of sight before it was lifted up to the window. Once or twice there's been a false bottom over a trap door, so that I could be lowered down, though this has entailed the risk of a sheet or some other garment getting caught in the stage trap and giving the game away.

Here in Mexico I was first confronted with a small box. No way could I have got into it. 'A basket,' demanded Tito. 'A big basket.' They came back with one that might just have been large enough for my eldest son. 'A basket big enough for Falstaff,' Tito explained. 'A wardrobe basket for costumes, a skip.' Nothing. So he sent them to make one.

Back came the most beautiful custom-built chest. About five or six feet long, three wide and three deep. Solid wood, with just one handle at either end. It appeared just in time for the dress rehearsal and, without thinking, I clambered into it. I have to spend several minutes in there, but nobody had thought to provide air holes. I began to knock on the lid and shout, but the music being played while Ford is conducting his frantic search for the suspected lover simply drowned me out. Gasping for breath, I had to force the lid up with my shoulders, and this was quite a feat because Quickly was sitting on the basket.

Falstaffs in the past would simply step or climb into the laundry basket to hide from Ford, but Carl Ebert and I decided at Glyndebourne that it would be more in keeping with Falstaff's character if he were to be pushed, lifted or otherwise forced into the basket by the three ladies in the room with him. To achieve this, I would sit on one corner of the open basket, and brace my arms on two sides. Alice and Meg lifted my legs up and I would topple backwards into the basket.

Once inside, I then had to turn on to my knees ready to crawl out through the false side, or drop down through the trapdoor. It took a tremendous effort in my padding and costume, and with all the loose linen in the basket, but I always thought it worthwhile to achieve the effect.

The Mexican chest had no escape mechanism. And two handles were insufficient for the purposes of lifting it with me inside. Even with extra handles fitted on, it took eight of them to lift it to the window. And what then? There was a drop of six feet or so from the windowsill to the stage floor, and I was still to be inside. After a hasty conference with Tito Capobianco we came up with the solution of two greased planks nailed to the windowsill out of sight, down which the chest would slide to the backstage beyond.

'Take a chance, Geraint,' implored Tito. There was no time to rehearse anything between dress rehearsal and performance, but I agreed to go along with the risk. On the first night I was bundled into my 'coffin', hoisted to the window and tipped over on to the greased planks, which promptly transferred their grease to the underside of the chest so that, even after it hit the floor it continued sliding into the distance, fortunately coming to a halt before it collided with anything. But that was the first and last time I ever agreed to stay inside, not knowing what might happen to me when it went through the window.

Preparations for *Don Pasquale* weren't much smoother. Again there was no set to speak of. Tito had to uncover what was left around in store, something from this opera, something from that. While he was trying to get it together he asked me, as a favour, to help with the directing, saying I knew the opera. Actually, my experience of it amounted to no more than the few performances in Buenos Aires I've described, but there was an Italian in the cast who knew it quite well, so between us we managed a kind of collective production which Tito polished at the last moment.

At the dress rehearsal I was still without the necessary dressing-gown for one of my scenes and the only waistcoat available was some 18th-century fashion which came below my hips. 'It'll all be ready tomorrow,' I was promised. The last *mañana* came, and it still wasn't ready. Tito exploded, pulled money from his own pocket, gave it to my dresser, who was also in charge of the wardrobe, and sent her out to buy a dressing-gown, *any* dressing-gown, provided it fitted, while I cut the waistcoat with scissors and tried to pin it up.

Half an hour to curtain-call, ladies and gentlemen, but we made it – even with a dressing-gown in the most horrific colour, and a waistcoat pinned into position!

There were other problems also, most of them centred on the soprano who sang Norina. She was a local girl, light-skinned and very beautiful, but it was soon clear that she knew practically nothing of the role. At every rehearsal she was still learning the words from the score, and when she came unprepared to the dress rehearsal I made some enquiries about her. I was in Mexico for the first time and knew nothing of her, but it transpired she was the protégée of a wealthy donor to the opera who was expecting her to sing.

It wasn't for me to make a fuss in that situation. She'd made a couple of films, I was told, so I gave her the benefit of the doubt. Came the first night and it was obvious she simply wasn't equal to the part. She was replaced before the next performance by another soprano who knew what she was about, but before this I'd been approached for an interview. I blew off steam about the hopeless first soprano, who I reckoned had ruined the performance, and of course my words were printed in the next day's papers. I was never asked back to Mexico City after this visit.

I'd been warned about the high altitude in Mexico before I went there, and that it might make me short of breath. The Royal Ballet had already performed there and had been provided with oxygen cylinders at the side of the stage and the same arrangements were made for us. As it happened, I never needed the oxygen, because I decided to acclimatise myself while the rehearsals were taking place by doing some jogging. At that time it wasn't quite as fashionable a pursuit as it is now, so I used to go out at night, around ten o'clock, to a particular area where nobody much would see me. Anyway, I wasn't sure about using the cylinders. I like to know what's happening inside my body, and I was always careful about treatments. I never risked sprays if my voice wasn't in good shape – you never know what might happen to the vocal cords or to the muscles around them.

At one small reception I was sitting out in the garden with Carlo Felice Cillario, the conductor, when we heard a young man singing from an upstairs window. I was very impressed with the sound of him, and Cillario told me the singer had asked to audition. Would I hear him too? We did so, and Cillario mentioned that Glyndebourne wanted a tenor to sing Werther in Massenet's opera. He asked if I thought this man would be worth considering.

'He's just about ideal,' I said. 'He's young, a good presence, a bit heavy maybe, but a lovely voice. You say he's had some experience, and I think he could do it. What did you say his name is?'

'Domingo,' said Cillario. 'Placido Domingo. When you get back, will you tell Glyndebourne about him?'

So I did. But Glyndebourne were apparently no longer interested, even though Cillario was conducting their *Werther*, and that was the last we heard of Domingo for several more years, whereas we might have had the pleasure of hearing him right at the outset of his spectacular career. We've worked together a few times since he came to the top, and I found him still the friendly but dedicated person he was that time in Mexico City. He knew he wanted to sing opera, and he set out to achieve it, with determination but without brashness. He had a humility about singing as a career, and was the kind of personality that made you sympathetic and anxious to help.

After the audition in Mexico we saw more of each other there. He told me that at one time he'd thought of taking up professional bullfighting, becoming a toreador. I felt that was more of an idle dream, a form of hero-worship, but I went along with him a couple of times to watch a bullfight. I wasn't sure I wanted to, but I recognised it as part of the Spanish sporting culture, and I wanted to discover what it was all about. Of course there's cruelty in it, and I didn't like the way the animal was goaded by the picadors and the spears at the outset, but I was thrilled by and admired the courage, and the artistry, that went into the toreador's performance.

Now I realised what Escamillo sings about in *Carmen* and related my performance on stage to what was happening in front of my eyes at the *corrida*. What I saw was an immensely brave showman who was literally risking his life. It was like a ballet, but a ballet to the death. There's no death on my side of the footlights. Singers aim for what perfection they can, but if they fall short there's usually another chance. If a toreador falls short of perfection, it can cost him his life. Their technique is an art too, but their lives and not just their careers depend on what they risk each time they go into the arena.

The very name of the Metropolitan Opera House, New York, has the same kind of glamour for us in Britain as that of Covent Garden has for many Americans. As with San Francisco, I remembered my youthful film-going days, and the films I'd seen featuring not only New York itself but often stars of the Metropolitan Opera there, like Ezio Pinza and Lawrence Tibbett. So when I was first approached about singing there, I really felt I'd arrived.

My agent at the time was Howard Hartog, of Ingpen and Williams, who told me there was a message asking if I would be available to sing Falstaff at the Met between certain dates, in a new production by Franco Zeffirelli. I was indeed free, and I made sure the dates stayed that way. But time went on, and no further word came. The next thing I heard was that somebody else was cast instead, so I swallowed my disappointment and went off to keep my dates in San Francisco.

What should I next receive from New York but a letter from Franco telling me that things there weren't going too well, and calling me every name under the sun for 'not being available' when he'd asked for me! I'd no idea where that message had come from, but I was pretty annoyed with the Met anyway for keeping me dangling, and then never giving me a final decision. So when I finished on the West Coast I decided to stop over in New York for a few days on my way back.

My very efficient agent there, Ann Colbert, was as mystified as I was, so I arranged an appointment with the Met's general manager, Rudolf Bing. When we met in his office I told him outright that I thought it unprofessional, not to say rude, to have asked if I would be free for *Falstaff*, and then never to have sent any reply when I'd held myself ready. He called in his assistant, Bob Hermann, and they both flatly denied having made any enquiries about me at all.

I found this very strange, so I made ready to leave. Bing stopped me, took a book from a shelf and, running his finger down a certain page, enquired in the most patronising way: 'Well, now, what operas do you do?'

This was adding insult to injury, and I began to get very angry. After all, I'd been singing at Covent Garden since 1948, at Glyndebourne since 1950, and at San Francisco and Chicago, so as an Intendant who had himself been at Glyndebourne and the Edinburgh Festival before he went to New York, he must have known or read something about my professional work. This time I did take my leave, saying as I did so:

'Mr Bing, I've not come here looking for work. I've plenty of it, thank you. Thank you for seeing me. Good day.' And I left.

Maybe, I thought, that's it for me at the Met. But now I'd had an encouraging success with Falstaff in San Francisco, and the next time I performed there, word had gone round and some of the New York and other East Coast critics came out to hear me. That was flattering anyway, but so also were the reviews they wrote in the New York papers, calling me 'the best Falstaff we have' and asking why I hadn't been engaged there. For other roles, too.

Now came an official message from the Met, via Ann Colbert, inviting me to sing Falstaff after all, with Leonard Bernstein conducting. The invitation could not have come at a worse time for me personally. I was still suffering from the mystery illness that had affected my voice and made such a fiasco of my Rigoletto at Covent Garden, and I was very worried that my New York debut, now that it was actually arranged, might be spoiled in the same way.

It was Ann Colbert who came to the rescue. She persuaded me to go to New York anyway, so that even if the worst happened and I had to cancel, I would at least have shown willing in the first place. But she'd also talked to a doctor about my trouble and the symptoms. He was an elderly Viennese who said he'd come across this particular virus only three times before, but he thought he could treat it if I would give him time, at least a few weeks.

The soonest I could go there was about four weeks ahead of my debut, and this I did, starting the treatment as soon as I arrived. Two weeks later I knew I was much better and was ready to start rehearsals, but the doctor warned me I still shouldn't sing until he said so. For some days I worked without really using the voice, but then came the day of the first orchestral rehearsal with Leonard Bernstein who, up to that moment, didn't know what my singing was like.

I explained this to the doctor. 'Why don't you do the clever thing,' he said. 'Tell Maestro Bernstein you have a cold, that you'll sing the first scene for him properly, but then you'll mark the part, if he will agree.'

This was a new idea for me then, though I could see the sense of it. Afterwards I always reckoned that wherever I went for the first time, the first ten minutes or so of singing at a full rehearsal should always be the very best, so that everybody knows what you can do. I did this with Bernstein, whom I'd never previously met, though I'd once or twice been mistaken for him by autograph hunters, especially if they'd only seen him on the television or in photographs (we later had a good laugh about this, and he told me to sign his name if I felt like it).

He agreed that I should sing only the first scene fully, but when we performed it for that first run-through with the orchestra, I was agreeably surprised how well the voice sounded after the problems I'd had with it. At the end of that scene the orchestral players themselves applauded and Bernstein smiled at me: 'Save your voice now. We know what you can do.' I was very grateful.

Coming into an existing production meant that I was given no stage rehearsal. I simply didn't know what the set looked like before the first night. I was in my dressing-room a good two hours beforehand, as I always was for Falstaff – I needed a long time to dress and make up. To make things worse, the senior dresser, who had been at the Met for many years, had died suddenly a few days before, and his son had taken over.

Dressing me for Falstaff the first time would be difficult for anybody, and I've no doubt he was upset and nervous. Even so, we were late, and getting later. Met performances always started on time and 'Beginners' were called. That was me, and I was still only half-ready. Bing came to find out what was happening to me, and I apologised. Then Bernstein looked in because he was now ready to start. Eventually, five minutes late, I made my way to the stage, down the worn stone steps of the 'old' Met (before the Lincoln Center days).

I now saw the stage set for the first time. 'There's the door,' I thought to myself. 'And that's the table.' I just had time to take note of these details when I heard applause, Bernstein started the orchestra and the curtain went up as I scuttled to the seat where I should have been sitting. I was away, with no time to think about anything. Certainly no time to be nervous.

I've already described the excitement after I sang my first Falstaff at Glyndebourne, and then the elation of the performances with the same company in Paris, but that was surpassed by the New York reception. At the end of the first scene I'd no sooner sung the top note before starting to chase Bardolph and Pistol around the stage than the audience seemed to explode. I needn't have sung another note then. I couldn't hear the orchestra anyway, there was such volume of applause. And only then did I start to feel nervous, because I woke up to the fact that I was singing at the Met for the first time.

The rest of the performance went no less splendidly, I'm glad to say. Sometimes, when the adrenalin has been running high in a performance, the applause is little more than a background and I would be hardly conscious of it. But on this particular night I was certainly conscious of it; I knew what I was about and I wallowed in it and the thrill it brought. When the opera was finished the audience just got to their feet and swarmed down towards the orchestra pit, the better to shout and applaud. Brenda and Ann Colbert were more or less left alone at the back of the stalls, they later told me, tears of delight streaming down their faces.

I lost count of the curtain-calls. But after a good many of them Bernstein took me on with him, just the two of us. And it all seemed to start over again until I began to feel quite drunk with the huge excitement of it. There was a party to follow, and Ann Colbert had invited some of the British celebrities like Edith Evans, John Gielgud, Emlyn Williams and Alicia Markova, who were already enjoying a success in the New York theatre; and a number of musicians including Artur Rubinstein, Isaac Stern, Georg Solti and Terry McEwan. Now, for the first time, I felt I belonged to what had been called the British invasion of Broadway. Especially when, time and again, people would say to me: 'My God! We've had Sutherland as Lucia and now you as Falstaff. What else have they got for us over there?'

My euphoria lasted for some days after that as I was recognised in the street and congratulated or asked to sign an autograph. It reminded me of Vienna, where the same thing happened. One New York taxi-driver was all attention when I asked for the Metropolitan Opera House. 'You a singer?,' he asked, and when I said I was, he pressed the matter further.

'What are you then? Bass? Tenor? Baritone?'

I admitted to baritone.

'So what's your name then?'

'Evans,' I told him, thinking it wouldn't mean much to him.

'Gee!' he cried happily. 'You're the Falstaff. I heard you on the matinée broadcast. Quite a performance.'

He earned his tip, and it was another reminder of how much those Texaco Saturday broadcasts from the Met have done over many years to popularise opera.

I returned to sing Falstaff in the next two seasons, and then some of my other roles: Figaro, Leporello, Beckmesser, and Pizarro in Beethoven's *Fidelio*, which I'd already sung in San Francisco. It had been a success there, though I think this may have been due more to the production and the lighting than to me. I did what I could with the role, certainly, and I don't think I was bad, but I didn't count myself a top-line Pizarro in the way that I thought of Hans Hotter and others like him.

The New York production wasn't nearly so kind. I had to sing Pizarro's main aria from a kind of platform set well back on the stage, and I felt I really needed to be further downstage to have contact with the audience. From my point of view I didn't think it a success, even though Karl Böhm was conducting and we got on very well.

In the same opera I found myself singing against two of the biggest voices you were likely to hear: Birgit Nilsson and Jon Vickers, as Leonore and Florestan. I ask you! There was I in the dungeon scene standing between those two, wondering what on earth I was doing there! They were singing full out, Böhm was bringing up the orchestra fortissimo as well, and I knew it was useless for me to compete with them. Any sound I could make would be covered.

So at the climax of the ensemble in these performances I actually didn't make any sound. I mouthed the words silently and let them get on with it until the moment came for me to be heard on my own. Then I had plenty of voice left and I gave it all I had, as if my voice really was as big as theirs. And nobody knew I'd kept quiet and only pretended to sing just before that; nobody missed me. I rather enjoyed those performances.

Brenda and Huw were with me during the time of the *Fidelio* rehearsals, which were in December, leaving Alun at school at home. After they returned, not long before Christmas, Brenda asked Alun what he most wanted for a Christmas present. 'To go to New York and be with Daddy,' he replied, and he insisted that was what he wanted more than anything. So at the age of twelve he made the flight alone and I met him at the airport.

Alun was great company for the week or so he was with me. I took him sightseeing, and I saw more of New York than I ever had done until then. We looked at some of the big galleries and museums, and spent two days in the United Nations building, where we heard some of the debates. I also arranged for him to spend three days at an American school before they broke up for Christmas.

There was nearly a week without any rehearsal for me over the Christmas holiday, so Alun and I flew home together on a flight arriving in London on Christmas Eve, on which we found ourselves the only passengers. We had the entire attention of the stewardesses, who made a great fuss of Alun. Usually I made a point of not eating too much and not drinking any alcohol on flights because I felt better without it, but this time I thought we could afford to celebrate Christmas, so champagne was enjoyed by all.

It was the best start to Christmas that any child could have had, only marred by a sudden panic over the Atlantic when a message told the pilot to divert to Manchester because there was snow at Heathrow. Brenda was told about the change and arranged for us to be met in Manchester instead, then the conditions at Heathrow improved and we learned we'd be landing there after all.

Although for many years I was usually somewhere in America round about Christmas, I tried never to accept an engagement that would keep me away from the family celebration we always enjoyed so much. Other singers with families were the same, and we would persuade the director or conductor to finish in time for us to get home, however far we had to travel.

Once it seemed as if I'd be unlucky. We were rehearsing *Peter Grimes* in New York before and after Christmas, and the schedule was pretty tight. Jon Vickers decided he'd go home to Canada, even if it meant only being there for Christmas Day, and I made up my mind to do the same. So once more I took the Christmas Eve flight, and arrived home in time to surprise Brenda and the children. On Boxing Day I flew back to New York, but it was worth it to have Christmas Day at home.

When I first sang Leporello at the Met the Don Giovanni was Cesare Siepi, with whom I'd sung in the same opera at Covent Garden a few years before, and what a splendid Don he was. We had a good rapport and worked together very happily, but things were not as easy with Elisabeth Schwarzkopf, who was to sing Elvira. It was intended to be her debut there, although it wasn't a new production, and I was surprised that so distinguished a singer hadn't sung at the Met before this.

One day I was rehearsing the 'Catalogue aria', which Leporello sings to Elvira, when we were interrupted by Schwarzkopf's husband, Walter Legge. He came on stage to dispute with the director Elvira's movements at certain moments during my aria. I kept out of it, not knowing that everything on stage could be heard over the intercom in Rudolf Bing's office. A few minutes later Bing appeared and asked Legge to leave the stage. The rehearsal went on as before, but after the first night Schwarzkopf cancelled the rest of her performances and Pilar Lorengar took her place.

Apart from this the *Don Giovanni* performances went well, including the portrayal of a beautifully stylish Ottavio by the veteran Jan Peerce. I couldn't help being distracted, though, by one episode in the production, which had been around for some years. During the supper scene at the end, when Don Giovanni is swaggering about his conquests before the stone statue comes to claim him, who should appear but four shapely girls swaying their way across the stage in harem pants and brief tops. *Kismet* had come to *Don Giovanni*, the showbiz touch looking absurdly out of place.

Mr Bing's habit of keeping his office loudspeaker tuned to the stage during rehearsals helped to pacify me on the only occasion I threatened to walk out. It happened during the stage rehearsals for *Wozzeck*, when I was taken aback by the quick curtain to end the barrack-room scene where Wozzeck is kicked and beaten by the Drum-Major. Berg had specified a *slow* curtain here, and even included four empty bars to be conducted: one of the most dramatic silences that I know in an opera. This I saw Kleiber rehearsing to perfection at Covent Garden, and the effect was ruined if the curtain came in too quickly.

The first time it happened I let it pass, thinking that they were maybe wanting to save stage time. When it happened again, I asked the director about it but he shrugged it off. At the dress rehearsal, the same thing happened. By now I was so angry I was boiling over. 'If that's the way you want it,' I told the director, 'you come and play Wozzeck.' And I walked off.

The altercation was heard by Bing, and he came to my dressing-room to ask what the problem was. I pointed out to him what was written in the score and he promised to look into it. I was glad Colin Davis was conducting as he felt as strongly as I did and supported me all the way. When the first night performance eventually took place, the slow curtain and the silence were both reinstated, though it was not as perfect as it ought to have been with proper rehearsal.

At the Met one usually sang five or six performances of each opera. Seldom more. And these were often spread over many weeks, which meant that singers were kept hanging round from one performance to the next. Not very economical and, for us, often very boring once the first excitement of New York had worn off, especially as it became less and less safe to walk about alone at night, even for some harmless window-shopping.

Outside Central Park one day I noticed an old man being grabbed round the collar by a youth, who was demanding money. Passers-by were avoiding them, but I could see the man was really frightened. I couldn't let this happen, so I turned back and put on my deepest voice: 'What's going on here? Leave him alone.' At which the youngster swore at me, took a couple of steps backwards, and drew a flick-knife.

Now the people did stop to watch as we circled each other while I wondered what on earth I should do next. Thoughts of unarmed combat from my wartime training came flooding back as the youth made a couple of lunges at me with the knife. Nobody else did anything except a couple of building workers on a job next to the Mayflower Hotel. They must have seen what was happening from above, and came down. One took a cardboard box from a trash can to put over one arm and challenged the knifer, who just ran away. So for that matter, did his intended victim. 'The kid was high with dope,' said the worker who came over, and I was never more grateful than for their timely intervention.

About this time the old Metropolitan closed its doors and the bright and glittering 'new' Met opened in Lincoln Center. It is a marvellous theatre for facilities, but it took some getting used to in performance. I missed the old-world feeling that put me in mind of Covent Garden or La Scala, the atmosphere of history. The Lincoln Center house seemed empty and bare by comparison. It still had to build its tradition and, until it did, it gave the sensation of being *nouveau riche*, although one must compliment New York on this marvellous centre for the arts.

Sometimes I've sat in the auditorium to watch a rehearsal or performance and wished I had blinkers, so as not to be distracted by the modern chandeliers and other furnishings all around. The acoustics were certainly pretty good, although I felt a lack of focus from the stage, as if one's tone was being diffused in all directions instead of being projected directly out to the audience. By now, of course, there'll be a new generation going to the Met who won't have any experience of the older house with which to compare it. And what they hear will sound as good to them as it did before to their parents in the older house. I hope.

My first appearance at Lincoln Center (where the opera house first opened in September 1966) was in a new production of *Peter Grimes* early in 1967. Vickers sang Grimes, and the director was Tyrone Guthrie, with whom I was delighted to be working again.

Solti was due to conduct, and I gathered some problem arose over Lucine Amara, who was to sing Ellen Orford. Bing maintained that he needed to have a resident singer for the role, when Vickers and myself, Guthrie and Solti were all 'guests', and in fairness I think he was right. When we came to the performance, I knew he was right, because Lucine sang a very expressive Ellen indeed.

By that time we had a different conductor. Solti had withdrawn. Bing and Hermann asked my opinion about a replacement, mentioning three possible names, and it was decided to invite Colin Davis. He was new to the house, and he had a major success with those performances, as did Jon Vickers, with Guthrie to mould his stage character.

Colin's only problem was an assistant conductor in charge of the off-stage music who fussed continuously over each detail. He kept popping out from behind the scene to check this point or that, each time bringing the rest of the rehearsal to a standstill. Eventually, Colin could stand no more. 'Get out!' he cried to his tormentor. 'Go home!'

The man was so flabbergasted, he backed away and hit his head on a lamp, putting himself out of action for a good few days. Colin was embarrassed, of course, and apologetic. But the rehearsals did go more smoothly in his absence.

Although the *Peter Grimes* production was very successful, Guthrie wasn't too happy about it. It was presented as a stage within a stage, with the next scene built on trolleys at the side, designed to be wheeled into position with the minimum of delay. The time and expense of scene-changing saved by this method, however, was counterbalanced by the need to act within the limits of the movable part of the scene. Back at Covent Garden, Guthrie had created an unforgettable effect when he had the chorus running downstage and massing themselves at the footlights, and he felt he couldn't do that on this set. 'If you ever direct *Peter Grimes*,' he told me then, 'do it on the flat.'

That was my last visit to sing at the New York Metropolitan. I'd gained a tremendous amount of experience from it and I could feel, in a humble way, that I had become, for a few years, part of a great and continuing tradition. For me, of course, this was stronger in the old Metropolitan Opera House which I'd come to know and love in its last years. Now and again, as I did at Covent Garden, I stood alone on that stage with the curtain open and the house quite empty, in absolute silence, thinking of all the great singers who'd been part of its fabric of history.

Believe me, the silence was deafening.

CHAPTER SIX

Going Places

A telephone call one day in the early spring of 1960 initiated travels in a different direction. The call was from Sandor Gorlinsky, well-known in London as a leading agent for singers and other artists. Could I, he wanted to know, be available to sing Figaro at La Scala, Milan, with Von Karajan conducting?

I could hardly believe my ears. To sing at La Scala is still one of the summits for any singer, and I fairly bubbled with excitement. The dates he mentioned were in May, and happily I was free to take them. It transpired that Tito Gobbi had been engaged for the role but had become unwell and had to cancel, and somewhere along the line somebody had pointed to me. I was very ready, and very willing, and when word got about that I'd been asked to do this there was a lot of support and encouragement from friends and colleagues in the profession.

The time came, and I made my way to Milan and to the famous opera house, where one of the first persons to contact me was Boris Christoff. I admired him as the great performer he was, and much appreciated the fact that he and his wife took the trouble to come looking for me and to greet me. 'Here's our telephone number,' they said. 'If you want to know anything, if you need anything, if you have any problems, don't be afraid to call us.'

As I knew nobody in Milan apart from some of the cast, that was a marvellous kindness. It helped to give me some confidence, as did the fact that the cast included my Glyndebourne friends, Graziella Sciutti as Susanna and Sena Jurinac as the Countess. Christa Ludwig was to sing Cherubino, and I also met a new Count Almaviva in Eberhard Waecnter. We worked well together.

I soon became known for the hundreds of telegrams that were sent me from friends and well-wishers at home. At the opera house it came to be known as 'the Evans mail', and when I went in at the stage door the two attendants there would pull open desk drawers stacked with telegrams to give to me. They came from all parts of Britain, from people I knew and from many I didn't, and I was greatly touched by this extraordinary interest and support.

Four generations: Geraint with *(l to r)* his grandfather, great-grandfather and father

At home with Brenda and their two sons, Alun and Huw

Main picture: Singing with the British Forces Network chorus in Hamburg
Inset: Geraint and Brenda on their wedding day

Main picture: Geraint as Dr Bartolo in *The Barber of Seville* in Chicago, 1969
Inset: Backstage in Salzburg with Olivera Miljakovic

As Tonio in the Zeffirelli production of *I pagliacci* at Covent Garden, 1959

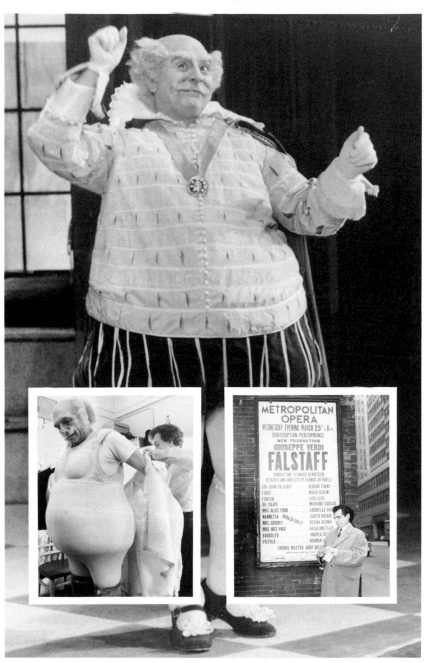

Main picture: Falstaff: Sir Osbert Lancaster's design for the Glyndebourne production, 1958. *Left-hand insert:* Dressing for the part. *Right-hand insert:* Debut at the Met, 1964

Figaro – one of Geraint's most famous roles: with Graziella Sciutti in Milan (above) with Evelyn Lear in Salzburg (below)

Main picture: Bottom in *A Midsummer Night's Dream* at Covent Garden
Inset: Zeffirelli's first production of *Don Giovanni* at Covent Garden

Working with Herbert von Karajan on a recording of *Die Meistersinger* in Dresden

L'elisir d'amore for HRH Prince Charles following a performance at Covent Garden

There had been other singers from Britain at La Scala before me, but this was the first time since Eva Turner in *Turandot* thirty-five years before that a leading role was being sung by somebody from these islands. 'Un inglese cantare Figaro alla Scala,' was the astonished remark I heard going round backstage.

Later I was told that a group of stage-hands were heard discussing me at a nearby café. They were puzzled because they thought I sang the Italian well enough, I even looked like an Italian, yet with a name like mine they couldn't make out where I came from. Obviously I wasn't from anywhere round about, and after some heated discussion as to my origins, they eventually came to the conclusion that I *must* be Sicilian!

The rehearsals were few enough when I was feeling very much the new boy, and I had only one piano call with Von Karajan before orchestral rehearsals. It was our first meeting, and I was pretty much in awe of him, thanks to the reputation he'd already acquired in the continental opera houses and on the concert platform. I soon realised that his first demand was for a singer to know his music thoroughly, that his rehearsal was to satisfy himself of this by going over just a few passages, and that if I hadn't known what I was about, I would have had it.

In my dressing-room before the first night performance I had my first encounter with Signor Claque. I didn't speak much Italian then, and had no idea who this elegantly dressed man might be, with his brown fedora and silver-topped cane. I thought at first that he had simply come to wish me luck, that he might even be the Intendant, whom I hadn't then met.

After some very inconclusive remarks from his point of view he went on to talk to Waechter in the next dressing-room, and only then did one of the other singers tell us who he was: the leader of the regular claque in the upper galleries. In return for a cash payment, they would ensure that the singer had plenty of applause in the right places.

The system had a long tradition in Italy, but Waechter and I were new to it. We had a quick discussion and refused to go along with it until Graziella explained what it meant to the Italian singers. She also said there was serious concern that the claque might just as soon turn hostile and start some demonstration against us if we didn't give them something.

So in order to smooth things out and not provoke anything untoward, I agreed, for the first and only time, to 'pay claque'. Waechter supported me and we each handed over a bundle of lire notes, though we had no idea about the usual scale of payment and didn't know that the lire we passed over came to no more than a pound or two. The gesture was nevertheless accepted, though I didn't feel any better about it except to know that the others thought it helpful.

The first performance went very well, so far as I could tell. I enjoyed singing on that stage – the acoustics were marvellous and I felt that they enhanced the voice, from a singer's point of view. I can't speak for the audience, because I never sat in the auditorium then, nor have I since. I was, however, a little disturbed by people moving in and out of the stage boxes. At La Scala the nearest boxes to the stage actually overlap it, and as I moved about the stage I was aware of people opening chocolates and eating them, while others, just one or two, came and went, going out for the recitative passages, in which they weren't a bit interested, and coming back for a well-known aria.

I didn't let it affect me unduly, though, and I felt reasonably happy when we took our calls, even though Von Karajan said not a word. Early on in the performance I'd been a bit shaken when, in the middle of the first act, I looked to him for my cue to begin Figaro's aria 'Se vuol ballare'. And there I saw Von Karajan leaning back against the rail of his podium with his arms resting along it, and giving the beat by just waggling one finger.

For me at this point the important signal was the conductor's upbeat before the aria, which set the tempo and helped me to begin the emphatic '*Se* vuol ballare' right on the downbeat. With Von Karajan content just to waggle a finger I hardly saw any upbeat at all. I just came in when I thought I should and, thank God, it was right on the downbeat. Whether perhaps the nervousness about this made my adrenalin work more that evening I'm not sure, but the rest of the performance certainly went well.

As Von Karajan passed me in the wings on his way to the pit for the third performance, I took courage and asked him about the tempo for 'Se vuol ballare'. I hoped he would give me a bigger upbeat to start it, because I'd now come in twice by what I thought was more good luck than judgment, and I was afraid I might get more nervous about it. But Karajan didn't wait to hear. He just dismissed my question with a wave of the hand as if to say, 'Don't worry', and went on his way, leaving me to cope as best I could. Thank God it was right every night.

It wasn't until we were taking calls after the third performance that Von Karajan made some complimentary remark to me about my performance, which put me more at ease. A singer who doesn't get some kind of acknowledgement, even just a word or two, is apt to think the worst.

Brenda had flown out to be with me in Milan for the first night, and she was getting ready to leave the hotel for the theatre on her own when she had a call from a London music critic who was staying at the same hotel, offering to escort her. She was feeling nervous anyway and was grateful for the company, and that was how we first came to know Noël Goodwin, then of the *Daily Express*, who took a particular interest in the progress of British singers abroad. He accompanied Brenda to the performance, we met afterwards, and we've remained friends ever since.

Another friend we made on that occasion was Stanley Blair, an importer of Italian clothes who was on a business trip in Milan, and who came up to us as we were waiting to cross a street. He introduced himself and said how much he had enjoyed the previous night's performance, and that he was making sure he heard another performance as well. Again it was a pleasure to have somebody make themselves known in a strange city, not to mention the handsome compliment he paid me.

Stanley came to other performances of mine, in Salzburg as well. Here we went for a meal after one performance, then strolled to one of the bridges to look for a taxi. As we crossed the bridge, what should we see but a girl about to jump. Without thinking I ran to grab her as she fell, almost taking me with her until Stanley came to help and we lifted her back over the barrier. The next moment she simply ran away, leaving us shaking with the fright she'd given us.

Strolling around Milan, window-shopping and feeling pleased that all seemed to be going well, Brenda and I were accosted near the opera house by a ticket tout. We politely declined his tickets, but I suppose we looked like tourists and he persisted, saying in broken English: 'A good performance. See, there is an Englishman singing,' pointing to a poster on the wall above him.

As we walked on he kept pace with us, trying to make a sale, until Brenda pointed to me and said: 'He *is* the Englishman who is singing the Figaro.'

Now he seemed even more delighted than if we'd paid over the odds for his tickets. He beamed and talked very fast and shook our hands, and he must have pointed me out to his friend, another tout, because after that they would be hanging round each time I walked the short distance from the hotel to the theatre, hailing me and shouting good wishes for the performance.

I was more concerned by the stage-hands in the theatre, and the dressers in their white coats, who congregated in the wings to hear this 'Englishman' singing Figaro. So far as I was concerned, this was *their* audition of a newcomer, and believe me, if you can persuade them that you can bring off the performance, then you're well on the way, because they know better than most which are the good and not-so-good singers. To pass their test is quite an achievement.

I had one more audition to meet on that visit: my father. The Pontypridd Male Voice Choir, without my knowing it, had clubbed together to pay his fare to Milan so that he could hear his son sing at La Scala and give me a surprise. It was a wonderful gesture on their part, although I couldn't accept their generosity. A choir never has enough funds for its main work, let alone for extras of this kind. Nevertheless I saw to it that my father came to Milan, although it gave me added responsibility on top of the inevitable tensions of the performances.

My father had never flown before, and he'd seldom been further from Wales than an occasional visit to London. I went home to collect him during a gap between performances, and we flew back to Milan together. He stayed with me at the hotel, excited by all the new experiences, and when I needed to sleep for a couple of hours in the afternoon before my performance, he decided he'd take a walk round. To help him, I drew a map of the streets near the hotel, but still worried about him as he didn't understand any Italian. I also felt concerned that evening because he was on his own in the opera house. But of course he was all right; he enjoyed the performance, he talked a lot about it afterwards, when we flew home again together, and his chest was ten feet wide.

I'm sure I'd have felt just as good if it hadn't been for that business of 'paying claque'. The whole principle of it sickened me, and I knew there'd been many attempts to get rid of it, though without complete success. There were still singers who would be played off one against the other in the claque's favours, and I later heard that it was going on at the Metropolitan Opera in New York as well.

As for me, it was the first and last time I 'paid claque'. I decided that I'd rather be booed, I'd rather face anything that was thrown at me, and I never went along with the system again. For all that it flourished over the years, I don't for one moment think that it had any real effect on the standard of singing. It focussed attention on this singer or that, dispensing plaudits or hostility irrespective of the real merits of the performance. The singer, in my opinion and whatever the circumstances, is there to give the best performance possible, whether it is a big part or a lesser one, and no amount of claque is going to change the nature of individual talent.

From now on, after Milan, I began to feel that British singers were and should be accepted on equal terms with their foreign counterparts. Just as we felt it an honour to be asked to Milan or Vienna, for instance, so foreigners came to look on Covent Garden as part of the same league, as another centre of operatic distinction.

As I've found from experience, singers can usually be helped by a good agent, not necessarily their own. I mentioned Sandor Gorlinsky, who first approached me about La Scala even though I wasn't 'on his books', and although I've never been one of 'his' artists, he's always been friendly and helpful whenever we've met in many places around the world. The same with Lies Askonas and John Coast, who often took the trouble to come round after a performance and to make encouraging remarks.

My own first regular agent was Joan Ingpen, of Ingpen and Williams, who also managed my singing teacher, Theo Hermann, through whom I was introduced to her. She looked after me very well indeed in the early years of my career, and the success of her own later career is a tribute to her personality and expertise: at Covent Garden in charge of operatic planning under Solti; then at the Paris Opéra in a similar capacity, and in recent years she's been at the Metropolitan Opera, New York.

Her agency in London passed to Howard Hartog, with whom I stayed for a while before deciding to handle things on my own. I don't think one can lay down too many hard and fast rules about agents, but it is certainly helpful to have one at the start of a career and, later on, to fix the details of travel, accommodation and dates when things start to get busy. An agent can also be most valuable in negotiating fees. A good manager knows how much is being asked and paid around the world, and can save the artist embarrassment of having to 'market' his reputation.

In my case I had a couple of years managing myself and it was beginning to become rather tiresome when I learned through John Pritchard that his friend and manager, Basil Horsfield, was planning to start an agency. Feeling that he might be very helpful, I went along at John's suggestion and we became more or less his first clients. I remained with Basil and his partner John Davern for a number of years, and had much help from them both.

In my early days I had suffered from the fact that there was one agency which virtually had the monopoly of oratorio and music society bookings in places out of London. More than once I found that a society or concert organisation had asked for me and been told that I wasn't available, when in fact I was free and would have been happy to take the engagements. The agency would take the date for a singer who was already on its books, without passing the enquiry on to me or my own agent.

My first American agent was somebody who didn't even trouble to meet me. I can't remember her name now, but I do recall that all I ever had from her was a letter saying she would represent me, and then the charge for her commission. I've no time for that sort of agent and soon moved on a recommendation to Ann Colbert in New York; she represented some of the best in our profession, including Joan Sutherland, Marilyn Horne, Luigi Alva, Dietrich Fischer-Dieskau, Hermann Prey, Georg Solti and others.

Every good agent will treat each artist individually. One may have all the attributes and yet still feel desperately nervous and unsure, so that his confidence needs building up. Another will be neurotic and temperamental and need calming down. It's part of a good agent's job to handle as many different kinds of personality as there are clients, but the one thing an agent must never do is to over-sell, to put forward a singer for an unsuitable role, for instance. I've known careers suffer a serious setback because a manager has tried to advance a singer in the wrong way, getting roles which the singer doesn't want to refuse but which are simply not the right ones.

Of course, a singer must, by the same token, give the agent a chance to do what's possible. It takes a couple of years to circulate a reputation properly, to market a talent and obtain engagements, so a singer should, I believe, be prepared to stay with an agent for at least three years. But even though an agent may have done a good job, making the client's name known in various opera houses or with concert societies, it's surprising how often an engagement will eventually come about through word of mouth, through one singer speaking about another, or through a conductor or director recommending a singer they've worked with and liked.

My own first invitation to Vienna was one I turned down. Not because I didn't want to go there; in fact, I was as thrilled to be asked there as I was to Milan, but the circumstances were rather different. It was to sing a Figaro or Leporello, I forget which, about a week before Christmas. I happened to mention this casually to Rudolf Kempe at Covent Garden one day, feeling quite pleased at the prospect, and he warned me that there would be very few rehearsals and, if it was the week before Christmas, there wouldn't be any at all.

I was dismayed to hear this, because I certainly didn't want to make my Vienna debut unrehearsed, and without knowing exactly what I would need to do before going on stage. So I told Vienna I wasn't available for that date, wondering as I did so how long it might be before they'd ask me again. No sooner did my message reach them, however, than I had another letter asking me to come in

March instead, for a series of *Figaro* performances. This time I accepted, not knowing that my debut would turn out to be in something quite different. Or that it would still be unrehearsed.

I went to Vienna in good time, but after a few days there was still no word of my rehearsals. A visit to the Staatsoper seemed necessary, so about midday I went along to see what I could find out. As I made my way to the office, who should I encounter but Paul Hager, whom I'd come to know well in San Francisco, and Von Karajan himself. Paul now pointed to me and cried: 'Schaunard!'

For a moment I'd no idea what he was getting at, but then he explained that Hans Braun was ill, and there was no cover for Schaunard in *La Bohème* that night. Nobody else was available. Would I sing it?

Would I? I hadn't sung the part for a long while. Besides, it wasn't the kind of role in which I particularly wanted to make my Vienna debut. I said this to Von Karajan, but all he replied was: 'Ece-vans, you will do it for me?' Paul also did his best to persuade me, and the upshot was that I agreed to go on, provided I could have a répétiteur for the afternoon to go through the role and refresh my memory.

So there I was in March 1961, treading the Staatsoper stage for the first time, in an opera for which I hadn't been engaged, a role I hadn't sung for some time and a production for which I hadn't been rehearsed. Not, you might think, an auspicious way to make a debut. After the first act, however, word got round that Von Karajan, who wasn't conducting that production, had taken the unusual step, for him, of going into the auditorium to see some of the performance. How much he saw I don't know, but others were very surprised that he'd gone in at all.

Nobody was more surprised than I when, at the end of the performance, his secretary, Matoni, came to my dressing-room with a message that Von Karajan wanted me to join the Vienna State Opera as a permanent member.

I was flabbergasted! For a while I thought how marvellous that could be. Somebody in the opera house must have known or overheard this, though, because next morning in London some papers carried a Press agency report that I'd been asked by Von Karajan to join the Vienna State Opera and would probably accept.

David Webster at Covent Garden saw the report. Brenda was telephoned: 'What is this? What's he doing?' Eventually I was able to sort it out by deciding to stay with the Covent Garden Company and go to Vienna as a guest if they wanted me. I did so quite often, singing not only the Figaro I was first asked to do, but Leporello, Papageno, Beckmesser, and Tonio in *I pagliacci* as well as Falstaff.

I never cared for hit-or-miss performances as a rule, but there was one hit in Vienna I wouldn't have missed. I'd done my contract performances of Figaro when, after the curtain-calls at the end of the last one, Von Karajan called to me: 'What are you doing next Saturday?' He explained that there was to be a gala at which the German Chancellor was to be the guest of the Austrian President. 'I would like you to sing Figaro for me,' he said.

I tried quickly to think of my commitments. I remembered I was to be interviewed by John Freeman on his TV programme, *Face to Face*, that Friday night, and I was keen to do that. So I told Von Karajan about it, and said: 'It's rather a risk. I'd have to come out on Saturday, and what if there's a fog, or some other airport delay?' (I hated travelling on the day of a performance in any case.)

'I take that chance,' he said.

The TV interview went well enough, I thought, but it went on very late, then I had to go home, snatch some sleep, and still get to Heathrow in time to take the eight o'clock breakfast flight to Frankfurt, where there was a connection to Vienna. Sure enough, there was a flight delay from Heathrow, and I missed my connecting flight from Frankfurt. Eventually, I reached Vienna about one o'clock or one-thirty in the afternoon, and went straight to the opera house to let them know I'd arrived.

No rehearsal, of course, but Von Karajan had gathered together such an experienced cast that we could take the performance straight through. I'd only ever worked with Sena Jurinac previously as the Countess, and here she was singing Cherubino which she hadn't done for some years. Lisa della Casa was the Countess; Oskar Cerwenka was Bartolo, and my Susanna was Hilde Gueden, then a mature artist who nevertheless looked beautiful in the part and sang enchantingly. The Count was Eberhard Waechter, or 'Herr Baron', as he is known (he is a Baron in his own right – maybe this was why he made such a good aristocrat).

Not having a rehearsal made us concentrate the more, and with the resulting tension it was a really brilliant performance. Practically all that went wrong, as I recall, was when Susanna and I accidentally bumped into each other during the last act in the garden, where the comings and goings can be accident-prone even when they are rehearsed.

It was a gambler's performance. And because we worked together instinctively, it succeeded. But only a cast like that could have brought it off, and it could probably never have been repeated. I don't think I'd have wanted to try.

The only moment when I felt bothered was when I heard the

orchestra play the German national anthem. I hadn't heard it since the war years, when it meant something I didn't want to remember, and it still sent a shiver down my back for a moment, though the wounds had been healed. Music, I've always believed, plays a major part in bringing people together, whatever the quarrel.

The gala was a big diplomatic event, of course, and I noticed that, as elsewhere, singers from other countries were visited in their dressing-rooms by their Ambassador or Consul, but nobody at all from the British Embassy made themselves known to me. I'm bound to say this has been disturbingly typical wherever I've been throughout the world. Time and again I've been invited along to receptions at the German Embassy, the Austrian Embassy, the French Embassy, the Polish Embassy, and others besides, because their nationals have been in the cast of an opera with me. And I'm hard put to remember any occasion when I've been able to reciprocate through the British Embassy. Certainly no more than a couple of times during the whole of my career. I know I'm not the only British artist who is very conscious of this. Our Embassy in Warsaw was a shining exception in this respect, as I was later to discover, but usually nobody wanted to know about singers, much to the embarrassment of myself and others from Britain on numerous occasions.

When I asked why this should be, the usual excuse was that Embassy staffs were concerned with trade and commerce. To which I'd say that we, too, did our bit for the balance of payments, even if we did only go round the world singing.

An incident which stays in my mind is of a lunch in Buenos Aires given by the English Speaking Union while I happened to be singing there. It was in honour of Lord Denning and Lady Denning, and although I'd been there some time, it was the first occasion I'd met our Ambassador and his wife. This lady said she didn't know I was in Buenos Aires, although all the newspapers had already carried news or reviews of my performances.

'You should have come to the Embassy and signed the visitors' book,' she told me. 'Like Sir Malcolm Sargent does.' And then she added, in a rather offhand way: 'We must invite you to the Embassy for supper one evening. And you can give us a few songs.'

At this I felt justifiably annoyed. 'Madam,' I told her, 'I don't sing for my supper.' Nor was I ever asked to the Embassy.

It's a sad commentary on our foreign relations that so little interest is shown in the arts and British artists, who actually do much more than is realised to bring respect for Britain.

My next invitation to Vienna was to sing Papageno in *The Magic*

Flute. Talk about coals to Newcastle! On the one hand I was tremendously honoured to be asked to do this in the city (and in some performances in the actual theatre, the Theater an der Wien) where it all began, in the last year of Mozart's life. At the same time, it was a nerve-wracking experience to follow in the tradition of Emanuel Schikaneder, who wrote the part for himself to play in a local and colloquial style.

I thought I'd have a go at it, nevertheless, provided I could be sure of at least a few rehearsals, to which the Vienna management agreed. I went there on a Monday, with an agreement to sing Leporello on Friday and Papageno early the next week, I think on the Tuesday. Rehearsals were indeed arranged and my main concern was to improve my German, especially in the speaking lines, while one of the répétiteurs gave me one or two lines to say in the Vienna dialect, which made it the more interesting.

Anton Dermota was to sing Tamino, and he was marvellous when we got to the performance, but the only other singer I did much rehearsal with was a very young Gundula Janowitz, who at that time was covering the Papagena role. Little did either of us realise what a future career she would have as the major international star she soon became.

I worked hard at my rehearsals for three days and on the third day, Thursday, I told my répétiteur that I wouldn't come in the following day as I would be singing in *Don Giovanni* and wanted to take it easy during the day.

To which he replied: 'Nein. Es ist *Die Zauberflöte* morgen' (It's *The Magic Flute* tomorrow).

I nearly died. We argued, but he insisted, so I went to check and found indeed that the performances had been changed, though nobody had thought to warn me. My first Viennese Papageno was to be the next night.

If that's what had to be, it had to be. I did the performance, and a much better performance than I had expected, terrified as I was, except for a couple of minor incidents.

One involved Papageno disappearing at one point down a trapdoor in the stage. The trap was pointed out to me, but when the actual time came, just as I was going to position myself on the trapdoor, the stage light went out. With only a spotlight, I simply couldn't be certain if I was in the right place or not. Rather than risk being caught in the wrong place, maybe with one leg on the trap and the other not, I took myself off into the wings. The trap opened with no Papageno on it, but I wasn't taking any chances.

The other moment I remember was my first sight of Papagena

without the 'old woman' disguise in which we first meet. I'd rehearsed with Gundula, but the part was sung by Olivera Miljakovic and when she first stepped from the stage 'nest' as the young girl intended for me, I've never done such an involuntary double-take in my life. Not only was she stunningly beautiful, but she was wearing a costume somewhat briefer than the Bunny-girl outfit.

I must have gawped. The audience roared. And it was a totally genuine reaction on my part at seeing a kind of pin-up Papagena come to life.

After a couple of Papageno performances I still wasn't feeling too happy in the role. I went to the management office and they sent me on to Von Karajan.

'Maestro,' I told him, 'I can't play Papageno any more.'

'Why not?'

'I'm just too nervous. Here am I singing Papageno in Vienna where he's one of your own characters. I just don't think I can be right for it.'

'You're doing very well. I'm told you're doing a very fine performance. I am 'chief' here and I want you to sing it.' And with that he sent me away.

I went on doing what I could with it, but when I remembered singers like Erich Kunz and Willi Fassbaender, who could pick up on whatever was topical and political in Vienna at the time and make some improvised comment on it, I felt I couldn't help being at a disadvantage. All I could do was say what I'd specially learned, and that wasn't as effective. So even though I was asked back to sing more performances of Papageno I didn't do so, and kept to Figaro and Leporello, and Guglielmo in *Così*.

Word soon gets round in Vienna as to who is singing at the Opera and who the newcomers are. I was made aware of this when, on what I think was only my second day there, I went into a nearby restaurant, and a smiling head waiter greeted me saying:

'Guten tag, Herr Kammersänger.'

Totally unused to such a title, I looked round to see who'd followed me in, until I realised the compliment was meant for me.

As well as the Mozart roles in Vienna, I sang Tonio in *I pagliacci*, which I've already mentioned. I don't think now I'd have accepted it if I'd remembered about the slightly higher pitch in use, but happily I was in good form and all went well, as also happened when I sang Beckmesser there.

It nevertheless meant that I worked with some fine colleagues. The David role in *Die Meistersinger* was sung by Murray Dickie, the Scottish tenor who became a regular member of the Vienna State

Opera as early as 1952. He settled there and had a distinguished career as a valued member of the company, becoming a *Kammersänger*. He helped me to find my feet right from my first visit there, as did Paul Schoeffler, who was again singing Sachs. He and his beautiful English wife, Mary, made me feel very welcome, as indeed did Ljuba Welitsch when she took the trouble to telephone me at the opera house soon after I arrived.

Paul took me to some of the outer districts of Vienna, including the 'Heurige' taverns to taste the new wine, where I think I should perhaps have spat out more than I drank. I was very glad not to be singing the next day.

Yet even with two such friends to work with in *Die Meistersinger*, I was still astonished at the risks the management took in using newcomers in important roles with little if any rehearsal. In my own case as Beckmesser I only had the chance to look at the set for each act on the night of the performance, and it was left to me to figure out then just how and where on the stage I was going to perform. I'd never even walked through the part before I was expected to sing it in a production I knew nothing about.

In these circumstances, what worried me more than anything was the distance I'd be from the prompter during Beckmesser's serenade in the second act. With three verses to sing there's always the chance that you move into the wrong one, and that can throw you completely. The prompter can help a good deal to keep you right, but not if Eva's window on the stage set is so far back that you can't hear him. When it came to the performance I had to decide in the space of a few seconds how to place myself on the stage so that it would look as if I were serenading Eva, yet at the same time be within earshot of the prompter.

As with Papageno, I was conscious that the Beckmesser role had its own tradition for the Viennese audiences, who were going to judge me pretty severely if I didn't match up to it. And that meant I had to pull out all the stops, to do better than the best where they were concerned. Fortunately I was accepted, and it was good to be asked back. I went about three years in succession, then there was a gap in the late 1960s when the dates didn't work out. In 1969, though, I was able to go there for *Falstaff*, in an existing Visconti production to which I quite looked forward. Until I was on that stage.

As usual there was practically no rehearsal. I had a kind of run-through in one of the rehearsal rooms with some chairs representing the props, but when I first saw the stage set I was totally dismayed. There was so little on the stage that Falstaff was dwarfed by his surroundings. Instead of being larger than life I was submerged and had to work hard to project the character across the footlights.

Nor was this all. In the second act, when Falstaff goes to change for his assignation with Alice, and leaves Ford alone on stage to sing his celebrated monologue, jealous and wrathful, I could hardly believe what happened. While doing my quick change of costume in the wings, a second set of the clothes I'd been wearing was being tossed on the stage as Ford began to sing. It took all the attention away from him for absolutely no reason at all, and I was furious about it. Visconti production or not, I begged them not to let it happen again. It was the only serious disagreement I had in Vienna.

Maybe this affected my attitude to these Falstaff performances. The role was, after all, my particular pride and joy: I loved playing it and I naturally wanted to be successful in it wherever I was. Yet in Vienna, it wasn't a production I could respect and in which I could feel comfortable. The opera, for me, was diminished by it.

It was while I was singing Falstaff in Vienna that I had a most exciting message in a telegram from Brenda, although I didn't at first realise what it meant: 'CONGRATULATIONS STOP SIR STOP I AM VERY PROUD FOR YOU.'

I thought perhaps there had been some flattering report at home about me singing Falstaff and put it on one side. I usually called home every few days, to keep in touch with the family and to check on messages and engagements, but it was another couple of days before I did so again.

Brenda was furious. 'Where have you been?,' she demanded. 'I've been waiting for you to call for two days. Didn't you get my telegram?'

'Yes.'

'Well, didn't you understand what it meant?'

Now I was puzzled. Had I forgotten a birthday, an anniversary? Was it something to do with singing Sir John Falstaff, I asked.

'Think again,' said Brenda. She was desperately trying to work out a way of telling me on the telephone that word had been sent to notify me that I was to receive a knighthood. I had to confirm my acceptance within fourteen days, but of course it had to be kept entirely confidential until it was formally announced.

She tried again. 'You remember that message you had in 1959, when you received that honour?' I realised she meant the CBE. 'Well, it's the next one up.'

'God! No!,' I cried. And it was such a shock that, without thinking, I put the phone down.

It took me the next two or three hours to get the connection back so that I could speak to Brenda again. As the news sank in I was bursting to tell somebody about it, but of course I couldn't do so, whereas if I'd been at home I could at least have had a talk with my wife. For this, if for nothing else, the Vienna *Falstaff* is enshrined in my memory.

Meanwhile, I received my first invitation to the Salzburg Festival in 1962, the year after my Vienna debut. It was to sing Figaro in a new production of the opera in Mozart's birthplace, and this would open the festival that year. I was thrilled at the prospect, and eagerly looked forward to what I'd been told was a Mecca for festival-goers. To me, when I experienced it, the Salzburg Festival combined something of the community spirit I'd previously found among the artists at Glyndebourne, with the wider musical scope of the Edinburgh Festival, and there was a certain reminder of the Scottish city in seeing the old palace of the Prince-Archbishops perched on its high hill, like the Edinburgh castle on its rock, with the town clustered round its foot.

As a first-time singer at Salzburg my fee wasn't exactly generous, and I had to find reasonable lodgings for the several weeks of rehearsal and performances. I came across a small *pension* close by the side of the Mönchsberg on which the palace was built, and I soon came to enjoy the walks up the mountain, or down by the side of the river that tumbled through the centre of the town, or into the town itself, past the market stalls where I'd stop to buy some fruit.

Mozart's birthplace was there to be visited, as it is by almost everybody who goes to Salzburg, but Salzburg is less forthcoming about his burial, as if it were a continuing embarrassment that so great a musical genius went, at the end of his short life, to an unmarked grave. Neverthless I felt the festival to be warm and welcoming and there were several friends among the *Figaro* cast: Sena Jurinac, Graziella Sciutti, Evelyn Lear and others. We soon began going to a little coffee shop between rehearsals, and the atmosphere was very much like that of the Glyndebourne 'family' again. Later there were other, new friends like Lucia Popp, whom I helped to find her way around Salzburg when she first arrived and with whom I often worked when her career took wing.

From time to time during rehearsals I saw a distinguished white-haired gentleman coming round backstage and wishing all the singers good-day. One morning several of us were sitting outside our dressing-rooms having a break and drinking coffee when this same person sat down among us and carried on a lively conversation, chatting and tapping an arm or a knee in a warm and friendly way, and I suppose the others just assumed I knew him too.

They were highly amused when, after he'd gone, I asked Sena who he was. 'Don't you know?' she asked incredulously. 'That's Dr Nekola. He's the Director of the festival.' I'd no idea, and felt more than a bit embarrassed. Eventually I came to know Dr Tassilo Nekola very well, and found him a most charming man who always put you at your ease, and to whom you could talk in a very friendly way. But it was quite typical for a guest singer around the world not to meet anybody in charge unless you searched them out.

Except in San Francisco or Chicago, where a representative from the opera always met you at the airport and made you feel welcome as soon as you stepped off the plane, a singer was usually very much left to fend for himself. I would go to the opera house, find a company office and let them know I'd arrived, look for an opera manager or one of the music staff to discover when and where I was supposed to rehearse and take it from there on my own.

It never occurred to me in that first year at Salzburg that I was building the same sort of regular association that I'd had with Glyndebourne, or that I'd be returning to Salzburg for nine consecutive years. For my first Figaro there I was directed by an experienced man of the theatre in Gustav Rudolf Sellner, another who liked to work constructively with the performer, never reluctant to try something a different way, or to find what suited the performer best.

Dietrich Fischer-Dieskau sang Count Almaviva, and we had long discussions about the master and servant relationship, and the confrontation between us in the third act, where I was concerned to make Figaro challenge the Count's authority, especially in relation to his designs on Susanna and the *droit de seigneur*. I think that between us we made it a very telling moment.

With Sellner's help we managed to overcome the lack of character in the set design, which tried to make a garden scene out of flat plastic sheets standing upright, staggered at intervals around the stage. Neither this nor the indoor scenes did the opera justice, and I was glad when, a few years later, they were replaced with a new production.

Heinz Wallberg, the newly appointed music director at Wiesbaden, was the conductor, and the performance went well, so far as I could tell from my involvement. Well enough, anyway, for the Austrian radio to ask me for an interview once they were sure I'd had a success.

The radio producer was quite candid about it. 'Forgive us for not asking you sooner,' he said, 'but we were worried about whether you would be accepted here, where there has never been a Figaro from Britain before. Had you not been successful, then the listeners need not have known too much, but now that you are, we'd like you to be interviewed.' And I was.

That was more than I ever had from our own BBC, who sent a television crew to Salzburg that year to make a documentary about the festival. They organised interviews with Sena, Graziella, and I think Evelyn Lear, and when Graziella asked me when I was doing mine, I had to say that I hadn't been asked for one. Graziella told me that she reminded them that there was a British Figaro that year. It was still quite rare for anybody from this country to be among the festival artists, but I never heard a single word from that BBC team. And that was a little hurtful.

Brenda wasn't with me in Salzburg that first year because she was heavily pregnant with our second child, who was due towards the end of August. I was very much the concerned father, of course, and flew home a couple of times when there was a break in performances. Still nothing happened, I sang the last of the Salzburg Figaros, and arranged to fly home the next day with only another day or so before going on to San Francisco.

Unknown to me at this point, Brenda had given birth to our second son. We had an Austrian au pair living with us at the time and Brenda asked her, with her fluent German, to telephone a message to the stage door at the Salzburg Festspielhaus and also to send a telegram announcing the birth. I'm still waiting for both messages.

Knowing that I was going back the day after my last performance anyway, I hadn't called home, and on the flight I settled down to look through *The Times*. I don't usually look at the births column, but we hadn't decided on any names for the infant, and I wondered what names other parents were giving their children. I looked down the list and noticed with a chuckle that Peter and Sylvia Ebert had had another baby, their fifth, I think. Their first had been born at about the same time as Alun. I had some catching up to do! Then, close underneath I read:

> EVANS. To Geraint and Brenda Evans, a son,
> Huw Grant. A brother for Alun . . .

The plane seemed to spin round. I had refused a drink earlier, but now I called the stewardess and said: 'I think I'll have that drink. And you'd better make it champagne all round. I've just read that I've become a father again.' The pilot sent back a message that he and the crew couldn't drink in flight, but they'd like to drink a toast when they went off duty.

We'd always agreed that our children should have Grant as a middle name, but we hadn't decided on another boy's name. I learned when I got home that this was actually Alun's choice. He watched the news on television, read then by Huw Thomas, and when his brother arrived he said to Brenda: 'I like the name Huw. Can't we call him Huw?' So Huw it was, and we decided we liked it too.

I hardly had time to see them when I did get back, as I was due in San Francisco a couple of days later. Indeed, my travels kept me away from home so much during the next ten years or so that it chiefly fell on Brenda to bring up the boys. It was often tough for her, especially as I was so seldom around even to do the ordinary family things like take them for picnics or watch them play cricket or rugby for their school. I sometimes wonder why they became such dedicated rugby players. For several years they were quite shy about me to others, and about the work I did, which didn't conform to any stereotyped job. One of them even used to tell people that his father worked in the Income Tax office in Bromley! I suppose it sounded more respectable than capering about the stage in San Francisco or Salzburg.

Another Salzburg personality I met on my first visit was Bernhard Paumgartner, a tall, lovable man and a distinguished academic who'd been connected with the festival since it began in 1920. Indeed, he composed and conducted the music for the festival's first productions of Hugo von Hofmannsthal's mystery play, *Jedermann*, which was performed every year, and after being Director of the Salzburg Mozarteum before and after the war years, he'd just become President of the festival, holding that post until he died in 1971.

Paumgartner once paid me a great compliment in a BBC television interview. I don't remember the exact words, but it was to the effect that he was sure that my characterisation of Figaro was the one Mozart would have wanted.

During the festival he would conduct morning concerts at the Mozarteum, and it was something of an honour to be asked to take part, as I was when I returned the next year. I sang two of the Mozart concert arias, and there was a harpist also performing. At the end of the programme a little girl came forward with a bouquet of flowers. She seemed to be making for me so I went towards her and bent down, only to see her by-passing me and going to the harpist instead. I had the presence of mind to pretend I was only helping her up a couple of steps she had to climb on the way, but I felt rather stupid, even so.

The 1966 festival brought a new production of *Figaro*, which I'd been asked to sing, and I was delighted to learn that it would be conducted by Karl Böhm and directed by Günther Rennert. I'd known Rennert since my days in Hamburg at the end of the war and had worked with him at Glyndebourne. He was a very dedicated director, so much so that he sometimes didn't know when to stop.

Once he was into a scene he'd keep at it for three or four hours without a break, not thinking about the time, or about the effect on us. Once or twice I tried to force him to break by asking if he'd like a cup of tea. Each time he refused, until his wife realised what I was up to and said to me quietly: 'Why don't you offer him a coffee? He doesn't drink tea.'

Next day I took her advice. 'Dr Rennert, would you like a coffee?' Almost without thinking he agreed, so I quickly brought him a coffee and put it in front of him. He had to stop work for a few minutes to drink it, and that way we managed to get a short break in the next few rehearsals. Sometimes I thought he over-rehearsed, going over the same things repeatedly, tiring the singers and, after a couple of weeks, bringing us to a peak too soon, exhausting us to such an extent that we couldn't help some deterioration setting in during the last few days before an opening.

Even when he was directing comedy, Rennert was always very serious about it, so that you began to wonder if it was meant to be comedy at all. Yet he was another director who was prepared to talk and discuss things with his cast, to try something an alternative way, provided it was within the framework he wanted for that opera.

His production of *Figaro* at Salzburg in 1966 was one of the best productions of that opera I've experienced. Susanna was Reri Grist and we had new singers, Ingvar Wixell and Claire Watson, as the Count and Countess. Rudolf Heinrich designed some very workable sets, and even went to the trouble of drawing a ground-plan of the Almaviva mansion for the programme-book so that audiences could relate one scene to another on the stage.

Böhm, of course, was wonderful in Mozart. And after a performance has gone well, I've seen him doing a little side-skip into the air with both feet clear of the ground to show his delight, as he came behind the curtain for his call.

One of those *Figaro* performances was also the only time I've seen him get really mad. Just before the last, happy ensemble starts in the finale, when everything has been sorted out among the different characters, there's a beautiful passage for the orchestra alone which seems to epitomise that spirit of understanding and forgiveness. No matter what production you're in, at this point everybody on stage stays absolutely still, and Böhm liked to phrase that passage as if it were a perfect jewel which, in musical terms, it is. But on this occasion one of the violins made a horrible scratching noise, destroying completely the mood created by the music. Whether a string had broken or a peg worked loose, I don't know, but I thought for a moment Böhm would have a stroke on the spot. Instead he kept the beat going, at the same time swearing furiously at the unfortunate player.

The following year Hermann Prey came to sing the Count. He was based at Munich, where Rennert that year became Intendant in charge of the Bavarian State Opera. Prey arrived with very little time to rehearse and, although the rest of the cast had sung the production the previous year, it was essential that we rehearsed as much as possible for our own good, as well as doing what we could to help him. But one day we were called for ten o'clock in costume but no make-up, which meant being at the theatre half an hour earlier to get ourselves ready. Twelve hours later, we were still on the stage, still in costume, having had no proper break all day and little to eat.

At ten past ten Rennert decided to finish. 'Thank you very much,' he said. 'Don't forget ten o'clock rehearsal tomorrow morning.' By this time we were all exhausted, and pretty annoyed that we'd been put in this situation for the sake of one singer. The last two hours, at least, of that day's work hadn't meant a thing because we were so tired. And for the first time I was angry with Rennert and spoke my mind:

'Are you sure we've finished, Dr Rennert?' I said. 'Because we've been in this theatre since nine-thirty this morning without you giving a thought to whether we've had anything to eat, or how tired we might be. I think what you've asked us to do today is disgusting. It's when people are treated like this without consideration that strikes start happening.'

He was pretty taken aback at this outburst, and probably quite annoyed as well. 'I'm sorry, I'm sorry,' he said, but I'm not sure that the words meant much, and it was a bit late for that anyway. I noticed, however, that the only person who spoke out in support of my protest was the stage manager, and he was as forceful as I was. None of the other singers said a word, even though I knew they felt as I did, and I suppose I can't blame them too much. Several of them regularly sang in Munich, and Rennert was the new Intendant there.

Earlier in the rehearsals he'd come to me and asked if I would sing Figaro for him in Munich some time the next year. I told him I'd like to, but later, after the Salzburg performances were over, I had a letter from him telling me that owing to unforeseen circumstances, my services as Figaro wouldn't be required.

I was sorry about that. I should have liked to sing Figaro in Munich, but at the same time I felt I was right to have made my protest when I did, not only for myself but for the other artists as well, and for those who followed us. How different it was from being outspoken at Covent Garden, where you could speak your mind and not risk being penalised for it.

I came to realise over the years that the best results are produced when rehearsals are concentrated into a certain number of hours, otherwise you begin to lose focus, you can't absorb what the director is saying and you just don't respond. When the time came for me to direct *Figaro* at Edinburgh some years later, with Ileana Cotrubas, Teresa Berganza, Heather Harper and Fischer-Dieskau, we put this to good effect, having a proper break and finishing about three-thirty.

Rehearsing for Herbert von Karajan, as I did for the new production of *Don Giovanni* he directed as well as conducted at the 1968 festival, produced a different problem. On the whole he favoured very dark stage lighting, as I discovered when I first made my way from the old Festspielhaus to the new and much bigger Festspielhaus alongside.

It had been open for a few years but I'd never yet sung there. The new *Don Giovanni* was to be given in it, though, so I thought I'd look in on one of the rehearsals for *Il trovatore*, in which Leontyne Price was singing. I found my way from one theatre to the other through many doors without going outside the building and stood watching Ferrando singing his opening aria with the chorus, grouped in a dim light at one corner of the stage.

The stage in that theatre is exceptionally wide, the length of two cricket pitches end to end. I stood there quite casually for a few minutes, watching what was going on, and as my eyes became accustomed to the gloom I discovered I was actually standing in the middle of this vast stage. Von Karajan was rehearsing from the front and it was all so dark, absolutely nobody had seen me.

I mentioned this to Leontyne.

'Don't worry, darling,' she replied. 'It's so dark on that stage the only person they can see is me.' And she rolled the whites of her eyes in the blackness of her face.

It was exhilarating to work with Von Karajan on *Don Giovanni*, even though the low lighting did become a problem on occasion. I asked if I could have more light at one point because I really couldn't see where I was going.

'No, no,' he called back. 'I can see you fine.'

A few moments later he came on stage to demonstrate something to Nicolai Ghiaurov, who was singing the Don. Having done this he wanted me to understand, and looked round, calling for me.

'Here,' I said, practically at his feet. 'Now will you believe it's too dark?' And he had the grace to admit that maybe I was right.

Ghiaurov had problems during the early orchestral rehearsals in putting across the Don's 'Champagne aria' at Von Karajan's fast tempo. I suggested that instead of trying to sing every word fully, with his big voice, he should play with it more flexibly. The next time we rehearsed he did just this and it worked excellently, to the extent that the orchestra, and even Von Karajan, applauded him. He was so thrilled when he came off stage that he embraced me, kissing me on both cheeks and, with a big smile, said 'Thank you!'

Von Karajan greatly loved to demonstrate personally what he wanted us to do. At the early rehearsals we were without Rolando Panerai, who was to sing Masetto. Von Karajan would then take Masetto's part, thoroughly enjoying himself, and when Panerai arrived he was ready to show him just what he'd done in rehearsal.

The combination of dim lighting and sheer distance on that stage caused a number of problems. There was a time lag, or a lack of co-ordination in places, as happened at the dress rehearsal when Ghiaurov and Mirella Freni, who was Zerlina, finished their duet a whole bar after Von Karajan and the orchestra, as if they'd just lost touch.

I was a bit thrown myself at the start of Leporello's 'Madamina!', the 'Catalogue aria'. For the bar and a half of orchestral introduction Von Karajan had turned, as he often does, to face the instruments concerned (in this case the 'cellos) so his upper body was sideways to the stage. It was too dark to see any beat and I was too far away to hear the first bars. I looked to the prompter, but he couldn't hear any better.

Six bars later, however, I came in, fortunately with the right words in the right place. I'd sung it so often by then that the orchestral music was in my mind, even though I couldn't hear it properly. Incidents like this convinced me that the new Festspielhaus at Salzburg is simply too big for operas on the Mozart scale. Fine for the Coronation in *Boris Godunov*, and spectacular scenes like that, with big choruses, but some operatic adjustments just can't be made in those surroundings.

After my little scene with Günther Rennert a few years before, I was agreeably surprised when he came to me during Salzburg's 50th anniversary festival in 1970, when I was again singing Figaro with

Karl Böhm, and asked if I would sing Wozzeck in a new production they were planning for the following year. I took it as quite an honour that I should be approached in preference to the native German or Austrian singers who knew the role, and I accepted on the understanding that Rennert himself would direct. I may not have liked his rehearsal methods, but I always had great respect for him as a director, and I believed he could give me the confidence I'd need to sing Wozzeck there.

Böhm was to conduct the performances, but when the next year came and I arrived in Salzburg to rehearse Figaro first, I learned that Rennert was no longer involved in *Wozzeck* and Sellner was to direct it instead. Having worked with Sellner in my first year at Salzburg, I knew him to be another skilled and sympathetic director, so wasn't too concerned at Rennert's absence.

My main problem when we started rehearsals on that enormously wide stage was to keep in contact with Böhm's conducting. One scene would be played at one side of the stage and, after the short linking orchestral interlude, the next scene would perhaps be right on the other side. This meant that we were constantly trying to keep in touch with Böhm from the corner of an eye; hardly ever did we actually face him in stage centre.

It's difficult enough in *Wozzeck* to make the title role musically and visually convincing, without having to cope with long and oblique sightlines to observe the conductor, and after one or two rehearsals I started to feel more and more nervous about it. Anja Silja was singing Marie and the two of us decided to tell the prompter we'd take our cues from him at those points where, owing to the stage placing, we could see him better than Böhm. At which point the prompter confessed that he barely knew the opera, not having realised when he accepted the job in Salzburg that he'd be prompting *Wozzeck* but not wanting to risk being dismissed if he turned it down.

Anja and I just looked at each other but we didn't enquire further as to why there couldn't be another prompter who did know the work, but I explained to Böhm some of the difficulties we were having. and he was marvellous in helping us, making every effort to ensure that we could see his beat, wherever we were on the stage. Both of us were grateful for this and it was effective. By all accounts it was also very successful with the audiences.

Afterwards I was approached by one or two opera houses in Germany to sing Wozzeck there too, but in each case the dates didn't work out and I had to refuse. I'd also told the Salzburg Festival management some time previously that I wanted to make 1971 my last visit, for the simple reason that for nigh on twenty years my summers had been spent either at Glyndebourne or Salzburg, sometimes with Edinburgh added on as well. I thought it was time I had a proper summer holiday with my family, especially as the boys were growing up fast.

By now we'd bought ourselves a Welsh home at Aberaeron, on the coast of Cardigan Bay, between Cardigan and Aberystwyth. The house, which had once been a pub, was built in the early nineteenth century and overlooks the little tidal harbour. At first it was our holiday home, but it soon became clear that we wanted it to be more than that, and that eventually we wouldn't need or want a house in the London area. The boys had bought themselves a boat for sailing in the summer, and they had more fun there than they would have done if they'd just been hanging round Salzburg in their holidays. Brenda stayed to look after them, and came less often to Salzburg herself.

I didn't want to spoil what the boys enjoyed doing for themselves in the holidays. Indeed, I wanted to share more with them. As it was, I flew back from Salzburg whenever there were four or five days between performances, as often happened. I'd drive down to Aberaeron from Heathrow and back again, and even if it meant only a couple of days with my family I always felt it was worth it. Now I thought I should spend more of my summers there.

First of all, though, the Salzburg management pleaded with me to return the next year to sing Wozzeck again. It had been so successful, they planned to open the festival with it. I still thought it an honour to be asked and so I accepted, but definitely for the last time.

About a week before I was due back there to rehearse, I was in Wales filming a musical documentary programme for Harlech Television. One scene involved me dressing up as a Victorian country squire, with sideburns, heavy tweeds, gaiters and a cravat, and riding a horse, singing a song about the woman I'm about to meet.

I'd already recorded the song, so all I had to do was to mime the words while the horseback scene was shot in front of a big manor house in Abergavenny. The horse was a splendid animal, 17 hands high, a real gentleman farmer's mount. What it was that upset him I shall never know, but all of a sudden he reared on his hind legs and threw me, a good six feet backwards.

I landed on my back, my head hitting a lump of turf with such whiplash force that I was quite heavily concussed. I only learned later that there followed a scene of much consternation as an ambulance was called and I was taken to hospital, where I didn't fully regain consciousness for two to three days. I was there for a week, and among the messages I had was a telegram from Sir Harry Llewellyn, the champion show-jumper, sarcastically commenting on my poor horsemanship. The Abergavenny horses were known to be the best in the world!

There was a rather funny side to this episode. While I was lying outstretched in the emergency room waiting for an X-ray, one of the nurses recognised me and started gently smoothing the sides of my head, when all of a sudden there was a loud scream. People came dashing in, wondering what had happened, only to find the nurses now roaring with laughter. My side-burns (which had been stuck on) had come off in her hands! I was now doubtful when or if Salzburg would see me that year. I sent one message warning them, and another cancelling my engagement when I was advised by my doctors to rest completely for a couple of weeks at least.

Do you know, I don't think Salzburg believed me? I met Anja Silja in America later that year, and she asked me if the accident had really been as bad as reported. She sounded rather sceptical, and I had the impression the festival management felt the same. Especially as I'd previously said I wanted 1971 to be my last year, and had been very reluctant to change my mind.

I hope all the same they did understand it was genuine, because I had some wonderful times at Salzburg and many of the performances were among those I enjoyed the most in my entire career. I've always had warm memories of Dr Nekola, the festival director, and Professor Paumgartner, who died in 1971. I still hope to go back sometime during the festival and greet some of my friends there.

While I was singing in *Die Meistersinger* at Vienna in 1963 I was approached by Von Karajan who said he was planning to record the opera in the near future and would like me to sing the role of Beckmesser. I was very pleased to be asked, both because of the opportunity to work with him, and also because I hadn't had the chance to make many records.

Time went by and nothing happened. I'd almost forgotten about the project when, *six years later*, I had a letter from him saying the recording was now set for Dresden, in East Germany, and hoping I'd be free between the dates mentioned. I made certain that I would be and sent my acceptance. I was very pleased that he'd kept his word.

When the time came I flew to West Berlin, where I was met by a car driver who said he was to take me all the way to Dresden. We collected my visa for East Germany at Checkpoint Charlie without any trouble, but then the driver said he had to meet another passenger in the centre of East Berlin. We parked opposite a police station and he asked me to wait in the car. Fifteen minutes went by, then half an hour, and there was no sign of him.

The absence of people and traffic in the street gave an eerie and almost threatening quietness to the surroundings and soon I began to feel I'd been abandoned there. A policeman walked past the car, taking a hard look at me, then came back for another look. I started to feel quite nervous and wondered if I looked suspicious. Perhaps I should take a walk around, I thought, and then wondered where I would walk to anyway. After about an hour and a half my driver returned, but by then I was actually shaking with a kind of fear induced by the sinister silence all about.

We drove to Dresden, and went to my hotel, arriving at about ten o'clock at night. I was tired and didn't want to eat, so I went straight to bed. Next morning I went in search of breakfast. The hall porter showed me where to go.

As I pushed open the swing door of the breakfast room there was a partition screening it from my view. I began to wonder if I'd opened the right door. At home one would have heard the sounds of conversation, dishes rattling and so on. Here there was total silence. I poked my head round the screen and saw thirty or forty people at their breakfast tables, but not a whisper of talk, not a single cup and saucer rattling. It was uncanny, with a portrait of Lenin gazing down on the scene, a scene that I came to accept while I was there but which always set me on edge, wondering.

A car took me and other singers to the converted church which was the recording studio. As soon as we started a run-through I could tell the acoustics were particularly good, warm and mellow for the voices and orchestra alike. During a break, or when we weren't needed, we'd sit at one side of the studio, outside the control box, talking freely about anything that came to mind.

One of the assembled company always had very little to say. We thought he belonged to the engineers but when, after a couple of days, somebody asked them who he was, they denied all knowledge of him. 'Isn't he one of your singers?' they asked in return. Then it dawned on us that he was the listening post for the Government, noting and no doubt reporting on all that we said.

He made his position clear only once, after the recording finished. It had taken only about four and a half days, half the sessions that had been set aside for it. I think Von Karajan wanted it to sound spontaneous and many of what we thought were run-throughs turned out to be actual takes. We didn't know this at the time, however, and if you listen carefully there are a few mistakes here and there, one of them in my own part.

I suppose it's arguable whether one should have studio perfection for gramophone records, with every little blemish corrected and patched over, or whether a sense of actual performance is preferred. *Die Meistersinger* turned out to be a very good album, I thought, and I'll say that I've seldom heard an orchestra play so magnificently as the Dresden State Opera orchestra did in those sessions. I'd never heard them before, and they made a fantastic sound.

Von Karajan was quite overcome by this, and after the sessions were over he made a speech of thanks to the musicians, praising their work under such difficult circumstances. His words had many of them in tears. I understood a little of what he said, but the German singers with me commented on what a marvellous speech it was. The studio microphones had been left on while he spoke, and René Kollo, the tenor who sang Walther von Stolzing, asked the engineer in charge if he could have a tape of the speech. One or two others then made the same request, and I thought it would be interesting to have a copy as well. Then what should happen but that the party agent, the mysterious unknown among us, came round and declared that nobody was to have a tape of the speech; it would not be allowed. I'm not sure if anyone managed to get one after all, but I certainly didn't press for mine. I still had to get home, and when I did return I was held at Checkpoint Charlie for two hours while they examined everything I had: I'm convinced they were searching for that tape!

During the time we were recording in Dresden we were given sizeable sums of East Deutschmarks in cash for our expenses. It was more than I needed for day-to-day living, but although I would walk round the shops occasionally there was nothing there to buy. I was approached one day by a black market currency operator who wanted to offer me a deal for my marks, but I knew what kind of trouble that could land me in if I were found out, and I refused.

Yet here were these wads of East German marks, several hundred of them. There was nothing to spend them on, and currency restrictions prevented one from changing more than about five pounds' worth when crossing the border to the West. In the end I gave them away, to the elderly couple who acted as caretakers for the converted studio in the church. They were decidedly suspicious at first, but I told them it was to thank them very much and left as quickly as I could.

I hoped it wouldn't put me wrong, or them. I just wanted to be rid of the money which was of no use to me, though it might be to them. I was glad indeed to get back across the border into West Berlin and on my way home.

My only other visit to Eastern Europe was to Warsaw, and in some ways that was a much pleasanter affair.

It started with a call from Regina Resnik. She'd been talking to the Polish conductor, Kazimir Kord, about the possibility of making some guest appearances with the Warsaw opera company, and they had decided to stage *Falstaff*, which had never been given in Warsaw. Kord had seen a performance of mine somewhere and asked her to sound me out about singing it. Regina was to direct it as well as singing Quickly, and her husband, Arbit Blatas, would design the opera.

The idea sounded attractive to me, with a group of us going there, and when I saw that I could manage the dates (they were set for early in 1975) I agreed. This time I wasn't so apprehensive about visiting Eastern Europe, because I'd already met a number of Polish emigrants when I sang at the Chicago Lyric Opera, where they made up practically the entire chorus, and found them so warm and friendly that I welcomed the chance to visit their homeland.

The arrangements were made and I flew to Warsaw (Brenda was to join me a few days later). When I landed there was quite a reception committee at the airport, about eight or nine people, including the Intendant from the opera house and other members of his staff. Also present was the head of the airport police, who asked for my passport and visa.

Now although I'd spoken to the Polish Embassy in London about my trip, nothing had been said directly to me about a visa, and I rather thought it would be waiting for me when I arrived, as it had been on my visit to Dresden. I handed the police officer my passport, and when he asked again for the visa I replied, 'Why, isn't it here waiting for me?'

At this the police officer looked at me. The reception committee looked at me. There was a deathly hush. They looked uncomfortable, and I felt even more uncomfortable, because it dawned on me that I should perhaps have done something about it. To try and pass it off, I fell back on a commonplace remark yet a very true one: 'Well, does it matter?' I asked. 'Music hath no bounds.'

Most of them understood, and smiled. Even the police chief half-smiled. Having taken my passport he said something in Polish; the rest of the party came forward to welcome me, and in about three minutes I had my visa, stamped and signed. Next day the Warsaw papers carried my picture with the caption translated into Polish: 'Music hath no bounds.'

I was taken to a hotel and shown to a very luxurious room with a high dome to it, plenty of light, but very, very cold. It was January after all. Looking round, it wasn't difficult to spot two little microphone 'bugs' and no doubt there were others. Before Brenda joined me I asked for somewhere warmer and another room was found, not so big and elegant, but comfortable enough. Whether that was bugged too I didn't much care, but I did warn Brenda about it when she arrived a few days later. It's odd what an effect the idea of being spied on can have – just the thought of microphones affected Brenda in such a way that she wasn't only afraid for what she might say, but she also insisted on keeping the lights turned off when she dressed or undressed. We decided to speak to each other only in Welsh and I couldn't resist saying in English to one of these microphones, 'Sort that one out!'

Ten years previously Warsaw's national opera house, known as the Wielki Theatre, had been reopened after being completely destroyed by fire in 1945, and it now had some of the best facilities I've ever seen: not only the latest technical equipment for the stage and the best of backstage accommodation for the artists, but even a sick bay, with three beds and a doctor and nurse in full-time attendance.

Yet when I saw some of the other productions in the opera repertory, it seemed to me that they were at least thirty years behind in the style of their staging. Regina and I hadn't taken this into account and when we started to work on *Falstaff* we took it from our own western standpoint, with the style that was current in Covent Garden and the American companies. It was particularly encouraging to find the singers and staff there responding enthusiastically to our ideas, as if it were a relief to try something new. What with the new style of acting and different approach to stagecraft, it was as if they were making a new start in terms of production and stage personality.

Among the local singers was a baritone for the role of Ford who, I was told, was a fine artist. Yet he seemed nervous and unforthcoming, and after making enquiries we discovered that he'd been kept back and not given any major roles for about ten years. All the same, it was a good voice, and Regina suggested I should work hard with him and try to give him confidence. So I did.

By the first night he was a changed man. He smiled, he was more sure of himself, and he was well received by the audience. The general response to the opera and to the company could hardly have been more enthusiastic. During the second performance this baritone came to me in the interval with a flask, to offer me a drink as a friendly gesture. He poured me a vodka in a little aluminium cup, and another for himself, saying whatever is the Polish for 'Cheers!' and throwing it back quickly.

I did the same, and gasped. I'd never drunk spirits like it. I swear it was 120° proof, or some such. It burned my throat and all the rest of my vocal apparatus, so that when the stage call came for the next act, I couldn't talk, let alone sing. I gulped down as much water as I could to lubricate the mechanism, and somehow managed to get the voice back just in time. Next interval, and the one after that, my friend returned with his flask. Rather that offend him I accepted his drinks, but I made sure that I was standing close to a washbasin: as he threw back his vodka, I threw mine, very discreetly, into the basin. I dared not risk another drink of that strength!

Another performance found Regina ill with a gastric upset. The same happened to me later on. Each time we were given medicine which settled the system so that we could continue singing, but Arbit Blatas was convinced he had the solution: 'You and Regina have not been drinking vodka,' he said to me. 'Brenda and I have drunk the vodka, and you see, we are not ill!'

My birthday, which is in February, fell during this visit. After one performance, as the audience was applauding, the orchestra stood to applaud as well, looking up at the stage and chanting their greeting, 'Stolat! Stolat!' I thought it was something to do with the conductor, but he stood back and only then did I tumble to the fact that they were wishing me a happy birthday. The audience sang 'Happy Birthday' and never have I had so many bouquets of flowers presented to me.

During the five weeks we were in Warsaw, Brenda and I enjoyed a wonderfully warm association with the Polish company and some delightful hospitality. The opera's principal singers each had a flat close to the opera house, provided for them by the government. But the flats were tiny and on the occasions when we were invited to dinner with one or other or them, what they gave us to eat amounted, I am sure, to virtually the whole of their food allowance for the week.

The resident singers couldn't afford to miss performances for fear of being penalised. One soprano had sung *La traviata* one night, and was due to sing Frasquita in *Carmen* the next. She wasn't well and had problems with her voice, but she simply dared not refuse the Frasquita in case she found herself replaced for later performances as well.

I heard a number of very fine voices in that Warsaw company, most of whom would have liked to sing in the West. Unfortunately they were never given permission to do so, because their Minister of Culture and the Arts, whom I met once or twice, totally disapproved of the idea for ideological reasons and refused to allow the Polish singers to take Western engagements. How Regina and I came to be invited to Warsaw in such a situation I never knew, but we were the first singers from the West to perform there since the beginning of that regime.

Our fees were paid in Polish zlotys, and of course I knew beforehand that I wouldn't be able to bring any money back with me. It meant a financial loss, but I accepted that for the sake of the experience and the pleasure of it.

It happened that Regina's original call about Warsaw had come on a day when I was at a dinner with Lord Eccles, who was then the Minister for the Arts in Britain. I put this point about the currency from Poland to him. He felt it would be a political and diplomatic advantage if I accepted the invitation to Poland, and he promised to look into the financial question on my behalf. Later, however, before I left, he got in touch to say, very apologetically, that nothing could be done.

This meant that I had pockets full of zlotys, even after paying for the hotel. There was little enough to spend them on, apart from some furs that Brenda and I had seen. My last performance there was on a Friday night, so we decided to stay on Saturday and shop for furs, taking the Sunday flight home.

Just our luck! The Saturday in question turned to to be a public holiday of some kind, and the shops were closed. We took a walk round just the same, and in one fur shop we saw a light on and a man inside. I tapped on the window to attract his attention and pointed to some furs. He looked pretty suspicious, so I hauled out a wad of zlotys, pointed to Brenda and back to the furs.

Now he gave us a big smile, rather like Aladdin's cave, because all his teeth were gold-capped. He opened up the shop and was delighted when we spent quite a lot of zlotys on behalf of Brenda and my sisters. I'd already bought myself a leather fur coat in the market, though it had quite likely fallen off a wagon at the border: it was the kind of coat the Russians used to say had won them the war. We gave away what remained of our zlotys, some to the driver of the car who took me around, and some to our girl interpreter, to whom Brenda also gave some of her clothes.

The day we left Warsaw there was another committee to see us off, with flowers and presents. The flight was delayed a couple of hours, and when the call came we joined the queue for the bus that would take us to the aircraft. As we stood there, the police chief who'd fixed my visa when I arrived came up and motioned us to a different door, while somebody took charge of our hand baggage.

I thought he was just giving us preference as visitors and putting us on the bus first. Instead of which the bus started up with just the police officer and ourselves on it, and when it passed the waiting line of other passengers I just cringed in embarrassment, hoping nobody would see who we were.

The incident seemed to me characteristic of a system which ostensibly put so much store by 'equality' but which was in fact no more equal than any other. Human beings are fallible, and I doubt whether any ideal of equality is attainable. It certainly wasn't the case in Poland, where it didn't take long to discover that the more senior or more active party members qualified for preferential treatment. When we accepted one invitation to dinner it was noticeable that they had a bigger flat with more furnishings than the other members of the company; they could afford a better meal and run a bigger car than her opera colleagues, even though her ranking in the company was the same as theirs.

Just before I was due to leave Warsaw, I had a message from the opera management that the company had been invited to take this *Falstaff* production to Moscow, and would I sing it there with them? Regina had been asked as well, both to sing Quickly and to mount the production, so after verifying the dates I told them I would be very honoured to go with them.

Time went by and I heard nothing more. Eventually Regina called me to say the arrangement was off: the Soviet authorities didn't want Western guests with a Polish company. *Falstaff* went to Moscow, with our parts sung by the local singers who'd covered them while we were there.

Regina and I both left our costumes behind for them to use. I was later told that they're now on display in a Warsaw museum, and I'm proud that I should have left something of me in Poland to support the wonderful affection I feel for the people we met there.

The hospitality and friendship they showed to us is unforgettable and we left with heavy hearts under the smiles because we sensed a continuing tragedy, a continuing conflict between the system and the faith of a people which gave them strength and kept them together. We came back to our freedom of speech and opinion, while the friends we left there had to make do with what they could get, and to watch what they said at all times. Not for nothing were their churches filled to capacity. Their faith was the bond that united them, and the anchor of their existence.

CHAPTER SEVEN

Right for the Part

STUDIES IN INTERPRETATION

Before I discuss my interpretations of some of the roles with which I have become most closely associated, let me say in a more general sense that opera singers, like other stage performers, do aim to give their best. We want to be liked by you, the public, who often pay quite a lot of money to hear us. We are professionals who take a pride in what we do, and we work pretty hard aiming for perfection. When you show pleasure with your applause, we love it. Genuine applause is our food and drink, just as it is for a cricketer, say, who scores a century. We all want to score centuries, and tip our caps to you. Nobody *wants* to be out for a duck.

Sometimes I've sat in an audience and been carried away by a performer to such an extent that I've had to applaud there and then, even if it might be the 'wrong' place. So the music is beautiful. So we should wait until it stops. But if our emotions are thrilled or deeply touched, why should we force ourselves to repress them? I don't believe that audiences should. My view is that the singers perform in order to stimulate such a response and should always welcome genuine applause even if it does sometimes come at unexpected moments. The composer concerned, whether Verdi, Puccini or anybody else, would surely have welcomed such recognition with warmth and pride.

I also believe that a singer should try to look right for the part. I sang Mozart's Figaro over nearly thirty years, and I prepared for most of those performances by going on a diet some weeks ahead. After all, Figaro is a young man, and I wanted at least to look presentable, especially as his habitual costume of breeches and a cummerbund can exaggerate many a physical defect. A voice in a million will sometimes be accepted even if its owner doesn't look the part, but it behoves the rest of us to recognise that audiences want us to look credible as well as to sound right.

My ideas about Figaro changed and developed from the time I first sang the role, in January 1949. On the advice of Percy Heming at Covent Garden I read the Beaumarchais play, so I had some idea of the character before starting to rehearse. I soon found, though, that Mozart and da Ponte between them had, to some extent, softened the edges of what is actually quite a cruel and bitter play. Only later did I come to incorporate some touches of this in my approach. At first it was all comedy, gaiety and youthful spirit.

I think my impressions of eighteenth-century social graces were coloured by memories of pre-war or wartime films of costume comedies, in which the men minced about foppishly, waving a handkerchief delicately in one hand and wearing heavy make-up with the inevitable beauty-spot on one cheek. Percy Heming, as I've told elsewhere, tried to give me a semblance of period manners according to his view, but Peter Brook, who directed my first Figaro, wanted me to discard all these ideas and simply let the character grow from inside as we worked on it.

Thanks to his guidance and help from the rest of the cast, with Elisabeth Schwarzkopf as my first Susanna representing what I thought to be the 'real' Viennese Mozart tradition, we built up a credible character for me, and I believe I gave a creditable performance. I was a pretty exuberant Figaro to begin with, but when, some time later, I re-read Beaumarchais, I began to feel that something of his revolutionary spirit was missing from my characterisation.

That was after I'd been singing Figaro for six or seven years and had given well over a hundred performances. I asked David Webster if I could have a rest from it and perhaps look at it from a different aspect. He was very clever in his response. Not only did he go along with my request, but he immediately suggested that I took on the Count instead. This suited me very well and I sang Count Almaviva at several performances in 1957 and 1958, first with Forbes Robinson in his Figaro debut and then with the American, James Pease.

During this time I made two discoveries. One was that Figaro needed to be played more seriously and with more revolutionary intent than I'd been doing. The other was that the Count was actually an easier role to play because he's seen in relation to several different foils: Cherubino, Figaro, Susanna, the Countess and even Antonio the gardener. He can thus vary his vocal and expressive character according to the circumstances of each of them, whereas Figaro has to be serious and single-minded in his determination to outwit the Count and marry Susanna before his employer can seduce her.

The opportunity to make Figaro much more resolute and rebellious came when I first went to Salzburg to sing in a new production there directed by Gustav Rudolf Sellner, with Dietrich Fischer-

Dieskau as the Count. I've already said that Sellner was an excellent man of the theatre, always ready to discuss new ideas, and Fischer-Dieskau was likewise eager to strengthen his interpretation.

The three of us talked round the characters, their feelings and motives, and at my suggestion we made the scene before the third-act finale, when the Count believes he has compromised Figaro, a moment of direct confrontation, the servant challenging his master to his face, perhaps for the first time. The incident is trivial: somebody has jumped down from the Countess's window and damaged the gardener's flower-beds. Figaro says it was he and the Count believes it was Cherubino. 'Perché no?' demands Figaro. 'If I can do it, why shouldn't he?' The way this is done can make Figaro suddenly seem very dangerous in the implied threat to his master's authority.

We played it this way and, by doing so, helped to suggest more of the revolutionary undercurrent in the story. From then on I played the Figaro role more seriously and looked for ways to give it this added character. For instance, I would also ask whichever Count I was performing with to create another moment of tension near the end of the opening scene: while the servants are singing his praises as their noble protector of innocence and chastity, he is trying to postpone Figaro's betrothal to Susanna. At this point I like to have the Count and Figaro look fixedly at each other for a moment, absolutely still while the chorus is still singing, so that they convey the opposition of their intentions. Even though he has already renounced the *droit de seigneur*, the Count still wants to make love to Susanna. As Figaro says to the Countess in the next act, 'It's very natural and, if Susanna consents, very possible,' but at this first point of confrontation I wanted Figaro to glare his defiance: 'You're not going to have her.'

My advice to any young singer about to tackle Figaro would be to approach the role in this way. Of course he'd have to grow into it, but he should have in mind from the outset that Figaro is a fighter. He's fighting *against* the privilege that he fears may be wrongly used: the traditional rights of the Lord of the Manor. He's fighting *for* Susanna: fighting for her life, in a way, certainly for her virtue, and for all that means to their own life together.

He also has to fight *not* to marry Marcellina. Unless he were simply to run away there is, to me, a very real chance at one point in the third act when, without the money to pay his debt, Figaro might yet have to marry the woman who is, though so far unknown, his mother. That's a terrible thought to have in mind, a real touch of Greek tragedy, and I would play Figaro's dilemma at this point very seriously indeed, with a sense of despair; there is a moment of numb shock before Figaro grasps the truth of the revelation about his parentage, and only then does he begin to see the funny side of it.

The audience will always find the situation amusing; no matter what the performance is like, from the moment that Bartolo first tells Figaro that Marcellina is his mother and Marcellina names Bartolo as his father. The audience laughs and the Count also responds instantly, realising that his plot to grab Susanna away from Figaro has collapsed. But Figaro is the last one to see the comic side of the situation, though when he does so it's because it seems, to him, like a happy ending, until the last act brings back the doubts and despair as a result of the plot by Susanna and the Countess against the Count.

Figaro is a long part for a singer, and it needs careful pacing. Musically it lies well for a bass or bass-baritone, or even a baritone, although it would often happen that in ensembles with Bartolo, who is a true bass, I would sing his notes and he would take mine where the words are the same, either because the tessitura was too high for a particular bass, or even because the change would improve Figaro's sound. 'What line are you singing?' was often one of the first questions to be settled at rehearsals.

Pacing oneself for Figaro is important in relation to the last act. Not only does he have to move around a lot, hiding here and popping out there, with a good deal of recitative that should come across very clearly, but he also has an important aria which must be sung directly to the audience. Most of Figaro's arias are written in such a way that they express his feelings half to the audience and half to the characters on stage, but 'Aprite un po' quegli occhi' is addressed directly to the audience, telling the men to open their eyes to their women folk: they're as foolish as Figaro if they think they can trust them. It's a style of aria that demands a different approach from the singer, and Mozart uses it again for Alfonso in *Così* and Papageno in *The Magic Flute*.

Susanna has a comparable problem when, at the end of a long and pretty active role, she has to sing the wonderful aria, 'Deh, vieni', an invocation to happiness which she's privately addressing to Figaro while he's suspiciously thinking it's meant for the Count. I've known Susannas who worry about this all through the opera, terrified that in spite of having to give their all throughout the first three acts, they still have to make a success of that last aria.

Sometimes I think the opera should have been called *Susanna*, because she's in many ways the more decisive character. Figaro is an honest-to-goodness person who acts according to his lights, but Susanna is the clever schemer who plants the seed of suspicion in

Figaro's mind. If you look at the story, it's she who's more involved than Figaro with the various intrigues. I see her as the type of woman who loves her man but also wants to make him a little jealous, so that he in turn becomes more attentive or protective.

I've been lucky to work with the finest Susannas of the time – Graziella Sciutti, Mirella Freni and Reri Grist – all of them delightful personalities as well as wonderful singers who understand that Mozart operas depend on teamwork, not on individual star quality. No matter how talented each singer may be, unless he or she is prepared to become part of a collective ensemble working together, no Mozart opera will succeed. Likewise, the more responsive they are to each other, the better the production will become.

I had to rely a great deal on this spirit of co-operation when I directed *The Marriage of Figaro* for the Edinburgh Festival in 1975. We had a marvellous cast, including Ileana Cotrubas (Susanna), Heather Harper (Countess), Teresa Berganza (Cherubino) and Dietrich Fischer-Dieskau (the Count), and Daniel Barenboim conducted. When the Festival Director, Peter Diamand, asked me to direct the production, however, he gave me a budget figure which must have been one of the smallest allocated to any director for that opera.

There would be nothing elaborate in the way of decor, that was for sure. I discussed this with the designer, John Fraser, and we agreed on certain essential elements – doors, trees, and so on. For the rest, he had to temper his ideas in accordance with the size of the budget, and although I thought some of the colours were not quite as effective as they'd looked on the little model he built, I felt his designs were extremely resourceful.

This meant that we in the cast would have to compensate for these limitations with our personalities, and I'd have to encourage this in directing them. Fortunately we'd all worked together before, and I knew their capabilities in performance. For instance, when Teresa Berganza asked me what I wanted her to do on her first entry, when she sings Cherubino's 'Non sò più', I said she should do nothing but sing. She looked puzzled.

'I mean nothing,' I told her. 'Just get the feel of it, the expressiveness, and sing it. You don't have to "do" anything: it's there in the music. The way you sing it and your facial expressions, with those lovely big eyes, say it all.'

'Oh, thank God,' she responded. 'At other times I've been asked to run round here, kneel there, and sit down somewhere else. Now I can concentrate on singing alone, and singing it well.'

I'm convinced that the singer and the music between them should convey much more than they're often allowed to do by some directors. I shall never forget a performance of *Carmen* with Regina Resnik, who sang the role so seductively with so little movement, even though you might think it essential for a character of such volatile temperament to be almost flamboyant. Nevertheless, Regina said all that needed to be said about that woman and her feelings through the music she sang.

I thought the same principle should apply to Count Almaviva during his duet with Susanna in Act 2, when she's pretended to agree to an assignation with him in the garden that night. Fischer-Dieskau, of course, is a big man with a big voice, and I wanted him to make the role seem boyish and spoiled rather than assertive. 'Think of Baron Ochs,' I suggested, remembering the *Rosenkavalier* character's roving eye for anything in skirts. And for the first time in my experience, the spoiled boy came through in Fischer-Dieskau's portrait of the Count, especially the petulance of the aria, 'Vedrò mentr' io sospiro', when he questions why he should have to yield the woman he wants to a serf.

Because it wasn't an elaborate production, I wanted the emphasis on personality and I think this came across. One review questioned why Antonio the gardener should appear from the Countess's boudoir balcony with his broken plants in a flower-pot. As it happened, I borrowed this from Peter Brook's Covent Garden production 25 years earlier; it seemed much more logical to me that the gardener should climb a ladder to the balcony from where Cherubino had jumped down a short while before, than that he should trail his broken flowers through the house in order to make his complaint. Having heard the Count's voice through the window, the gardener decides to get his grievance settled right away.

On the other hand, nobody noticed that in the opening scene I had the doors to the Count's and Countess's apartments barricaded across, because the room between had fallen into disuse and was now intended as somewhere for Figaro and Susanna when they married. More than this, the barricade effectively prevented Cherubino's escape when he came to flirt with Susanna and was trapped in her room by the Count's arrival. Otherwise, I've always wondered why he should stay in hiding when he might escape through one of the other doors. My way, I'm sure, made more dramatic sense.

Having stressed that the production should be dependent on music and personality, I was delighted with the way Daniel Barenboim complemented it in his conducting. I could feel the audience in the King's Theatre responding each night, feel them smiling, feel them enjoying the comedy as they were meant to enjoy it, without all the paraphernalia of unnecessarily complicated sets or overwhelming props. Sets are meant to enhance the production, not to dominate it, and sets that diminish the human scale of the performers, as many now seem to do, to my mind detract from rather than support the opera. The same thing applies to costumes that impede a singer's movements or breathing, however accurate they are historically.

I quickly realised that Figaro is neither a man-of-the-world in terms of experience, nor yet is he a dim country yokel. His view of life may be limited, but it is absolutely clear and guileless; he is a man on whom a bright, intelligent girl would feel she could depend. The same goes for Masetto in *Don Giovanni*, which I played before taking on Leporello. Masetto and Zerlina parallel Figaro and Susanna: Masetto and Figaro are virtually one and the same person.

I was lucky to have Carl Ebert directing me when I first played Masetto at Glyndebourne: he had no sympathy with the commonplace idea of Masetto as a stupid bumpkin. If Zerlina was sufficiently attractive to stop Don Giovanni in his tracks, she would never be wasting her attentions on a Masetto who didn't have something to offer. But if Masetto is played with the same clear-sighted sincerity as Figaro, reliable and warm-hearted, the relationship becomes much more convincing.

Leporello, which I began to sing very soon after Masetto, is a different kind of role entirely. He's not a nice character at all, just the opposite, in fact. He's ready to pick up whatever Don Giovanni might discard, whether it's a leg of chicken, his clothes, or even a woman. He has a love–hate relationship with his master, one moment wanting to imitate him and resenting the fact that he can never be like him, and fawning on him the next. Indeed, Leporello is rather like a dog, and once I'd built up a little experience of the role, I would ask whoever was singing the Don to throw me down during our first recitative, and make as if to kick me like a dog.

In learning any role, I was most concerned to listen to what the music could tell me about it. It's advisable never to be too dogmatic about a character before you know the music, because it might well tell you something different. Right from the opening scene of *Don Giovanni* there's much to absorb. 'Here am I keeping watch, slaving night and day, and nothing pleases him,' grumbles Leporello in his opening lines. So we're told of his feelings immediately, but if he's that fed up, why doesn't he leave Giovanni and find another master? Because he's a coward.

Leporello should never be played in a tidy, clean costume. I wanted to look dishevelled and decidedly grubby, with stains down the front of my clothes, and I even put dirt in my fingernails if I were singing on film or television. I wore dark, greasy-looking make-up, a wig that was cut to give a slightly sinister appearance, and later I added that Mexican brigand's moustache, drooping at the corners, and every producer seemed to prefer this approach to the comic servant stereotype.

To my mind, in most productions the Don is dressed too elegantly as well. The opera is about the end of a 'rake's progress', in a sense, and I would have him dressed in a way that suggests he's down to his last penny before retribution catches up with him. He's spent himself and his money in the pursuit of women, of some kind of ideal that exists perhaps only in his imagination, and now he no longer knows or cares much what he's chasing or which way to turn next. So at one moment he kicks at Leporello like a dog, and the next puts his arms about him. It's hardly surprising that Leporello doesn't know where he stands.

All this can and should be established in the opening scene, and then Leporello has a further chance to show his necessary vulgarity, his grubby mind, if you like, when he sings the 'Catalogue aria', the list he's kept of his master's conquests, to the distraught Donna Elvira. I would creep behind her during the recitative, and speculate why she's come in search of the Don. Is it a first love she can't forget? Is she pregnant, perhaps? And now my master wants nothing more to do with her; she's in despair, and maybe this is *my* chance to have her.

Nasty, I know, but the opera is absolutely about good and evil, and shouldn't be afraid to show it. Sometimes I've thought I'd like to see a production designed in the style of those old Biblical prints about good and evil, the righteous and the wicked. The 'Catalogue aria' shows Leporello being very wicked. Elvira is already in despair, and he's putting the knife in and twisting it to make her discomfiture the worse, telling her that she's neither the Don's first nor last love, that there have been hundreds more, in one country after another and, in Spain, 'mille e tre' (a thousand and three). We have to accept da Ponte's poetic licence at this point: maybe it was his own wishful thinking?

I would never hurry this aria because it's the only major aria that Leporello has in the entire opera – from then on he's heard chiefly in duets or ensembles. Besides, there's such a wealth of character in the lines themselves that it's essential to colour the voice to emphasise them. The legato second part of it, from 'Nella bionda', I would take pride in phrasing exactly like the violins carrying the melody, consciously looking down from the stage to the orchestra, if it were possible.

The unfortunate Elvira also has her part to play during this aria, even though she's silent. It's better for her *not* to face front all the time (as some sopranos are inclined to do). Leporello is singing not to an expressionless statue, but to a human being, and hurting her as he does so. It's important for her to react to this, and she is most effective, in my view, if she has her back to the audience and her head down, feeling the pain, and turning her head occasionally to let them see her anguish. Without an Elvira who can respond, who knows when to sit and when to turn, the whole scene can fall disastrously flat.

The catalogue itself, the list that Leporello supposedly reads from, is a vital prop, and I hated the caricature version with a lot of linked pages that he was supposed to throw half across the stage. It wasn't so bad with a few linked pages that dropped perhaps to my knees when I opened them, so that I could pretend to enjoy reading them again as I folded them back, but best of all I preferred just a small notebook, wetting my finger when I turned the page as I listed one country's total after another.

I know it's said that in spite of this record of sexual prowess, the opera doesn't allow the Don a single further success, but he does come close to it with Zerlina. That's why the recitative before their duet, 'Là ci darem la mano', is to me one of the key passages in the opera. It's the only time that the Don is heard actively attempting a seduction and much of the opera's success depends on the way he sings it. Few indeed, in my experience, have been able to make it so totally captivating as Mario Petri did at Glyndebourne.

When I tried out the title role in Dublin, as I've previously mentioned, the performance was in English, and though I did my best to phrase it as I remembered Petri doing, it didn't come off. The words somehow didn't have the warmth of the sun in them, and if you look at the libretto with any album of records of the opera, you'll see that the Italian has a much more romantic and poetic quality to it which no English equivalent can really match.

It's strange to recall now that my first Leporello performances were also in English, with the then Sadler's Wells Opera, the only time I sang with them. And whereas I believe *The Marriage of Figaro* and *The Magic Flute* can be given successfully in English, especially in the Edward Dent translation, which avoids making it sound too colloquial, to me his version of *Don Giovanni* doesn't succeed in the same way, nor does any other I know. All my good intentions about the seriousness of Leporello, the seediness of his character and behaviour, came to nothing because practically everything I had to utter in English was greeted with laughter. As with Verdi's *Falstaff*, it's the flavour of the words that counts, and you can't afford to lose the garlic.

On the whole I found Leporello as comfortable to sing as Figaro, the part lying as well for the voice. Of course, he's not such a central figure as Figaro – Leporello should be a good feed for the Don, and he has to adjust his performance to that of the latter. The better he does so, the more dog-like he is, the more successful both roles become.

I had one problem, in our opening duet in the second act, when I had to repeat the word 'Sì' very fast several times. I mentioned this to Sesto Bruscantini, who knew the role as well as anybody, and even he admitted that although he was Italian, he sometimes came adrift in this passage. 'I'd sing the first few,' he told me, 'then fake the rest by putting in a "z" sound to link them together.' If an Italian has problems here, I thought, what hope for me? But indeed this came off very successfully.

Otherwise, I never like to hurry recitative. There are some conductors who pay little attention to it, treating it as little more than a linking passage to the next aria or ensemble, but to me it's always important. For one thing, recitative conveys a lot of information, so it invites you to colour it accordingly, even to exaggerate the colour at times, and it's worth taking some trouble over this. In Mozart it's particularly important to create the right atmosphere for the next musical number, and the end of the recitative needs a sensitive delivery in order to lead directly and effortlessly into whatever comes next.

A steady tempo, avoiding any sense of rushing, is often desirable in other places. Fritz Busch at Glyndebourne would always hold the tempo back for the ballroom scene at the end of the first act in *Don Giovanni*. 'Hold the reins,' he would say, and proceed to build the tension of the scene from within a steady tempo, whereas a conductor who set a quicker tempo (as several did) found that it just accelerated the activity without increasing the tension.

The only place where I felt the need to modify my Leporello character was in the second-act sextet after Don Giovanni has persuaded Leporello to exchange cloaks and hats, and sends him off with Elvira as if he himself were escorting her. I would bring some comedy into this mock serenade, which I had to mime in view of Elvira while the Don sang it. My unmasking in the next scene, however, surrounded by five angry people who've been tricked by the disguise, was best sung without much emphasis of character but with feeling for the music, like the long phrase on Leporello's plea, 'Perdon, perdono', when he reveals who is actually under Don Giovanni's hat.

It doesn't matter if the audience chuckles at this, as they often do, any more than if they do the same in the graveyard scene later on when Leporello is ordered by the Don to invite the statue of the murdered Commendatore to supper. What does matter here is that the scene should be played for real, with a sincere terror on Leporello's part of the blasphemy he is committing and the possible consequences it might bring about. However casual the Don seems, Leporello must show himself an abject coward again, scared out of his wits.

He should convey the same sense of character in the final scene, too. There can be a moment of unforced comedy when Leporello helps himself to a chicken leg after the Don has been served his dinner and the servant is caught with his mouth full, but this is provided for in the libretto and the comedy arises out of the situation. Apart from that, I would never otherwise play this scene for laughs in any sense: no hiding under the table and peeping from under the tablecloth, as I've sometimes seen happen. I tried only to show by the way I sang and played that Leporello is absolutely terrified the moment he sights the statue.

During the very last notes of that scene, when the Don cries out as he disappears into the hellfire, Leporello also sings a last long-drawn 'Aaaahh' as he sees what happens to his master. Just then I felt he should show a glimmer of courage or bravado, and I would stretch out my hand as if I wanted somehow to save my master. Otherwise I would be a very serious Leporello all through the opera. Imitating the Don in the serenade to Elvira, and disclosing my own identity in the sextet soon after, were the only touches of comedy I put into it. Leporello doesn't change as a character and he must be consistent.

In the opera as a whole I would sometimes feel a touch of jealousy over the two tenor arias for Don Ottavio, 'Dalla sua pace', and 'Il mio tesoro', which to me are Mozart at his most beautiful. I was first thrilled by them at Glyndebourne, when I heard them sung by Leopold Simoneau, who had such style and a lovely *mezzo voce*. Later on, Stuart Burrows also sang them most beautifully. I heard many fine tenors sing them at one time or another, but these two singers gave me the greatest pleasure.

Among the Dons I worked with, Mario Petri and Cesare Siepi were outstanding for their beauty of voice and force of character, and I also enjoyed Tito Gobbi for a different reason. He was perhaps rather staid for the role, which was not one he often sang, I think, and I had to adjust to that, but we were both always looking for ways to improve presentation. Even at the side of the stage during a performance we would discuss a new idea and we would say: 'Let's try that out tonight.' I enjoyed that: it meant the characters didn't get stereotyped; it kept our brains active; it made us feel we were doing something different for each performance, and if it worked we kept it in.

The secret of a successful *Don Giovanni* production is that it should flow from one scene to the next as smoothly as possible, not come to a sudden stop after each scene. This is where I found John Piper's designs for Carl Ebert's Glyndebourne production in the 1950s so successful, when I was singing Leporello for the first time there, whereas Franco Zeffirelli's Covent Garden staging in the early 1960s, excellent as it was in many respects, suffered from the long delays while the sets were changed. I remember Rudolf Kempe getting impatient with it at one of the revivals: 'We could have done another couple of operas while we waited,' he declared.

The last production in which I sang at Covent Garden was absolutely useless as a stage design. It had a set built so far back that we couldn't work in it: perhaps during the sextet I'd wander to the back for a moment, but for the rest of the opera it didn't mean a thing because it didn't serve any useful purpose, either for us or for the audience. We might as well have given the opera as a concert, and I really think it would have been more successful.

The Glyndebourne company did just that the first time a BBC Promenade concert at the Royal Albert Hall was given over to a single opera in 1961. Moran Caplat had the idea of putting the singers on a small raised platform behind the orchestra; we came and went according to our cues, instead of sitting in a row across the front of the main platform, and we dressed to suit our parts. György Melis as the Don wore tails; I wore a dinner jacket. Anna and Elvira (Gerda Scheyrer and Ilva Ligabue) wore long dresses; Mirella Freni as Zerlina a short cocktail dress. With John Pritchard conducting, it worked a great deal better than some theatre productions.

I've long thought there should be more consideration of the technical problems involved in staging opera, more consultation before large sums of money, often thousands of pounds, are spent on sets and designs that turn out to be unworkable, sometimes downright dangerous. Built-up sets involving scaffolding, for instance, either have to be braced from all angles to make them secure, which often means there's little space left to move on stage, or else you risk having them wobble and shake and terrify the singers when the producer expects them to climb up and down the structures.

When I remember the old Covent Garden sets for *Die Meistersinger* and *La Bohème*, which dated right back to 1908 or thereabouts, I realise how splendidly these conveyed the right illusion but at the same time gave the singers room to move and bring character alive without risking life and limb. Of course there must be changes, but production teams should be wary of being too clever: the set for the 1977 Covent Garden production of *La fanciulla del West* was so elaborate that it couldn't all be accommodated on stage, and what there was left little enough room for anybody to move.

I don't believe it's necessary to construct sets in such naturalistic detail. All that's needed is the suggestion of period, place and time. Nothing is worse than having scenery impeding an entry, not least when sixty or seventy chorus singers all have to get on stage, sometimes swarming in from unrealistic directions. I believe that audiences would rather be convinced by the artists and their performances than any amount of pseudo-scenery. Many operas can be very successful with nothing but drapes on the stage, or gauzes such as John Piper devised for *The Magic Flute* in 1956.

Papageno in *The Magic Flute* was always one of the roles I most enjoyed. For this I had quite a lot of preparation in my early years at Covent Garden when I sang Second Priest or Second Man in Armour, and could therefore observe what a fine singer like Jess Walters made of Papageno's role. Or when I saw Erich Kunz, who was equally excellent though his style was quite different. At the same time I wanted to create my own character and not just rely on imitation, even if sometimes there were details in another singer's interpretation which were worth borrowing and incorporating into one's own.

Believe me, the worst thing any singer can do is to go to the first rehearsal with a blank mind about his role. I'm convinced that you should always make a foundation of character from your own judgement, from reading, and from listening to others. Then you have something for the director to work on, and the better the foundation the easier it is to be flexible and adapt to his suggestions, or to other singers in the cast. No matter how close to perfection the singing alone may be, it's still not enough without the requisite character to support it.

I look on Papageno as a role that most young baritones should at least learn to portray, even if they do no more than rehearse it to themselves and never sing it on stage. First, it demands a certain style of singing, a style that never calls for fortissimo voice but always requires warmth and a firmness of line, as well as often surprisingly delicate inflexions. Secondly, the physical appearance and stature play a part in achieving credibility. And thirdly, there needs to be a fellow-feeling for the kind of person that Papageno represents; one shouldn't be embarrassed by his naïvety and innocence.

These were the qualities I tried to find. I wanted to make Papageno the child of nature the fable suggests. I tried to identify with a boy in early adolescence, who has seen few other human beings and is therefore basically shy, but who has begun to feel a need for something that is still outside his experience, as we all do in puberty. What Papageno really wants beyond his food and drink is a girl. He doesn't know this, or why it should be so, and it only crystallises for him towards the end of the opera, but the feeling should be apparent from the beginning.

Papageno is essentially a lovable character. The audience needs to feel this, and he in turn wants them actively on his side. I'm sure this was in Schikaneder's mind when he wrote the role for himself to play at the original performances in Vienna. When I went there to play it, singing and speaking in German, of course, I'd be given some topical remarks to make in Viennese dialect, just as Schikaneder might have done.

Something similar happened in San Francisco, where the opera was sung in English. I'd go round before each performance, talking to stage staff and dressers (many of these were local school-teachers), asking about topical gossip and comments, and I'd collect perhaps as many as twenty possible throwaway lines, from which I'd choose just a few of the best to use on stage. The audience there loved it; they felt part of the opera because the remarks involved them. Yet at Covent Garden, Peter Hall and others seemed afraid for me to make topical references in English. Once or twice I risked it, but the idea was never really accepted here in spite of our music-hall tradition.

Papageno isn't the same central focus of attention in the opera that Figaro is, or even Leporello in *Don Giovanni*. In *The Magic Flute* each principal has his or her turn to hold the centre stage, but some of the most important parts of Papageno's role occur in his scenes with other characters rather than when he is on his own: with Tamino, of course, and with Pamina, the Queen of Night, Sarastro, Mono-statos, the Priest and, eventually, Papagena. On every occasion his character provides a contrast to theirs, and the more elation he feels inside himself, the better it is communicated to the audience, particularly as much of his part is conversational.

My only problem with Papageno's lines was to avoid mixing up the three verses and refrain of 'Ein Mädchen oder Weibchen', one of the few solo passages, where Papageno thinks longingly of a girlfriend or a wife. Trouble with verses went right back to my youth, when I could remember all manner of stories, but never verses that repeated the same pattern. I had similar problems with Beckmesser's serenade in *Die Meistersinger*, and my last hurdle before I finally quit the operatic stage will be to get Dulcamara's verses right in the last scene of Donizetti's *L'elisir d'amore*.

With the Papageno aria, though, the difficulty only arose in the English version. I was all right in German at this point, except on one occasion when Klemperer was conducting at Covent Garden. He'd told me at the dress rehearsal that before I sang the last verse he wanted me to break in with a spoken remark, 'Jetzt mit Variationen' (Now, with variations). When it came to the first performance, however, I couldn't for the life of me remember what that German phrase was. So in the midst of my two German verses I suddenly broke into English, and in a deliberately emphatic way said: 'Now, with variations.' At this the audience roared. Klemperer hadn't realised I'd made the remark in English and asked the orchestra leader, Charles Taylor, what I'd said. When he realised, Klemperer started to laugh too, and laugh loudly. The audience stopped laughing at me and laughed at him instead. The whole performance came to a halt until we all stopped laughing. It was a great moment, and although I was happy to perform Papageno in German, it confirmed my view that *The Magic Flute* needs to be sung in the language of its audience. This was one reason I did not sing later Covent Garden performances in German.

Klemperer had a fantastic sense of tempo. Sometimes it might seem to be slow, but it would always be all of a piece with the performance as he phrased it. Nor did he vary from one performance to another as some conductors do. I once asked a répétiteur to time my arias in *The Magic Flute* with a stopwatch at three successive Klemperer performances and all three were exactly the same, an incredible musical consistency. I loved working with him and we all had a deep respect for his experience and his artistry. He knew the works intimately, seldom needed a score, and he often brought out details in the orchestra I'd never known were there until he made me hear them. And all this in spite of a few seconds' cat-nap he sometimes took in the middle of a performance!

During the recording of *Figaro*, I really did feel I needed to sing something more quickly than the tempo he set, but I didn't know how to go about asking him. Just to ask, 'Please can we have it quicker?' wouldn't get me anywhere. So I tried a different approach:

'Dr Klemperer, I can't phrase this as I should phrase it. I'm not as young as you.'

He laughed. 'I know what you want me to do,' he said. 'You want me to play it quicker, no?'

'If you will, I'm sure I can do it better.'

'We'll see. We'll see,' was all he would say. But when it came to the take, he did move that little bit faster and it made all the difference to me.

I wasn't the only one to have problems with his slow tempi. The other singers were also affected and, if you listen to a passage in isolation, it can sound very slow indeed. Yet overall it is a fantastic performance, and listening to those records later made me realise there are musical colourings and shades of expression in *The Marriage of Figaro* that I'd never heard before.

I've said before that character starts from the feet upwards: shoes too tight for Beckmesser; boots too big for Wozzeck. For trotting about as Papageno I wore ballet slippers or, in America, Indian moccasins with feathers in them, which suited the part excellently.

The two best Papageno costumes I wore were the work of Oliver Messel and John Piper respectively. Indeed, I think the former's overall design at Glyndebourne has never been bettered in any others I've been involved with or seen: it was truly beautiful. Both these great designers gave Papageno a bird-like appearance, on the principle that such a child of nature with nothing else to influence him would have copied the birds to some extent. At any rate, Oliver Messel gave me some fine plumage and a cock's tail at the back, and at my suggestion he had a string attached to this so that I could flick up the tail the moment I first caught sight of Papagena. It worked splendidly.

John Piper's costume was the one with a long peaked cap, like a bird's beak, and a jacket sweeping back to a tail. He readily shortened the peak when I pointed out that my face and expression would otherwise be hidden from all the upper seats at Covent Garden, and when I wondered if maybe the jacket could somehow have a more flowing line he agreed; he wired it so that it stiffened at the tail and gave the effect of a hint of cheekiness. This too looked good.

Papageno's panpipes and the magic bells he's given also have to be worked into the character he creates. Early on I had the idea of fingering the bells as if I were actually playing them, in time to the glockenspiel sounds from the pit, and I always preferred to see Tamino likewise pretend to play his magic flute. Some directors would have him walk round holding it at arm's length as if it were playing itself, but it's the sound the flute makes that creates the magic element, not the instrument alone, so I believe it's much more convincing if these instruments are seen to be 'played'.

The panpipes, of course, actually are played: five notes in an upwards scale. It was Klemperer who once suggested to me that it might occasionally be fun to reverse the direction and play the notes downwards, unexpectedly. I tried it and it drew a good laugh, so I'd sometimes do this for devilment, though never too often. There's also traditional licence for Papageno to vary the way he plays the one-two-three notes when he's intending to hang himself for the lack of a Papagena, and counts up to three as a last chance for her to appear. I might say 'two – two and a half – nearly three', or let the last pipe note dwindle despairingly away: several touches like this could make it different each time.

Of all the Mozart operas, *Così fan tutte* is the most dependent on teamwork, on ensemble, on those six characters who interact all the way through. On the surface it seems highly contrived and artificial: the two pairs of lovers who protest their deep devotion at the outset, only to exchange their partners when the men assume their 'foreign' disguise. It's absurd to believe they could realistically carry this off without being recognised, yet the music tells us it's no *opera buffa*, not just a farcical comedy of mistaken identity. So what is its purpose?

I believe that Mozart, within the conventions of his time, was trying to express the idea that it's possible to be genuinely in love with more than one person. I say this because of what the music tells us in relation to the words. The depth of feeling that comes across in the second act duets, for instance, when the women in turn succumb to the 'wrong' partners, suggests that they are genuinely falling in love. What's more, even though the men know that they are only playing a game, as proposed by Alfonso, the situation arouses a strong jealousy between them concerning the women's affections and their own inclinations.

The 'happy' ending also raises questions. Should we accept that there has in fact been a greater love for the second partner than for the first? Or, by returning to the first partner, that the first love is still the strongest and will remain so? These emotional aspects can be approached in so many different ways in production and perform-ance, and always leave something to ponder over when the opera is finished.

Despina, the lady's maid, takes care to keep herself fancy-free, and in this way she can be just as much a puppet-controller of those who become vulnerable through their affections, as is Alfonso the philosopher-cynic. Alfonso is shown as having the idea, but Despina is the means by which he carries it through. She has the licence for farce, for there's no other way for her to dress up as a doctor in one act and a lawyer in the next and put on a funny voice and expect to be credible. And in the first of these scenes the men, Ferrando and Guglielmo, also have to respond to her with broad comedy to make it work at all.

In any case it's essential for the words to be clear, whatever the language used. If it's sung in English, then I'd hope that the version has an elegance of style comparable to the music, not like some translations which try to be colloquial and only cheapen the music. When I first sang Alfonso as a student, we used a nineteenth-century text by the Reverend Marmaduke Brown. It was old-fashioned in some ways, of course, but it didn't betray the music. In America, on occasion, I didn't hesitate to replace lines from one version with those from another if I thought I was keeping better faith with the musical style, and with Mozart.

Coming back to Alfonso later in my career I kept in mind the model of Paul Schoeffler, whom I thought was one of the best ever interpreters of the role. Although he was by no means young, he had a natural elegance and dignity which suited the role, and he combined this with a certain wickedness of expression, the knowing, debonair man of the world. He'd arrived at this interpretation after a good deal of experience, and I see no harm in a younger singer modelling himself on such a good example, as I myself did.

Alfonso takes part with Fiordiligi and Dorabella in one of the opera's most beautiful numbers, the trio 'Soave sia il vento', calling on gentle breezes and calm seas for their loved ones after the two officers have supposedly been called to the wars. We would often dread this moment because its success depends absolutely on soft legato phrasing and blend of tone which sets a standard of vocal beauty for the rest of the opera. If we brought it off well, then we would be more confident for the rest of the performance.

Having sung so many performances of Guglielmo and then moved to Alfonso, I was often dangerously close to getting mixed up between the lines each character should be singing in the ensembles, but when this happened I usually managed to recover without disrupting the flow. Right from my first Guglielmo in Carl Ebert's production at Glyndebourne, though, I realised how much depended on refining the details of stagecraft like, for instance, the exchange of lockets between Guglielmo and Dorabella. It may seem a simple matter to take a chain from around her neck and replace it with one from around mine, but it's not so easy in practice. It had to be timed as we were singing so as not to interrupt the vocal line. I had to avoid catching the chain in her wig, or her costume, or in mine. I had to be sure not to fumble and take the wrong one when I held both chains together, putting one over one arm to keep it apart while I discreetly put the other round her neck. And withal it must be done with the necessary elegance. I remember rehearsing this over and over until it was right: in Mozart operas especially, it is always worth taking trouble over the finer details.

I learned that at Glyndebourne, where Carl Ebert's production was the best I've known for making clear the purpose of every movement, every gesture on the stage. John Copley's production at Covent Garden, the last I sang in, was also meticulous in this respect. But both of them were distinguished by that vital element of taste which is so important to the understanding of style.

It wasn't until I began working on Falstaff that I realised what a great role Verdi had made of it from his Shakespeare model. Even when the music is learned it's only a beginning: one has to think very hard indeed about how to portray the kind of character the music suggests without neglecting the Shakespearean aspects. I discussed these with one or two theatrical people, though I later had to discard some of those associations in the interests of musical character.

What I did keep in mind, however, was Prince Hal's contemptuous dismissal of Falstaff, the former courtier and companion, after he became King:

> 'I know thee not, old man. Fall to thy prayers.
> How ill white hairs become a fool and a jester!'
> (*Henry IV, Part 2*; Act 5, Scene 4)

This fate of Falstaff was in my thoughts from the start of the opera until I'd established the pathos of the sorry figure who, after being ducked in the Thames, then has to come to terms with himself.

First, though, it was a matter of building the physical character, and Osbert Lancaster's wonderful costume design for me at Glyndebourne, where I first sang the role, gave me the clue to understanding that a fat man looks pear-shaped. Singers usually wore a basket strapped round their middles to produce this effect, which only succeeded in making them look pregnant, and a dropped pregnancy at that. My padding began at the middle of my body and curved down to my thighs, so that it did give a pear-shaped silhouette.

At first it was made from kapok, but during the time I was using this at Glyndebourne, I noticed in a Woolworths store one day some squares of foam plastic, and wondered if these could be used to shape the padding more comfortably. Rosemary Wilkins, in the wardrobe department at Glyndebourne, and Harry Kellard, the property master, experimented with this foam plastic by shaping it on to a tailor's dummy like a sculpture. When they had it right, it was cut to shape and sewn together on a muslin base, then long cotton combinations were sewn over that, making a complete garment even down to slightly swollen ankles. A marvellous effect.

I also realised that fat men can often be very light on their feet, even dance quite elegantly, so I would have to give this impression if I was to think of pursuing the ladies, while at the same time developing the right kind of walk for such a figure. Because of the plumpness at the tops of his thighs, a fat man is forced to turn out his feet rather like a ballet dancer, and to develop this I would rehearse with a thick blanket slung between my legs, much to everybody else's amusement.

But it worked. And it helped me reach the point where Falstaff's movements and gestures became second nature when I was dressed for the part: the way to walk and sit; the way to relax with a hand resting on the tummy; the way to turn round. More than any other role I played, the physical sense of this had to become a part of me, and I rehearsed over and over until it grew into me. Carl Ebert appreciated the hard work I put into it, and thanks to him I acquired a wonderful foundation of character which served me for other productions.

My aim was to mix the wit of Shakespeare with the humour of Verdi, and that meant taking into account the differences of interpretation between one conductor and another. At times I felt baffled when one would assert that Toscanini took a phrase in such-and-such a way, and another would say, 'Oh no, when I worked with Toscanini he took it like this': the same phrase, done quite differently. I sometimes wondered who *hadn't* worked with Toscanini! After this happened a few times I took it into my head to persuade the conductor that the way *I* felt was also important, so why not try it the way I wanted it?

Take Falstaff's 'Quand' ero paggio', when he tries to ingratiate himself with Alice Ford and tells her that he used to be quite slim as a young man. Leonard Bernstein wanted this taken slowly, which he felt would be appropriate for an elderly Falstaff. To me, it's Falstaff recollecting what he was, picking up his tail and shooting a line, and rather overdoing it as one does when showing off. Gui and Giulini both had a theatrical feel for the episode in this way, and Solti took it even more quickly though still effectively, but there have been one or two who wanted it taken so fast that it became ridiculous.

Another instance was in Falstaff's 'Può l'onore . . .' in the opening scene, after he has rounded scathingly on Bardolph and Pistol for their protestations of honour. Gui at Glyndebourne had a natural feeling for the meaning of the words and music, not beating rigid time in a silent bar to link one phrase with the next, but shaping it with a sense of musical flow to support the expressive purpose of the words. I liked to sing this passage quite broadly and had my only slight disagreement with Solti about this, but I must say that nothing was more satisfying for me than my last Falstaff at Covent Garden with Solti conducting. Everything came together just as I'd always hoped it would, and these performances were the nearest to perfection that I could hope to achieve.

Verdi was clever in making a big impact with the person of Falstaff in the opening scene, then letting him take a rest offstage in scene two while the ladies were established: Alice Ford and Nanetta, Meg Page and Mistress Quickly. From then on, though, Falstaff is given a significant musical contribution in each of the remaining four scenes, and with the extra physical weight he carries in the costume it's essential to pace oneself vocally so as not to become exhausted too soon.

So much depends on that first scene, vocally and dramatically. Falstaff has to perform with the same force that Verdi launches his first chord, the moment the curtain goes up without any overture or preliminaries. He has to put across his character, his situation, his intentions, everything about him that the audience needs to know. A Falstaff who's not on form in this respect will find it very difficult to recover himself as the opera continues, because all his following scenes depend to some extent on what he shows himself to be at the outset.

I believe that he must be conceited enough to think that Alice and Meg (the 'merry wives' to whom he's written his letters) are actually interested in him in a romantic way, and not that they see him only as a ridiculous figure. Falstaff really believes he's doing them a favour in pressing his attentions on them and after writing his identical letters to each, he's quite sure that they'll both succumb to his advances. Which is why he's so furious with Bardolph and Pistol when they refuse to take his letters.

In that first production at Glyndebourne we took an immense amount of trouble to work out the moves at the point where Falstaff chases Bardolph and Pistol around the Garter Inn set. We rehearsed it over and over to make it seem natural, and it looked so good I tried to persuade other directors to retain as much of it as possible in the various other productions I sang around the world.

Sometimes an incident would go askew, as it once did at Covent Garden when the scenery or the furniture wasn't quite where it should have been. Zeffirelli had suggested that Bob Bowman, as

Bardolph, should climb from the back of the settle to the staircase to escape from Falstaff wielding a broom. On this occasion the settle was fractionally further away from the banisters than usual and poor Bob, being a short man, just missed being able to step across. He grabbed the staircase and was left dangling until Mike Langdon, as Pistol, grabbed him by the seat of his trousers to haul him over the banister.

Once at Glyndebourne, when I was chasing the two of them round the set with the broom, the handle came away from the rest of it, which flew into the air across the footlights and caught Vittorio Gui a glancing blow as he was conducting. A few inches to one side and it might equally have smashed the violin the orchestra leader was playing. Fortunately the maestro was not seriously hurt, though he was somewhat taken aback. He kept the performance going, and thereafter I tried always to make sure that the broom was securely fastened to its handle.

The only time I forgot to do this was at a performance in the Greek-style open-air amphitheatre at Berkeley in California. Came the moment when I flourished the broom, the end once more came away from the handle and travelled quite some distance through the air. We stopped altogether because we were terrified that it would hit somebody. But a man stood up in the audience and caught it in the air. A baseball catch. The whole audience applauded him – and ruined my scene!

Another important aspect of Falstaff is his desperate need for money. He doesn't even have enough to settle the bill for his lodgings at the tavern. So when Ford appears with a substantial money-bag to bribe him for a supposed introduction to Alice, Falstaff is hypnotised by sudden riches. He stares at the money more than he looks at Ford, and Ford in his turn, knowing Falstaff's circumstances, plays with him and his avarice, now dangling the money like a carrot to a donkey, now whisking it casually away from him as if it's of minor consequence, while Falstaff attempts to affect a subtle nonchalance. All this is of vital importance in the relationship between Falstaff and Ford.

The end of that scene is another significant moment for Falstaff, when he returns in all his finery to sally forth in amorous adventure, and affects a knightly courtesy to his visitor: 'Passate . . . Prego.' (After you . . . please.') 'Passate . . . Prego.' ('No, please . . . after you.')

Ford is mocking Falstaff at this moment, but Falstaff doesn't realise this. I would get annoyed that my visitor wasn't acting as a guest should, saying eventually: 'Passiamo insieme!' (Let's go together.)

In the next scene, when Falstaff presents himself to Alice in the genuine hope of seducing her, I would peacock around her with as much dignity and elegance as I could. I was the great lover, showing off, peeling off my gloves very slowly, with a hint of things to come, doffing my hat with elaborate courtesy. Then the music would express Falstaff's impatience, and he would start to chase Alice around the stage as if he couldn't hold himself back, as if he would gladly seduce her on the spot.

The test of any Falstaff, though, is in the sequel to this scene, after he's been dumped in the Thames in the linen basket and has somehow got himself back to the Garter Inn, his ego totally deflated. At this point the audience, hitherto amused, perhaps, at the stupid situations he's got himself into, should begin to feel some sympathy for this rather foolish old man, who is only now beginning to realise what an absurd figure he must seem.

Some productions required me to make an entrance looking as if I had that moment clambered out of the river, with clothes still wet, staggering and struggling to compose myself, and shouting for the innkeeper. I think that's entirely wrong. To me, the music conveys the nightmarish escape from drowning that Falstaff has just experienced. He sits clutching his blanket or whatever, giving a shudder at the orchestra's crescendo as if he were still recalling the sensation of drowning, then waking up and feeling cold, coming to terms with himself, his age, his portliness, his grey hairs, and calling for 'vin' caldo', mulled wine, to warm him.

At first he thinks that all that's left to enjoy is a draught of good wine, and I would cradle the jug or flask to my body as if it were a baby. But then after taking a deep drink of it and feeling the wine dilute the river water he'd presumably swallowed, Falstaff would feel his body coming to life again, and the flame of the candle begin to flicker once more. He wouldn't give in just yet. The music grows and grows, and Falstaff swells with it, recovering his confidence and feeling that he's not beaten yet; there's still blood surging in his veins.

Now Mistress Quickly appears, with the letter of assignation for Windsor Forest. At first Falstaff hates her for the trouble she's caused him, but when he reads the letter he recovers himself and even, at this point, begins to think he could take Quickly to bed as well.

The more sympathy the audience feels for Falstaff, the more they are on his side in the final scene, which should be shown as a cruel torment of Falstaff's pretensions. I would enter wearing the antlers on my head and, despite the fact that the audience sometimes laughed at the stupidity of my get-up, I was very serious about what I was doing, thinking about the assignation with Alice, even happy to die if I died while making love to this woman. And when the stage audience made fun of me and the children had beaten me with all the callousness of which children are capable, I would gather together all my dignity and remind them that if it weren't for me, they would have nothing to laugh at:

> 'Son' io, son' io, che vi fa scaltri,
> L'arguzia mia crea l'arguzia degl'altri.'*

After our final ensemble fugue ('Tutto nel mondo è burla'), I would ask the director if it were possible for Falstaff to stay on for a moment alone after the others have taken themselves off. Ford and the women should then come back to fetch him and invite him to join them for the celebration of Nanetta's betrothal, so that it reflected well on all of them in the end. There is so much that one can do with a role like Falstaff, but it's the inner thoughts that help to create a more convincing character.

This is equally true of Beckmesser, the crotchety Town Clerk in *Die Meistersinger*, who was a very different character from most of the roles I sang. When I was first asked to sing it I made a point of going to see a couple of performances by artists I knew were outstanding in the role at the time: Karl Schmitt-Walter at Bayreuth and Benno Kusche at Munich. I watched them carefully: Schmitt-Walter rather too placid in temperament, I thought, Benno perhaps a bit too much of an eccentric. Both nevertheless fine interpretations to admire, yet I knew I needed to create a different character of my own.

Neither Schmitt-Walter nor Kusche suggested to me why Beckmesser pockets the song he finds in Hans Sachs's workshop on the morning of the song contest instead of trying to put it back, thus creating an involuntary act of theft. I felt this to be vitally important to the role, far beyond Beckmesser's obvious irritability and spitefulness. We know that Wagner had in mind a certain critic of the time, one Eduard Hanslick, who had constantly attacked him in his writing, but there was more to it than just that. After all, Beckmesser couldn't have been a 'bad' man, otherwise he would never have become one of the Masters' guild. Nor would he have had a friendship with Sachs, who is basically warm and kind, and who must see something more in Beckmesser than what appears on the surface.

* This is roughly translated as follows:

> It's I alone who gives you pleasure,
> The wit of this man makes yours the better.

My instinct was therefore to portray a tremendous frustration within this man, apparently short-tempered and petulant, no longer very young, yet who has the audacity to believe that he can win the beautiful Eva for his wife. He is the Town Clerk, therefore he must be intelligent and educated, so what has caused him to be as he is? To explain this I invented my own background story for him: that he was the only son of a widowed mother whom he'd looked after, but who was afraid of losing him if he married so she created difficulties with his girlfriends, making him more and more repressed. Now his mother had died, and he was free for the first time to find a wife of his choice, although the years had slipped past and left him embittered and not a little jealous of others who were married with families of their own, and certainly of the handsome stranger who was distracting Eva's attention.

Having made up this story, it seemed to fit in quite well with the character I wanted to portray. I then thought about this man's appearance and started as always with the feet. I wore tight shoes, the discomfort helping me to feel irritable and forcing me to move in small steps and on the balls of my feet the whole time, with sharp, mincing movements. A fussy little man, although the fussiness shouldn't be overdone. Add to this a make-up in which I tried to give my features a naturally gloomy expression, drawing down the corners of the mouth. I emphasised this with a nervous gesture of the hand smoothing the hair downwards at the side of the face, and the essence of a character was there.

At the outset Beckmesser is first seen talking to Pogner, Eva's father, trying to ingratiate himself and asking Pogner to put in a good word for him with his daughter, who he's afraid might now think him too old to be her husband. Then he starts to get very worried indeed when the handsome (and younger) Walther von Stolzing turns up, saying he wants to join the Masters' guild, and is given a very friendly greeting by Pogner. Beckmesser instantly suspects a rival, and a dangerous one, his jealousy bubbling up as he asks himself, 'How can I stand a chance against this good-looking young fellow?'

This is what I mean by inner thoughts. This is what I made myself think in order to create a convincing outward character. How can I get this rival out of the way? Beckmesser's jealousy takes over when he 'marks' the song Walther sings as a candidate for the guild: he marks many more faults than he need do. When he shows this to the other Masters, he almost persuades them to reject Walther until Sachs reasons with them on the side of tolerance. Now Beckmesser, though he sings nothing for a while, must again suggest his inward thoughts: 'Why is Sachs supporting this stranger? I thought Sachs was a friend of mine.'

Beckmesser's relationship with Sachs is another crucial aspect of the opera. He obviously admires the cobbler-poet, whether for his poetry or for something else, and he likes to look on him as a friend. When Sachs makes his entrance in Act 1 and the other Masters are already there, I would get up and greet him effusively, exaggerating the handshaking a bit: 'Immer bei Sachs' ('Always near Sachs'), as Beckmesser sings a few bars later. Then in Act 2, when Beckmesser is almost beside himself at the way his hopeful serenade to Eva has been 'marked' by Sachs with blows of his shoemaker's hammer, I would also try to show that I was intimidated and just a bit frightened of him as well.

These are ways in which a singer can fill out the character suggested by the words and music, and show to the audience Beckmesser's feelings towards the man he admires more than anybody, whose friendship he wants to have and to keep. The depth of this feeling governs Beckmesser's crucial scene in Sachs's workshop at the start of Act 3, leading up to his pocketing of the song. Beckmesser has about four minutes alone in view of the audience, but doesn't utter a word: the music is saying all that needs to be said and, indeed, describing quite graphically what Beckmesser should be doing and thinking.

It is, in fact, one of the most exacting of mime scenes for a singer. I was fortunate to learn it first when Erich Witte, himself a distinguished tenor, directed the production at Covent Garden. He was able to take me through that scene, phrase by phrase, and suggest what it is the music is illustrating: Beckmesser's memories of the night before; the pain of the bruises from his buffeting in the street riot, and his embarrassment at what Sachs must think of him. All this and more needs to be carefully ingested and reflected on stage, to convey to the audience all these aspects of Beckmesser's character before his next action.

Traditionally, as the music pauses briefly before softly taking up the theme of the Prize Song, Beckmesser looks out of the workshop window to the square, perhaps even greets somebody, before turning back to the table and lighting on the song just as the orchestra plays the theme. Sachs enters while Beckmesser is reading it and, in his embarrassment, as he is too far from the table to put it back, he tucks it surreptitiously in his pocket: he *steals* it. This is, however, not a deliberate theft but an involuntary reflex action to cover his lack of courage to return it. When, a few moments later, he takes it from his pocket, it's to accuse Sachs of wanting to enter the contest, and although he affects to disdain it himself, he's only too delighted when Sachs makes him a present of it, 'Damit Ihr kein Dieb' ('So that you're not named a thief').

In spite of his ill-fated serenade the night before, Beckmesser is still out to win Eva with the song he thinks Sachs has written. I would show him badly affected by nerves, stumbling as he mounts the competitor's rostrum, getting the lute the wrong way round, sneaking another look at the verses, mopping his brow, any or all of this provided it's done as a natural outcome of the situation, not as a bid for laughs. One performance might be more successful than another, but the song itself I would sing as beautifully as I could, with entirely serious intent, the image becoming more pathetic as the jeers of the crowd increased.

To justify himself against their mockery, Beckmesser identifies Sachs as the author of the poem, but instead of throwing the paper into his lap, I went further, I crunched it up and flung it in his face. At this moment I would realise I'd gone too far: I'd insulted my friend in public, but I'd also humiliated myself, and all I could do was to creep away in shame. This was the moment when I had to make the audience feel sorry for Beckmesser, or else I didn't feel the performance had been a success.

In my last production at Covent Garden, directed by Hans Hartleb, he had the further suggestion that after Beckmesser has crept away in shame, he should come back to witness his rival's triumph and then be forgiven by Sachs and the other Masters, and be greeted as still being one of them. I thought it sounded a good idea, but only if it in no way disturbed Walther's singing of the Prize Song. We experimented with various timings for me to re-enter and found what seemed a good moment. It worked marvellously well, and underlined the all-round happy feeling at the end. Had I sung the role again, I would have tried to persuade any other director to keep this detail in to round off the Beckmesser role.

Beckmesser's vocal line in the music has its dangers. It's easy to sing too loudly too soon and find that one is exhausted long before the end. Tenors find Walther demanding, and Sachs is a marathon for any bass – the opera is about five hours without the intervals but I still say Beckmesser is the most dangerous role vocally, on account of the amount of colour that must go into it. Yet it must be sung as well as possible: the notes must be given their musical value and not spoken, or even half-spoken, which would destroy the effect.

I sang it first in English, then in German. When Reggie Goodall was preparing it in English for the Sadler's Wells Opera some time later, he asked if I would help his Beckmesser, Derek Hammond-Stroud, with his vocal characterisation. After listening to him sing Beckmesser's first entry in English, I asked if he knew it in German.

'I've started to learn it,' he said.

'So sing that in German for me.'

When he did he gave each note its full musical value.

'Now sing that in English the same way,' I told him. When he did so, the problem of stress and vocalising disappeared. It's important for the singer to sustain the musical line, to let the flow of sound come through the words. I was happy to pass on what I'd learned from experience about the benefit to the singer, as well as to the audience, of giving the notes their full value in musical terms, and I was delighted that Derek Hammond-Stroud turned out such a fine Beckmesser.

I've mentioned before that I always had difficulties learning verses, and Beckmesser's attempted serenade to Eva in the second act was a particular problem. I would often be terrified that I'd sing the verses in the wrong order, and then it would be difficult to get the lines back as they should be.

To think that after so many years, this is just what happened at one of my last Covent Garden performances. Colin Davis was conducting, the performance ground to a halt and we had to go back to the start of the serenade. One reason I couldn't save it, as I did one time in *Billy Budd* with my photographic memory for the score, was that I'd treated myself to a new *Meistersinger* score not long before, the old one having fallen to pieces. Between the two I'd confused myself, and my advice to any singer in this respect is: never throw an old score away.

Let me also say that an understanding Sachs can make all the difference in his workshop scene at the start of Act 3, where Beckmesser has to project across an orchestra playing fortissimo. The only way to do this is to come as far downstage as possible without actually stepping outside the set, and for Sachs to stand practically on the footlights with his back to the audience, so that one is singing out towards him as well as to the audience. I was lucky in usually having a Sachs who knew this and would 'feed' me in this way.

Singers need to pace roles like Beckmesser and Falstaff, just like a long-distance runner who times each lap in order to know where to put his maximum effort without tiring too soon. Identification with the character is also essential, thinking once again those inner thoughts that put one inside the skin, so to speak, though not to the extent of becoming so emotionally involved that you can't keep your own self separate. I've known some singers, sopranos in particular, who identify so deeply with a tragic character that they will break down in tears, which only means they can't go on singing as they should. It's the audience who should cry, not the singer.

Concentration is, of course, imperative, as one needs to give the right response to each situation even when one is not actually singing. My severest challenge in this respect was the title role in Alban Berg's *Wozzeck*, especially when, as often, its three terse Acts would be performed as fifteen consecutive scenes, with no interval.

When I started to learn Wozzeck I really had very little idea of how to play this extraordinary character, who was again so different from any others I'd played. I learned the notes. I memorised the words. I could hit out the phrases parrot-fashion, but there was no thought behind them. For a while, I think I was actually afraid of it. Then, when I knew it all musically, I tried to put together a character. I remembered watching Erich Kleiber rehearsing the opera for its first Covent Garden performances in 1952, and I called to mind Hermann Uhde and the simplicity he brought to the character of Wozzeck.

I felt I needed to have that same simplicity, but I also wanted to go deeper. The more I rehearsed and sang it, the more poetry I found in the man, which I wanted to bring out. It seemed to me that Wozzeck, the downtrodden, illiterate soldier of Georg Büchner's play which Berg set almost word for word, was the victim of his circumstances, his environment. Had he had any chance of education, he would have developed an innate artistic bent: I believe he would have been a poet. You can hear it in the words he uses, and you can sense it in the visions he describes.

Here was a man very much in love with Marie, the mother of his child, a man of simple sincerity and great dedication, suffering mentally and physically and practically sacrificing his life to keep his woman and child as best he could. Yet the more he worked himself to the bone for a few extra pennies to give her, the more frustrated he became that this was all he could do, until the frustration finally broke him and made him take the knife and kill her.

As for Wozzeck's poverty and humble circumstances, I felt I knew something of this from my own background. I was just old enough to remember as a boy the unemployed in the Welsh valleys, the men who tried by any means to buy a little bit more bread for their wives and children, and who went climbing to the old coal tips to scratch about for something to burn in their empty grates. This I knew, and while it may not have been the same sort of privation as Wozzeck's, I felt it helped me to know him.

When it came to portraying him in performance, I deliberately stylised the person so that he moved as little as possible. Cutting reeds with Andres in the second scene, experiencing strange visions ('A fire there, rising to Heaven and with a tumult of trumpets falling'), hearing and seeing things ('This place is accursed'), I stared around me but didn't move. The first time I sang it, in San Francisco, the production helped by having reeds so long that my head only just showed above them. And only at the end did I move, very slowly, as the score specifies.

In any case my movement as Wozzeck was again based on what I wore on my feet: jackboots, but a size too large. This meant that I could only plod, heavily and slowly, and this is how I wanted to show Wozzeck doggedly making his way from here to there, from the Captain to the Doctor to Marie, an endless monotonous trudge from one day to the next, with no sense that anything for him, neither work nor hunger nor anything else, would ever change until he died.

Wozzeck comes to Marie after she's given herself to the Drum Major, and he finds her trying on a pair of ear-rings. When she says she 'found them', Wozzeck remarks that he never 'found' anything like these, much less two together. He gives her the extra money he's earned, a coin from the Captain, a coin from the Doctor, and this should provide a moment of high pathos, the contrast between these two small coins earned by such soul-destroying effort and the glittering ear-rings so easily acquired. In a later scene, realising what she's done, I would lift my hand to strike Marie but then hold off, accepting that she is the stronger character.

It's an opera of stillness. The great moments aren't moments of action but moments of inaction. Like the tavern scene in Act 2, where there is singing and dancing, when Marie is in the Drum Major's arms and Wozzeck sits apart, absolutely divorced from all that is going on around him, retreating into his own private thoughts. I always asked for a table where I'd sit alone, staring out, not moving a muscle for about four minutes, not even blinking an eyelid. I'd be thinking once more to myself, and my thoughts could work like mental telepathy, forcing others to become aware of me, to turn and be magnetised by my stillness.

Stillness again, in those moments before Wozzeck kills Marie. They sit beside the pool like lovers who have quarrelled, each waiting for the other to make it up, to speak the first word, not moving. Marie senses that something is wrong. The audience should wonder what might happen. Only Wozzeck himself is calm, because I think it's only on the spur of the moment that something snaps inside him and makes him destroy all that he loves most in the world, the woman there beside him.

After the first few times I sang Wozzeck, I became quite worried because a kind of mental disturbance lingered after the performance was over. I'd have identified with the role to such an extent that it took a time to shake it off. People might come backstage to speak to me and I simply didn't know what they were saying. Later on, with more experience, I could unwind faster, but the concentration needed to perform this role meant that I was mentally more exhausted when it was over than after any other role. I was completely drained.

When I realised what this role entailed, I'd arrange with the stage manager wherever I was that nobody, but nobody, came on stage for three or four minutes before curtain-up. Nobody to ask if we had everything. No conductor to give his good wishes. Simply a total cut-off from everything else in the world beyond so that I could try to become Wozzeck in his own little world. When Richard Lewis sang the Captain, he felt the same. Sometimes the theatre staff thought I was a bit crazy, I know, but there was a reason for it.

Richard Lewis was again a captain, Captain Vere, when I took part in the American premiere of Britten's *Billy Budd* at Chicago in 1970, with Theodore Uppman in the title role as he was originally at Covent Garden. Benjamin Britten had revised the opera, writing it in two acts instead of four, and I played my first Claggart, the brutal Master-at-Arms who sets out to destroy Billy and his 'goodness', until the sailor strikes him dead. It was a role I felt had much depth to it.

My feeling about Claggart was that he had a homosexual element in him, feelings he had stifled or held back, or perhaps he wasn't even conscious of them until he met Billy. Then he became aware of a young man who deeply affected him and, because of their circumstances, affected him to the point of hatred.

That was how I tried to play Claggart. So when I first came in contact with Billy, in the scene below deck, I would draw the baton I carried slowly down his body, as if I wanted to touch him but this was the nearest I dare get to him. I asked Thomas Allen, when he sang Billy at Covent Garden, if he minded my doing this. He didn't object because he knew the effect I was after, and he said it felt nasty. Others I asked about it also said it seemed a thoroughly nasty gesture, one that could and did send shivers down their spines. They confirmed the effect I wanted.

Frederick Dalberg had been the original Claggart in 1951, a tall, imposing figure, as was Forbes Robinson, who to some extent expanded Dalberg's portrait. At first I played the part in the same vein, but I wanted to find a different way to command the stage in Claggart's scenes. Instead of playing him as the black-hearted character who is outwardly and obviously evil, I wanted to suggest that the evil was within him and only manifested itself in certain ways.

I was searching for some means to convey this when I remembered Charles Laughton in the old film of *Mutiny on the Bounty*. There was a man who could portray the image of evil with the lightest of touches. Just by his look, or his walk.

His walk! I had it!

So I started to practise a Charles Laughton walk, leaning slightly to one side and slightly back, swinging one loose arm. I rehearsed this over and over until I could hardly move. My back was killing me! It took me ten minutes or so at every performance before I could get into the stride ready to go on stage. Whether anybody else thought so or not, I felt I'd achieved a successful Claggart, and I was greatly encouraged to learn that a friend of Britten's had been heard to comment after a performance: 'I'm sure that's the Claggart Ben would like to have seen.'

It was a role I knew I'd been able to come to grips with. There were others in which I never achieved the same success, however hard I tried. One, for example, was the scheming marriage-broker, Kečal, in Smetana's *The Bartered Bride*. I tried to read something into him, to play him this way or that, but for me he remained just a con man, with nothing under the surface, and I never made a convincing character out of him.

Before curtain-up on certain roles, I would grow into each character by adopting his movements. I might practise some eighteenth-century gestures for Figaro, just to get the feeling right. Papageno wasn't such a problem, nor was Leporello. He's such a grubby character, I won't say it came naturally, but he was more easily assumed. The roles like Wozzeck, Falstaff, Beckmesser and Claggart really needed to be worked at, so that I was identifying with each of them from the feet upwards as soon as the performance began.

At another extreme were the multiple roles in *The Tales of Hoffmann*, a different character in each act, and different again in the Prologue and Epilogue. These had to be a matter of instant identification, because no sooner had I characterised one role than I had to be metamorphosed into the next, with no time at all to build anything. It was a question of convincing the audience that each character was a different person by the way he was immediately presented. I thoroughly enjoyed the challenge this represented.

The calmest of roles for me was that of Balstrode, the retired sea-captain in *Peter Grimes*, such an honest, straightforward, no-nonsense character. I had no difficulty in portraying him – all I did was to think of my grandfather.

Some roles require applied comedy, like Dulcamara for instance, the quack 'doctor' in *L'elisir d'amore*, whose bottled red wine is the love potion of the title. He's rather like Kečal in *The Bartered Bride* in that he's ready to seize any chance of making a quick buck. Dulcamara is basically a confidence trickster lording it over simple village folk, yet he is also genuinely concerned for the well-being of the community, and sympathetic to the hopes and desires of the heroine, Adina. Unlike Papageno, however, Dulcamara has no licence to indulge his comedy, or to exaggerate: it must all be played within realistic bounds.

Whereas Donizetti's Dulcamara is very much what one makes of it, in terms of comedy character, the humour in his other popular operatic comedy, *Don Pasquale*, grows naturally from the situation. What I made of the title role was a bachelor, well into middle-age who is seized by the possibility that he might yet have a young and beautiful bride. He weighs the excitement this can still arouse in him against the fears of how it might affect his present creature-comforts, his possessions, his self-indulgent way of life. It's a situation that still has its counterpart today, and it goes to show that even so artificial a comedy can bear some relevance to everyday life.

I've sometimes thought of my various roles in terms of drinks, the Donizetti comedies bubbling like Asti Spumante in contrast to the richer champagne of Mozart or the potent claret of Verdi and Puccini. To sing operas by the last two composers gave the opportunity to exhibit the finest quality of voice that one could command and, of course, nothing less than a beaker of matured sack for the old man, Sir John Falstaff. Nothing gave me greater pleasure than to sing the one long phrase of Amonasro in *Aida* with all the beauty of tone I could bring to it, and to sing this well was like savouring a draught of vintage claret.

Mozart was like champagne because any faking would always be exposed, but it was also, for me, a constant refresher course in the art of classic singing. Maybe Beckmesser was dry and rather neutral, like drinking soda-water, while Wozzeck was a shandy laced with rum, a mass-produced blandness lifted into a dizzying intoxication. All these roles are enhanced by the words, perhaps not so important in the heavily emotional situations of Verdi or Puccini, but absolutely necessary to understanding in Donizetti as much as in Mozart.

In this respect they resemble Britten's operas, which depend on the best possible relationship between word and music for each to be clear. Like composers before him, Britten knew just what different kinds of singers could achieve, and many of his greatest operatic roles were directly modelled on Sir Peter Pears. Even Berg, in his technique of *Sprechgesang*, or pitched speech, was well aware of the limits to vocal capabilities.

It seems to me now that many of today's composers no longer concern themselves with what is possible, practicable or even desirable for voices, forcing them to conform in some quite arbitrary way to a pre-arranged pattern of notes, rather than making the most of their individual capabilities. Singers will give everything of which they are capable, and often a little more, provided they can discover, in any composer's music, a testament of truth.

CHAPTER EIGHT

Sound and Sight

Radio, records, television and video all mean that a singer today gives a large proportion of his performances without an audience. Of course this increases the size of the public we reach many times over, but it requires differences of approach, of production and technique, as well as a realisation that one no longer has control over the end-product: the voice you hear is the result of balance, focus and studio direction by the technical wizards of sound and sight.

Since I first stood in front of a microphone in a BBC studio at Cardiff, waiting to go on the air for the first time, radio has become an integral part of my musical life. Certainly I couldn't begin to count the number of broadcasts I've made, many of them in Hamburg for the British Forces Network, but in my early days they taught me quite a few lessons about colouring the voice for this or that effect, as well as having to cope with matters like timing and placing.

Not long after I started at Covent Garden I went to Carmarthen to make a broadcast of Welsh folksongs which had been arranged by Idris Lewis, the music director for the BBC Welsh Region at the time. The Carmarthen studio was long and narrow, with the glass panel to the control room halfway down one of the longer sides. And it will tell you something of the way techniques have changed if I mention that, in order to get a satisfactory balance between my voice and the piano, I had to stand near a microphone at one end of the studio, while the piano was right at the other end, a good many feet away, and without an open lid.

We had our run-through and balancing test, and then we were on the air. I was singing one song, holding a manuscript sheet in front of me with the first verse on it, when I realised I'd left the several other typewritten verses on the piano lid. With some presence of mind, I thought, I made a diminuendo at the end of the first verse, stepped back a couple of paces, and ran as quickly and quietly as I could to grab the rest from the piano.

This meant crossing in front of the control room panel where the producer, Nan Davies, came close to a heart attack as she saw me whizz past and disappear just out of her line of vision. I later found she thought I had stage fright, or studio fright in this case, and had simply run off. She went to look for me in the corridor outside and fortunately stepped back into the control room and not into the studio itself, by which time I was back at the microphone and well into my next verse. I think it was one of her worst moments ever, as thoughts of fading out the broadcast chased through her mind.

I'd been singing mostly the Mozart roles when the BBC offered me a broadcast of Bartók's only opera, the one-act *Duke Bluebeard's Castle*. There are just two singers, Bluebeard and his wife, Judith, who forces him to unlock the seven doors in his castle and disclose their contents, before he sends her to join his previous wives. Joan Cross was the splendid Judith in that performance and I discovered what a truly great work it is. The symbolic and allegorical elements in the story are all expressed through the music, and it made ideal radio listening because you could use your own imagination to picture what was happening. At the same time, I found it bringing out an altogether nobler element in my own singing: whether this was a subconscious response to Bartók's vocal writing, or a deliberate effort to assume a kind of character that was new to me, I know that I brought a different tone colour to my voice. From then on I realised how important it was to colour the voice in various ways according to the kind of role I was singing. When I listened afterwards to the recording of *Duke Bluebeard's Castle*, I wondered if it was really my voice I was hearing. I impressed myself, and that takes some doing! Maybe I should have sung more roles of that kind – I certainly know that this was one of the most thrilling broadcasts in which I took part.

The conductor was Stanford Robinson and, although I was still pretty green in experience at that time, I felt that he was a conductor of exceptional ability. He was extremely skilled at balancing voices and orchestra, and he had a perceptive insight into the music. I never understood why somebody of his capabilities was not asked to conduct opera at Covent Garden or Sadler's Wells at that time, when good opera conductors weren't exactly thick on the ground, but he was a good BBC man and played an important part in furthering the interest of opera on radio and the BBC's reputation in presenting it.

Among the many broadcasts I made with him I remember o particular programme of operatic arias and the like when, during run-through a couple of hours before the broadcast was due, my voice deteriorating. By the time we finished, I was afrai

215

laryngitis and wouldn't be able to sing the programme. Stanford began to get very worried and the Covent Garden tenor, Raymond Nilsson, who was sharing the programme with me, suggested I should call in my throat specialist to see what he could do.

I didn't like to admit that I'd never consulted such a person, so I said I hadn't been in touch with him for ages. Raymond offered to call his own laryngologist, who duly came along to the studio, rigged up various gadgets and applied throat sprays and other treatments. About fifteen minutes before the broadcast was due he pronounced me fit to sing, and sing I did. But to be honest I don't think his medication did me any good at all – I felt my voice was, if anything, worse than it had been. From that time on, I made it a principle never to have medication I didn't know about before or during a performance. Any decision whether to sing or not would be mine alone, with no half measures.

Most of my major operatic roles I was also able to record for the gramophone, I'm glad to say, although I'd been singing some of them for a number of years before any recording opportunity came my way. There are few enough other records to my name: a couple of solo recitals, oratorio and opera arias respectively, some Mahler songs in *Des Knaben Wunderhorn*, a small part in Bach's *St Matthew Passion* with Klemperer, and larger parts in three of the Gilbert and Sullivan favourites which were among the first records I made.

I've told how my first encounter with Walter Legge at EMI was not exactly propitious as far as any hopes I might have for future recordings were concerned. It was a few years later, in the mid-1950s at Glyndebourne, when Sir Malcolm Sargent came backstage after a performance and, after complimenting me, said he would like me to participate in a series of Gilbert and Sullivan recordings he was about to make.

He mentioned some of the other singers he was asking and said that he planned to use the Glyndebourne Festival Chorus – this included some of the best students and other young singers acquiring early professional experience. The idea sounded promising. On the other hand, I had no experience of singing the Gilbert and Sullivan repertory, which has its own particular style, and when I thought it over I decided not to accept the offer. Besides, I wasn't sure it was the right thing for me to record at that time.

Nevertheless, Sir Malcolm persisted, even sending his secretary to me, while he was away in Scandinavia, with a message that he was planning to record Walton's *Belshazzar's Feast* and would like me the soloist in that as well. Now, this was an attractive carrot to dangle in front of me just then, and I thought it would be an added incentive to do the best I could. So I agreed to the Gilbert and Sullivan projects.

Don't misunderstand me. I'm not putting them down. I enjoy Gilbert and Sullivan as much as anybody in the theatre, but if I was going to record them I wanted to do the job properly and prepare myself accordingly. On the first day we were called to the studio, I thought we would spend some time rehearsing with Sir Malcolm, so that we would all agree on matters cf musical style and especially the colouring of the words, which I felt would be very important.

Instead, I was quite disconcerted to find that the rehearsal was to be no more than half an hour with Sir Malcolm at the piano before we started to record the full 'takes'. Some of the other singers weren't happy about this either, but we did what we could, and from my point of view I don't think the records turned out too badly. Indeed, there were some excellent performances from some of the other singers.

I took part in three recordings: as Ko-Ko in *The Mikado*, the Duke of Plaza-Toro in *The Gondoliers*, and Jack Point in *The Yeomen of the Guard*. While I was making the third of these, I heard that Sir Malcolm was indeed going to record *Belshazzar's Feast* next, as he'd said, but not with me as the soloist. Another singer had been booked.

When my recording sessions were finished I challenged him about this and had only some vague excuse in reply. I then told him I would not make any more of his Gilbert and Sullivan series. Fortunately they each had a separate contract, so I couldn't be forced to make the others. Although I had quite enjoyed making them, I dismissed any thought of doing any more and really felt badly cheated by the way things had turned out.

Soon after this I went to San Francisco for the first time, and what should I hear on the local radio there but that I was 'a Gilbert and Sullivan expert'. I'd gone there to sing Beckmesser in *Die Meister-singer*, and in my first interview I was asked how I related this to Gilbert and Sullivan. How indeed? I had to deny being any sort of expert in G & S, but these were all the records I had to my name at that time and I began to think that perhaps I hadn't been so wise to make them before I'd recorded any opera.

All that I'd done in this respect was the role of Ned Keene, the apothecary in *Peter Grimes*, when the opera was first recorded with Benjamin Britten conducting. Many years later, during the 1970 after Colin Davis conducted the opera in New York and then Covent Garden, I told him it was a shame that nobody was recor the opera with the cast we had then, which included Jon Vickers and Heather Harper, each so very successful in their respective roles (I was playing Balstrode).

Colin said there was no money to finance another recording, so I made my own enquiries and thought I might find a possible sponsor or two. I mentioned the idea to Decca Records (who had brought out the original recording), but before anything could be arranged, Philips started to take an interest because Colin was under contract to them. It didn't matter to me which company made the records so long as one of them did.

Plans went ahead with Philips and I was asked to keep open two groups of dates for recording Balstrode. Yet when I did eventually get a call from Colin's secretary requesting my presence at the studio, it was for a period when I was already engaged on the West Coast. It was suggested that I should fly back from California to record my part and then go out there again, all within seven days, but I decided this was too much. Except for coming back to be with my family at Christmastime on occasion, I've always avoided to-ing and fro-ing over long distances for engagements, and so I never did take part in that recording.

My first solo record came about in 1962 at the suggestion of a small company, Delysé, who proposed a selection of sacred music, mostly from oratorio, to be recorded in Llandaff Cathedral. I've always found this an exciting and uplifting place to sing in, even for a Methodist as I am. The idea went ahead and involved the BBC Welsh Orchestra, conducted by Mansel Thomas, and a chorus made up of the Shelly, Lyrian and Glendower Singers. I sang solos from Mendelssohn's *Elijah*, Handel's *Messiah* and *Judas Maccabeus*, and the Brahms *Requiem*, and I was rather pleased with the result.

The record went on sale as 'Geraint Evans sings in Llandaff Cathedral' and was generally well received and reviewed. I suppose I didn't listen to it again for several years but when I did, just before it was reissued in 1972, I thought to myself, 'Dammit, that wasn't a bad voice at all.' And I'm not ashamed to say so.

The only other solo record I made was an assortment of operatic arias which I recorded in Switzerland with Bryan Balkwill conducting the Suisse Romande Orchestra. There was more Handel (from *Berenice* and *Semele*); the main arias from my Mozart characters, Figaro, Leporello and Papageno; the Prologue to *I pagliacci* and Iago's 'Credo' from *Otello*; some Donizetti (from *Don Pasquale*) and Beethoven (Pizarro's aria from *Fidelio*), and the monologue of Bottom's dream from Britten's *A Midsummer Night's Dream*, all of which helped to show that I had quite a versatile range.

Also included was Falstaff's 'L'onore! Ladri!', when he rounds on his henchmen, Bardolph and Pistol, at the end of the first scene in Verdi's opera. The next year I was able to record the full work with Georg Solti in Rome for RCA-Victor. He wasn't at all well at the time, but he kept an iron control of himself and took the recording right through.

His musical judgment wasn't impaired. He pounced on a wrong note from the brass section in the scene outside the Garter Inn in the third act, when Falstaff is recovering from being dumped in the river Thames. To identify the culprit he made each player go through the phrase separately. The first few were note-perfect. Then he turned to the last player, who rather shamefacedly confessed he'd 'lost his lip', adding, 'You see, maestro, I've broken my false teeth.'

Amid the ensuing laughter, Solti quite kindly told the player not to attempt the phrase at all if he couldn't play it properly. I'm not sure what did happen in the end, but it all worked out for the final 'take'.

We had a splendid cast, including Ilva Ligabue, Mirella Freni and Giulietta Simionato, Alfredo Kraus and Robert Merrill, as well as my old friend from Covent Garden, John Lanigan, to sing Dr Caius. I was very delighted with the finished album and now feel sad that I never recorded anything more with Solti, who asked me not to take up the offer I had to record *Figaro* with Karl Böhm in order to be available for him. It was his intention to record the opera with the Covent Garden chorus and orchestra and I was made to feel my allegiance was to record with them. Unfortunately Solti never got around to it at that time, but it meant that I missed out with Böhm too, and who knows what might have happened had I accepted his offer!

On records and in the theatre I'd always sung Falstaff in Italian, but from time to time I was asked if I would sing it in English specially for television. The first invitation to do this came from Canada, then there was a second a couple of years later from the BBC. I turned them both down at the time, feeling that in spite of the Shakespearean basis for the opera I couldn't establish the feelings and phrasings of the role in the same way: the English version of that music somehow loses flavour.

When the BBC later asked me again about this, I changed my mind and decided to see what could be done to put the Verdi *Fal* into English for a TV audience. I asked that some of the lines standard translation should be rewritten in the interests effect, and Joan Cross and Eric Crozier agreed to do this Coleman to direct the production and Jimmy Lockhart

Basil was an outstanding director for me in this context, and his help was invaluable. He knew I wanted to get as much of the Italian flavour into the English version as I could, and at the same time he'd seen me perform it on stage and knew how the histrionics should be modified for television, where gestures and facial expressions have to be quite differently scaled. My theatre performance of Falstaff had to be calmed down, as it were, and Basil could achieve just that.

I worked very hard in rehearsal and the final result was eventually shown on Boxing Day, 1972. Among the effects we tried to achieve was a single continuous camera shot for the scene outside the Garter Inn in Act 3, where Falstaff staggers back from his ducking in the Thames and collapses into a chair, before beginning his monologue. I managed almost the whole scene without a change of camera until we came to the final 'take' when I reached the chair and realised the English words had vanished from my mind. I couldn't utter a syllable.

By then there was no time left to go over the whole scene again, so we had to make a break after all and start again with a different camera shot once I'd collected my wits. That was my only disappointment about that production and I really quite enjoyed putting it across in English. Regina Resnik was with me as Quickly, and Norman Bailey as Ford, and we all had the advantage of Eric Crozier being present at every rehearsal, so that he could and did alter a word here and there if we thought it needed changing, while watching what we had to be doing at the time. The librettist should more often be on the spot when an opera is being prepared for television, especially when the text has been translated.

My first TV opera was a BBC studio production of *Carmen* in about 1950, with Jean Madeira in the title role and Vic Oliver conducting. Some eyebrows were raised at the idea of a popular entertainer and comedian daring to conduct opera, but he actually had a great love for it and his enthusiasm overcame any shortcomings in technique. He used to direct a small company in the Rhondda in South Wales, where they were very successful, and of course his name was a draw to win a wider audience for opera on TV.

Our *Carmen* was pretty heavily cut for screen showing, but the staging was quite elaborate. I had to make my entrance as Escamillo wn a few steps from a door into a realistic-looking interior for s Pastia's tavern in Act 2. Above me was a fan, turning slowly in 'ing, but this wasn't switched on until the final 'take'. In those re was no stopping once a scene started, but as I came door wearing my toreador's hat I realised the fan-blades it off my head before I went down the steps.

It's surprising how quickly one reacts. I pretended the steps began before they actually did, bending my knees slightly as the camera moved from its long shot of me coming through the door into close-up, which I knew was the plotted move. The camera moved with me as if I were going down the steps and my hat safely missed the fan. Then I had to compensate by rising a little as I came to the second step and so on, so that I wasn't on my knees when I got to the bottom. Fortunately, it worked.

In the last act there was to be a close-up shot of Carmen and Escamillo kissing passionately before he goes into the bull-ring. Jean was an excellent Carmen, but neither of us were used to TV, and the first time we tried the kiss her rather large mouth was slightly open and looked even larger on camera. We had to try it differently but, when it came to the 'take', being nervous, she forgot, then remembered just as she moved into the kiss. So what the camera picked up was Carmen suddenly clamping her mouth shut as she was on the point of kissing Escamillo!

Over the years TV directors have recognised that it's best not to have close shots of an opera singer in full cry, whether man or woman, because it's never an attractive sight and certainly not very enticing for the viewer. I didn't take very easily to studio television, where there's no rapport with an audience, no relationship with anybody except the camera lens, the instrument in front of you. It took me a long time to acclimatise to the cold technicality of the environment and to realise how details are magnified by the camera. Raise one eyebrow too much and, on the small screen, it can look like a volcanic eruption.

This is where a performer becomes so dependent on the director for advice, and one of the most skilful I worked with was Patricia (Paddy) Foy, producer of many TV music programmes. In one of these there was an interview by John Freeman with illustrations cut in of operatic roles. I was also seen making up on camera: nothing elaborate, just a moustache and a few other touches to give an idea of character, but I believe it was the first time this had been seen on television and it caused quite a stir.

So also did my choice of a scene from *Wozzeck* as one of the illustrations, the second scene in the reeds, when Wozzeck hallucinates. On stage the facial expressions and vocal inflexion had to be assertive even overpowering, and with directorial help I had to find out how adjust this for the screen. Freeman wondered how viewers w take it, especially with the harsh music and the speech-son nique Berg calls for, but it transpired that this made quite th impact with the public in their reactions to the programr

It was at a BBC studio that I first met Norman Kay, the pianist and composer who later became music director for Harlech Television. I'd been broadcasting in *Riders to the Sea*, the one-act opera by Vaughan Williams based on the J. M. Synge tragedy of Irish fisherfolk. Mary Jarred and Margaret Ritchie were in the cast, and afterwards I was introduced to Norman, who'd been listening to the broadcast. After we'd talked I asked if he'd like to work with me on a regular basis as a répétiteur or coach.

He was keen to do so and we began a professional association which led to us becoming very good friends, as well as adding two successful new operas to the television repertory. Before these came about, however, having been impressed by Norman's skill in writing incidental music for BBC programmes, I invited him to compose something for me to sing in the 1964 Llandaff Festival.

The festival directors went along with this idea and the outcome was *King Herod*, a large-scale cantata for soprano, baritone, chorus and orchestra, which we premiered in Llandaff Cathedral. Heather Harper was my fellow soloist, and we had the Llandaff Choral Society and the BBC Welsh Orchestra. Norman wrote his own text, a dramatic portrait in three scenes showing Herod as an arrogant monarch, an angry tyrant undermined by prophecies he cannot understand, and insanely self-pitying in his diseased old age, the music vividly illustrating these different states of mind.

It lasted about forty minutes, as I recall, and it seemed to be enjoyed by the audience as well as generally well reviewed. I'm not sure the conductor was quite up to the demands of a first performance, but I was nevertheless very happy with it. I thought it would be a welcome addition to the choral concert repertory and regret very much that it's been so little heard since.

Not long after this, Norman was commissioned to compose *The Rose Affair* for BBC Television. Based on a play by Alun Owen, it was a version of the Beauty and the Beast fable, with myself as the rich but physically repulsive Betumain regenerated by the love of Anne Howells as Bella. John Cameron, Joseph Ward and Norman Lumsden were also in the cast, and it was directed by Peter Potter, with a young conductor then beginning to make his name, David Lloyd-Jones – he later went on to become artistic director of Opera North in Leeds.

The Rose Affair obtained a 'Highly Commended' award when it ~~entered~~ by the BBC for the Salzburg Opera Prize in 1968. A ~~tition~~ held every three years specifically for operas written for ~~medium~~, it has an international jury drawn from delegates to ~~national~~ Music Centre conferences held in Salzburg.

Twelve years later, the first prize in this competition was taken by Norman's next TV opera, *A Christmas Carol*, derived from the Charles Dickens story and commissioned for Harlech Television.

I had a splendid time playing Scrooge, with Gwynne Howell as Marley, and Ryland Davies and Elizabeth Gale as the Cratchits. The conductor was again David Lloyd-Jones, this time with the Philharmonia Ensemble, with whom Norman was able to develop a technique he devised for TV, the use of fewer instruments to obtain a fuller sound. I thought the television production made clever use of split scenes occupying separate parts of the screen at the same time, or superimposed one in front of the other, and Norman's music had a similar sort of ingenuity.

It seems strange to me that, in spite of these successes and of his other music for television, nobody asked Norman to follow them up with a work for the theatre. The problems attending any such venture are considerable, of course, what with the immense costs of production and performance, as well as the reluctance of many opera-goers to sample something they don't already know, but I'm sure a better scheme could be devised to make experiment more attractive.

Instead of spending such large sums on new operas at Covent Garden or the Coliseum for instance, I would like to see Sadler's Wells Theatre become a base where new works could be tried out on a more modest budget, and a virtue made of novelty for the public. And what an opportunity such a venture would afford for up-and-coming conductors and young singers. Then, if one or another of these productions was found to be successful, it could be taken over and, if necessary, more fully produced by one of the main companies, either in London or the regions. Otherwise these costly productions usually disappear after a few performances, never to be seen or heard again.

A system like this could have benefited another composer-friend, Alun Hoddinott, whom I persuaded to consider an opera after I came to know some of his orchestral music, which I thought had a dramatic flair. In due course he composed *The Beach at Falesá*, based on a story by Robert Louis Stevenson, as a commission for the Welsh National Opera, who premiered it at Cardiff in 1974. I took the role of a sinister South Seas trader terrorising the islanders, and Sandra Browne and Delme Bryn-Jones were the other leading singers in a production by Michael Geliot, with Richard Armstrong conducting.

This experience helped Alun to extend his operatic interest in *Murder, the Magician*, a short opera written for Harlech

1976. It had a libretto by John Morgan about a stage magician who discovers, *Pagliacci*-like, that his wife is having an affair and contrives to kill her lover during one of his tricks. Aided by a member of the Magic Circle, who coached me in performing the necessary illusions, this was another role I enjoyed tackling, with Elizabeth Gale and Ian Caley singing the other major roles.

Following this came two more Hoddinott operas in which I participated: *What the Old Man does is always right*, a children's opera originally composed for the 1977 Fishguard Festival and later adapted for TV, and in 1979 my last new role as the adventurer Jack Vandeleur in another Stevenson story, *The Rajah's Diamond*. This was commissioned by BBC Wales and the Welsh Arts Council to celebrate Alun's fiftieth birthday and Myfanwy Piper wrote the libretto.

This time the TV direction was once more in the skilled hands of Basil Coleman, and with Robin Stapleton conducting I thought it came across very successfully. I'm sure that more could be done with original operas specially written for television, using all the facilities of that medium, leaving the major classics to be performed in the theatre where they properly belong. This is a policy I've tried to encourage through my connection with Harlech TV and, with the spread of video-cassettes in recent years, including both major operas and ballets, there ought to be an increasing market for the future.

That same year, 1979, I found myself making a speech in front of the Queen and most of the Royal Family. I knew it was being televised and broadcast and this made me more nervous than any performance I sang. The occasion was the special concert at the Royal Festival Hall for the one hundredth birthday of Sir Robert Mayer, who was there to celebrate it in style as he promised he would be when he first asked me to take part in it a year before. I felt both affection for the man and admiration for his lifetime's achievement in music. I'd sung on many occasions at the Robert Mayer Children's Concerts, that astonishing series he began with his wife Dorothy in the year after I was born, and which continued regularly thereafter, except during the war. The Queen and Princess Margaret had both been taken to them by their Mother when they were children, and countless thousands of other young people had begun to enjoy classical music through the specially designed programmes and productions these concerts offered, at subsidised prices to make more accessible.

from my experience that Sir Robert had an extraordinary persuading people to support whatever he was intending to do. Whenever he asked me to sing at one of his concerts he somehow always knew already that I would be free on that date, and before he put the telephone down I would not only have agreed to perform, but he would have added, 'And you know you won't be paid for this!'

He was always very determined, very demanding and very reluctant to take No for an answer. Even so, I baulked when Lord Drogheda called me some months before the concert, which he was helping to organise, with Sir Robert's request not for me to sing but to give the address. I refused, gladly offering to sing instead. There were other calls, but still I would not agree, until one day I had a call from Sir Robert himself. Then I knew I was in for it and, sure enough, by the time I put the phone down, I had committed myself to making the speech.

Now began a panic to find something to say, when so much had been written about him already and was even then being put into more words for the occasion with articles by commentators like Richard Baker, Bernard Levin and others, infinitely more fluent than I would ever be. Still, I had my own knowledge of Sir Robert and his idiosyncrasies, and I collected further ideas for my speech from his office staff and his family.

One anecdote I included concerned an occasion a few years before, when Sir Robert went with his secretary to a reception supposedly organised to encourage fund-raising for the arts. Their hostess looked somewhat bemused when they arrived and Sir Robert was also puzzled by the fact that there seemed to be nobody he knew. He heard somebody say the Minister would be arriving in a few minutes and thought this would be the Minister for the Arts, so he sat on and waited.

Gradually it dawned on them that they must be at the wrong reception. The secretary made enquiries and discovered to his consternation that it was indeed another affair altogether, a party for a visiting Russian trade delegation. He reported this in some agitation to Sir Robert, but all he said was, 'Don't worry, my dear. Just say Shostakovich every so often and we'll be all right!'

Had I understood in advance the measure of that birthday occasion, though, I believe I would have been too frightened to go through with it. As well as the Royal Family, all the leading lights in my own profession were there, while on the platform were Dar Janet Baker, Sir Colin Davis, Yehudi Menuhin, Isaac Stern Simon Rattle with the London Philharmonic Orchestra, in th of celebration which had a special and unforgettable magic

Afterwards I realised how differently one can be af nerves. Because I wasn't singing this time, I thought pe less nervous, but whereas I knew how to control breathing and voice support for singing purposes, delivering a speech was quite another matter. My mouth became so dry that it was an increasing effort to get the words out, and by the end I was in a worse state of nerves than I had been when I started. I also discovered how nerves can affect others, when Janet Baker came off the platform to where I was standing in the ante-room, having listened to her singing so beautifully, and put her arms round me, saying, 'Hold me tight!' She was shaking with the reaction to nervous tension.

This tension can sometimes appear part way through a performance. I recall one occasion in San Diego, California, where I was singing Leporello in *Don Giovanni* and Victoria de los Angeles was Donna Anna. She was already a famous and experienced singer, but halfway through the evening she lost confidence and stood in the wings saying she couldn't go on again. When her cue came I took a risk and physically pushed her into the audience's view and she went through without any further hitch, thanking me later for acting as I did.

Perhaps helping others to overcome their difficulties, as well as providing encouragement, is one reason I so much enjoy giving master-classes, on television and around the country. I always thought the title somewhat pretentious, as they mainly consist of passing on hints, advice and information gleaned from other people and the experience of one's own career, passing them down the line to the next generation coming along. But master-class is what they came to be called and the name has stuck, all over the world.

I was first asked to do these master-classes in 1967 by Lord Dynevor, who was setting up a summer school at Dynevor Castle in Carmarthenshire. He'd had the idea from something he'd seen on television, when Carl Ebert had instructed some students in stagecraft for a few moments. I'd also seen this, together with the unforgettable Lotte Lehmann coaching aspiring opera singers in a series at the Wigmore Hall ('And to think, my dears,' she told a hopeful Octavian and Sophie, 'that I, an old woman, have to show young lovers how to kiss!').

Like those sessions, the Dynevor Castle classes were to be given in front of a public audience, and it's one of the essential but sometimes ᵗicky aspects of them that the student singers involved have to be ʰing, and able, to accept criticism in public. This is sometimes difficult than it sounds, if you don't happen to have faced it but in return I tried to make it a principle that any comments ould be constructive, and that I would take care never to student in public.

Happily my Dynevor classes went exceptionally well and I thoroughly enjoyed giving them. About two or three minutes from one of them were filmed by BBC Wales, who were making an hour-long documentary programme about me at the time. When this was shown, the couple of minutes or so of the master-class made such an impact with the viewers that Gethyn Stoodley Thomas, who was producing the programme, suggested to BBC Wales that I should do a series of classes specifically for TV. It became one of the most enjoyable and successful ventures I've ever been involved with on TV and Gethyn's enthusiasm encouraged me to carry on giving master-classes, which I have now done in this country and in America.

Not the least of the pleasures I experienced when organising the classes at the BBC was auditioning the young singers who came forward. Each of the classes dealt with a particular opera and we'd listen to perhaps two hundred singers in all. It was often very difficult to make the final choice, because there was so much talent around. I'm more than pleased to know that many of those I picked for these master-classes have since made successful careers. It's a thrill to think that I was the first to find something in them, or to hear something they'd already developed. I always hoped the classes would provide a useful shop window for them, and at the same time interest people in opera who might not otherwise have the opportunity to see it.

After one of the classes I gave at Sadler's Wells Theatre, to help raise money for the London Opera Centre, Sir Robert Mayer sent a cheque for a large amount and said he'd enjoyed one class so much he wanted to come to the next one, and that was when he was already well over ninety years old! Truly there are audiences for opera at any age from nine to ninety, and if one can but open a door for them to enter the world of infinite delight that it's been for me, then I will know it has all been worthwhile.

CHAPTER NINE

Excursions and Exits

However glad I was to keep a full engagement diary, and I count myself very fortunate in this respect, there were times when I was glad of a break, especially if it meant time to spend with the family. Even then there were often interruptions: a chance to sing something different, perhaps, or maybe a distress call to help a friend when somebody was ill. Brenda was sometimes cross with me for not knowing when to say 'No', but the warning signs about my own health were still some way in the future.

In the summer of 1965 I had the prospect of several weeks at home in Wales before setting out in August for my engagements in Buenos Aires and Mexico City. We went to the Opera Ball at Grosvenor House in London, where I was asked to be one of the judges, with Dame Eva Turner and Sir Osbert Lancaster, in awarding prizes for the best operatic costume. It made a change to watch a performance instead of being involved in it, and I relaxed at the thought of a rest from singing.

Not for long, though. The Handel Opera Society asked if I would sing the title role in their new production of *Saul* at Sadler's Wells in June. They'd done much good work in keeping Handel alive in the theatre, a medium for which he'd written many of his finest works, but where he was largely ignored by the established opera companies. I wanted to support the Society, even if it meant going against my good intentions of taking a break.

Besides, I confess I was tempted by the opportunity to sing a 'noble' role, after all the comic servants and other characters in my repertory. I didn't add much decoration to the vocal line in baroque style because I felt it diminished the strength of the character. What ̔e I did put in seemed to suit quite well, with Charles Farncombe ̔cting, and I enjoyed the challenge the production offered.

̔hief worry concerned throwing a javelin. The producer, ̔Geliot, and I decided to risk hurling it so that it stuck ̔ a pillar, in full view of the audience. I practised this over ̔, thinking I had to look convincing.

It worked very well at the dress rehearsal, and I prayed that nothing would go wrong on the first night to spoil the effect. Fortunately it worked again, bolstering my confidence, and I made sure the incident was successful at the rest of the performances. Regardless of how I sounded in the role, I reckon I scored a treble twenty with that javelin every time!

No sooner was I through with Handel at Sadler's Wells than I had a crisis call from Holland. Carlo Maria Giulini was conducting a new production of *Don Giovanni* at the Holland Festival and his Leporello, Paolo Montarsolo, had been taken ill. The call was to ask if I was available to sing instead and, if so, would I go there immediately.

My first instinct was to refuse, because it was getting close to my South American trip. Then I remembered how well I'd enjoyed working with Giulini before. The upshot was that I agreed to go, and took the first flight I could.

Giulini met me at Schiphol Airport and, as we drove to The Hague, where the opera was being performed, he forewarned me about the production. I could tell he wasn't at all happy about this, and as soon as I began rehearsing on the stage I knew why. It was one of those heavily stylised affairs which seemed to have little to do with the story and actually even worked against the music.

There was another jinx on the second night when Luigi Alva was taken ill. For his role as Don Ottavio they flew in Juan Oncina, who I hadn't seen since we were at Glyndebourne ten years previously. We had a happy reunion and, in spite of the staging, Giulini conducted a fine musical performance. I must say that I would have been more content if we had played against a backdrop of black curtains, instead of Mozart's musical implications being contradicted at every turn.

Although this production didn't concern me again after Holland, I wasn't surprised to learn that Giulini became increasingly unhappy about it and flatly refused to conduct if it went in its existing form to the Edinburgh Festival that year. He had his way, too. What the Edinburgh audiences saw was his own makeshift production on a bare stage, with the decor confined to projections of sky effects on the backcloth.

North of the border the Scottish Opera was a recent addition to the British musical scene. Inaugurated in 1962, it was already building gradual yet solid achievement as a regional company under Alexander Gibson (later Sir Alexander) as artistic director and principal conductor. From them came an invitation to sing Falstaff in a production they were planning for the spring of 1966 at the Theatre, Glasgow, their regular base at the time.

I was delighted to take this on, especially as the director was to be Peter Ebert. We both kept in mind the foundation of character that his father, Carl Ebert, 'the Prof', had laid down for the Glyndebourne production which had given me such a success, and we kept to that outline.

The first-night audience was very enthusiastic, but during rehearsals I'd picked up a cold which I couldn't shake off, and each performance became more of an effort. Nobody wants to give up without good reason. I suppose there are some roles where you can fight a passing infection and still sound well enough, but Falstaff isn't one of these. I knew that to keep singing was to risk putting my voice out of action altogether for two or three weeks so, much as I hated having to withdraw, I had to give up the last of the seven performances in my contract. Fortunately Robert Savoie was able to take it over and I went home to rest and recover. That was a great disappointment to me because I enjoyed working with the Scottish Opera.

Later the same year I appeared for the first time with my native company, the Welsh National Opera. I thought it odd in a way that I should have gone first to the Scottish, which had been founded when the Welsh company had been going for more than fifteen years, and that during all this time I'd never been asked to do anything by the opera management in my own country.

As far back as 1939, when I was having singing lessons with Idloes Owen in Cardiff, there was talk of setting up a Welsh company, if only for a few weeks each year. So many Welsh singers were then regular members of the Sadler's Wells and Carl Rosa companies, it seemed a good idea to bring them back with a proper opportunity to sing in their own land.

The war intervened, of course, but as soon as it was over the scheme was revived on the initiative of Idloes Owen. His name is hardly ever mentioned in this respect, but *he* was the one who was responsible for the formation of the company which gave the first of its regular seasons at Cardiff in 1946. Dr W. H. (Bill) Smith, who usually receives all the credit in operatic references, was brought in during the second season as a business administrator and fundraiser. He then became chairman of the management company for the next twenty years and a great success he made of it.

Regular seasons by the Welsh company continued in Cardiff after and by the mid-1950s productions were being toured to cities and, including London where the company appeared at the Wells Theatre. One of the glories in those early years was the chorus drawn from all over the region; they produced a magnificent sound like the best of the Welsh choirs. They gave up their weekends to rehearse and their holidays to perform until a professional chorus was formed in 1968.

It was only after Bryan Balkwill became the Welsh National Opera's music director in 1963 that he expressed his surprise one day that I'd never sung with the company.

'It's high time you did,' he declared. 'What would you like to sing and when could you do it?'

After thinking about it I suggested *Don Pasquale*, which I'd already started to learn because I'd hoped to sing it in Vienna until I found that the dates didn't work out. I thought Donizetti's comedy would be fun to do, and Bryan agreed.

'Fine,' he said. 'We'll do *Pasquale*. But you'll have to sing it in English.'

By the time the WNO staged their production, I'd already sung it in Italian in Buenos Aires, but I agreed to learn the English version because I recognised that comedy opera of this kind needs to be understood. This proved to be quite tricky in the quicker passages, and most difficult in Pasquale's patter-duet with Malatesta, where the Italian words trip very smoothly off the tongue. The greater number of consonants in English meant some really hard work to get the words out in time with the brisk musical pace.

Nevertheless, Michael Maurel and I managed to achieve the required effect. With Jennifer Eddy and Stuart Burrows singing the soprano and tenor roles, we had plenty of fun in a fairly straight-forward production directed by Dennis Maunder. The servants' chorus was still a non-professional body at that time and came in for special praise from the critics, one of whom wrote that he'd often heard the opera sung in English but this was the first time he'd understood every word.

For me it was a very good feeling to be singing at last with the Welsh company, even though it brought me one of those emergencies that every singer dreads but learns to cope with. I'd been in London between performances, and was on the train at Paddington one Friday, going back for my last Cardiff performance the next night, when I heard an announcement asking for Geraint Evans to go to the station-master's office.

My first thought was that something was wrong at home, and practically ran to the telephone. Instead it was a call from the o... management at Cardiff, who'd already spoken to Brenda and... told I would be at Paddington Station, asking if I could poss... Leporello in *Don Giovanni* that night because John Gibbs... ill.

'What language are you singing it in?' I asked.

'In English.'

'My God, I could never do it,' I said. 'It's years since I sang it in English, and I've been in so many Italian performances since then.'

'That's all right,' came the reply. 'We understand. You can do it in Italian.'

I just had time to agree and put the phone down when I heard the whistle for my train. I ran back even faster than I came, past the ticket-collector at the gate, who fortunately recognised me, and flung myself in to the nearest carriage just as the train started moving.

Walking back to where I'd left my belongings, I tried to calm down and get my breath back. Then I spent the whole journey going through the Leporello role in my mind. I hadn't sung it since some New York performances about eight months before and, of course, I had no score with me to help.

The train reached Cardiff about five minutes before the performance was due to start. There was a car to meet me and the curtain was held while I was rushed to the theatre and there scrambled into a costume and some make-up. Then I was on to start the first scene, perhaps twenty minutes late, in a set I'd never seen and a production I knew nothing about.

'Notte e giorno faticar,' I began, and a little later Don Giovanni called:

'Leporello, where are you?'

'Son' qui, per mia disgrazia. E voi?'

'I'm here.'

And so we continued, myself in Italian, everybody else in English.

I was greatly relieved that Don Giovanni was sung by Forbes Robinson, a Covent Garden colleague whose histrionic style I knew well and could respond to. Forbes has a knack for improvisation and he made the most of our language differences, even putting in two or three words of Welsh that he'd picked up. The audience enjoyed it tremendously and so, I must say, did we, even if the recitative did sound a bit awkward at times.

Shortly before this I had been back at Covent Garden, for the first time in more than a year, to sing Papageno in a new production of *The Magic Flute*. It was conducted by Georg Solti and directed by ~ter Hall, with whom I greatly looked forward to working. The ~night performance seemed to start very tensely and rather ~vely, but it eased with the warm and spontaneous applause ~ted my first entry. One review was kind enough to suggest ~ personal welcome back to me after such a long period ~refer to think it was a reaction to the idea Peter Hall and

I worked out for Papageno's entrance: I came on strutting across the width of the stage, towing a shopping-basket on wheels as my bird-basket, instead of having the basket strapped to my back as Papageno usually does.

The idea came to me at home one day when I noticed my small son, Huw, playing in the garden with his mother's shopping-basket. He was towing it proudly around with a cocky little walk, as if it held all his worldly goods. 'My goodness, that's Papageno!' I thought to myself, and wondered if we could use such a basket for the birdcage. During rehearsals I mentioned this to Peter Hall and demonstrated with the aid of a broom that was handy.

He liked the idea and, as a further refinement, we had two baskets prepared so that as I disappeared into the wings at one side, the second basket would be waiting there, facing in the opposite direction, and I could reappear in a split second towing the second basket. Had I waited to turn the first basket around, even that slight delay would have spoiled the effect. As it was, there was a gale of laughter from the audience, a smile spread across Solti's face, everybody began to relax and the opera was well away.

I enjoyed working with Peter Hall on this one occasion and am sorry he didn't do more at Covent Garden. He was another director who was never dogmatic about operatic staging; he was always ready to talk over ideas with the artists, and to reach a balance between what he had in mind and what was best for them. I'm sure his concern for the artist is a major part of his success in the theatre.

My admiration for him took a knock, I must admit, when I first saw the National Theatre production of *Amadeus*, Peter Shaffer's play about Mozart and Salieri. I was deeply shocked to see my idol portrayed as such a crude creature, however much was true to history. The Rimsky-Korsakov *Mozart and Salieri* which I had broadcast some years previously, with Alexander Young as Mozart and Stanford Robinson conducting, had none of this vulgarity. I just didn't want to see such a portrayal of Mozart and after about ten minutes I was ready to walk out, feeling I could take no more of it.

Brenda persuaded me to stay, insisting that I would be recognised if I left and that this could be embarrassing all round. I'm glad now that I did see the play through, because it was brilliantly performed and directed. Indeed, I went back to see it a second time, and th greatest irony of all was that I later found myself presenting *Evening Standard* Drama Award to Peter Shaffer for the best p the year.

I still had one reservation, even so. Why, I wonder, National Theatre stages such a play by a British auth

British director and a British cast, should we listen to the recording of a Mozart aria sung by a foreign singer? Why not a Welsh singer for instance?

As with Papageno, I try never to be content to play a role the same way simply because I've played it that way before. I like to have new ideas for a new production and credible reasons for whatever it is the character does.

For instance, when I next sang at Covent Garden, as Doctor Bartolo in Rossini's *The Barber of Seville*, I wanted to show a reason for his leaving the house in Act 1, thereby giving Rosina, his carefully protected ward, the chance to flirt from her balcony with Count Almaviva, whom she thinks is a doting student.

It occurred to me that Bartolo might well have a pet dog that needed to be taken for a walk, and when I happened to mention this to Peter Glossop (who was singing the Rossini Figaro for the first time on this occasion), he said, 'I've got just the dog for you.'

He and Joyce Blackham, to whom he was married at that time, were always ready to be helpful and Peter arrived for the next rehearsal with their fluffy white miniature poodle. It worked beautifully. Peter waited in the wings opposite, out of sight of the audience, and as soon as I came out of the 'house', locked the door and set the poodle down, it made straight for Peter and all I had to do was to follow it on a taut lead, as if it were taking *me* for the walk.

My Bartolo costume included a wig with a little bow clipped in the front of it, and I suggested we had a similar bow for the dog to wear. The audience enjoyed the fun of it, and somehow it enhanced the fussiness of the character.

I thought the idea of a dog for Bartolo was original to me but, a year or so later when I was in New York, I went to see the Metropolitan Opera's production of the comedy with Fernando Corena as Bartolo, and what should happen but that he should also make his entry with a pet dog. That vindicated my own idea because Corena was a past master at roles like this and a splendid performer in his own right, and the fact that he'd thought along the same lines as I had pleased me very much.

Back at Covent Garden, I enjoyed my performances in *The Barber* because we had such a good team, and it's an opera that depends on ~amwork. Peter Glossop was an excellent Figaro, the role ideally ~ing his voice, and Teresa Berganza and Luigi Alva were both ~ienced as Rosina and Almaviva respectively. Silvio Varviso, ~'d previously met in San Francisco, was a fine conductor and ~ colleague to work with.

~rs ago it was often said that Sadler's Wells should be

called 'Sadler's Welsh' because there were so many Welsh singers among the principals and chorus, but my next *Don Giovanni* at Covent Garden in the summer of 1967 could certainly have been called 'Dai Giovanni'. Five of the principals were Welsh: Gwyneth Jones (Donna Anna), Elizabeth Vaughan (Elvira), Stuart Burrows (Ottavio) and Delme Bryn-Jones (Masetto), with myself as Leporello. Tito Gobbi as the Don was the odd man out, and we thought we might give him a Welsh passport to make him one of us!

Soon after this the Welsh National Opera celebrated their twenty-fifth anniversary, and we had an idea that we might all to go Cardiff for *Don Giovanni*. Even the title role could be cast from Welsh stock for the occasion. The idea was put to the management who responded with a total lack of interest and it never went further. I still remember Stuart's bitter comment: 'My God! That would have been one of their finest and most valuable productions – because we would have sung it for half our usual fees!'

Among the coveted baritone roles in the international repertory is Scarpia, the venal police chief in Puccini's *Tosca*. I had heard some fine singers in this part in my time at Covent Garden, among them Tito Gobbi, Otakar Kraus, Gabriel Bacquier and Marko Rothmüller, and I was delighted when I was cast in it for the first time in 1968.

I think that Scarpia was Gobbi's greatest role, but Otakar was quite as evil in a different way. Between Kraus and Gobbi, Otakar had the bigger voice but Tito had a more incisive delivery. I had to think hard as to how I could be as effective as these two distinguished artists. Sena Jurinac sang Tosca and the Cavaradossi was Franco Tagliavini, whose height made me look shorter than I really am.

It was essential that I establish the evil of Scarpia immediately in a powerful first entry. To this end I worked hard to achieve the right colour for the voice and to perfect the arrogant strut of this dignified, cruel man as he stalked into the church in Act 1, on the trail of his escaped prisoner.

Here Scarpia encounters Tosca, who disdains the offer of his arm when she leaves. I'd seen Otakar at this point repeat the gesture with an imperious extra thrust of his arm, perhaps only by an inch or two, but with explosive effect. Tosca simply couldn't refuse, and the moment had such dramatic impact that I wanted to use it myself. I asked Otakar if I might copy it.

'Geraint,' he said, 'You pay me a great compliment. I'm flatte

So I did. Unfortunately there was very little time for prod rehearsal because both Jurinac and Tagliavini had been i event we had only about three days to work on the stagi like long enough for me to feel comfortable inside a create a full foundation for it, as well as fitting it to an existing production. I was accordingly very apprehensive when it came to the first night, although the performance itself brought a developing confidence.

I've always relied on Brenda for an honest opinion about any of my performances, especially in a new role, and when she said later that I'd made her flesh creep, I knew I hadn't given a dud performance.

Charles Mackerras, who conducted, also had encouraging things to say afterwards, and another friend, who had seen a good number of *Tosca* performances here and there, came backstage to my dressing-room to tell me what he thought.

'Well, I'm not saying you're as good as the others yet,' he told me, 'but a few more performances and you will be.'

That was praise indeed, and I'm really rather sorry that I was never asked to sing Scarpia again.

Yet a singer is often accepted in some roles much more than in others, and has to be prepared for this. It happened to me particularly with *The Marriage of Figaro*. Much as I enjoyed being Figaro, I would have liked to have sung the Count more often, although I recognised that regular opera-goers might find it disconcerting to look at Count Almaviva and see what they would know as Figaro's face. I did sing the Count again elsewhere, but I gave up the role at Covent Garden for this reason.

Every singer has to come to terms with certain individual limitations. To imagine you can make a success of every role in your vocal register is nonsense, and to become jealous of rival singers for their different achievements is to risk destroying your performance and, ultimately, yourself.

About a year before the investiture of Prince Charles as Prince of Wales in 1969 I was honoured to serve on a committee making the musical arrangements for the occasion. We had several meetings with the Duke of Norfolk who, as Earl Marshal, was in charge of State ceremonial and who had stage-managed the Coronation and other affairs. He was known to be a stickler for detail and I found him a most impressive character. He let others do the talking and seldom intervened, but when he did it was absolutely to the point and ouldn't be disputed.

One proposal we had was for a work to be commissioned from a h composer, and it was also suggested that it should include ng for me to sing as a soloist. Naturally I was flattered, but I ld not be fair to other Welsh singers, several of whom had quished service to Wales in one way or another.

here was a limit to the number of soloists who could be

involved in one work, but I reminded the committee of Vaughan Williams's *Serenade to Music*, which he wrote for sixteen specified solo singers, and suggested that something similar would be more appropriate for this occasion. Sir Arthur Bliss, then Master of the Queen's Music, supported the idea.

Together with the Earl Marshal, Sir Arthur backed another suggestion I made, that 'God Save the Queen' should be followed immediately by 'Mae Hen Wlad fy Nhadau', instead of keeping the Welsh National Anthem to the end of the ceremony. With so much feeling for Welsh nationalism at the time, it seemed to me that the two anthems should be heard as close together as possible instead of being widely separated, and I'm glad to say that is in fact what happened.

After our music committee had determined the important outlines, the Earl Marshal handed the chairmanship to the Earl of Snowdon, who also held the ceremonial office of Constable of Caernarvon Castle. He was an excellent chairman and organiser, although I had some difficulty thinking of him as Lord Snowdon. In my early days at Glyndebourne I had known him as Antony Armstrong-Jones, a nephew of the designer Oliver Messel, when he often came there to photograph the productions.

For the investiture, as Constable of the castle, he'd designed himself a very smart green ceremonial uniform. It provoked quite a few comments, some of them sharply mischievous, when he first wore it at the dress rehearsal for the ceremony.

As chairman of the music committee Lord Snowdon did an excellent job: everything was precisely arranged and timed, and on Investiture Day, 1 July, the ceremony ran almost exactly according to plan. We had a small group of Welsh solo singers and a large chorus chosen to represent the best of Welsh choral singing. They were joined by the BBC Welsh Orchestra and the music was conducted in turn by Roy Bohana, Arwel Hughes and Wyn Morris.

Among the music specially written for the occasion was *Rhapsody for a Prince* by Mansel Thomas, which he based on several Welsh folksongs including 'Dadl Dau', a ditty known to have been sung by an earlier Prince of Wales (who became Henry V) on his rollicking visits with Falstaff to the Boar's Head tavern. Alun Hoddinott's *Eryri* was a setting of both Welsh and English words by Sir Thomas Parry Williams, evocative of Snowdonia.

In spite of my protests, Alun had insisted on writing a short solo passage for me. It was only a dozen bars or so, but I wished he hadn't, for quite another reason than the one I've mentioned. Shortly before this I'd had a further official letter notifying me that my impending knighthood would be made public, along with the honours accorded to other Welsh people, on the day after the investiture.

To be involved with so many friends through that long day, knowing this was to happen and not being able to say a thing about it, was a stern exercise in restraint. It was in the back of my mind all through the ceremony and the singing, and at the celebration party later. A 'Gala Dance', this was called, but hardly anybody danced. We spent most of the time singing our hearts out, together with Harry Secombe and his wife Myra, who joined us.

It was a truly festive occasion and on our way home the next day, as we passed through the small, flag-bedecked villages, it was great to hear those thick North-Walian accents say of the Prince, 'There's a lovely boy he is.'

In September I was back with the Welsh National Opera for *Falstaff*. They now had a new music director in James Lockhart, who had succeeded Bryan Balkwill the year before. Jimmy was later to be the first British-born Generalmusikdirektor in a German opera house (at Cassel from 1972), and he'd worked as a répétiteur in Germany and at Glyndebourne and Covent Garden, where he was a resident conductor during the 1960s.

I'd privately urged Jimmy to apply for the Welsh appointment when I knew it was coming up. I knew his work and believed he had the right kind of experience, but I was somewhat taken aback when Sir David Webster asked me to see him one day and showed me a list of three names the Welsh National Opera were considering and asked my opinion. Why Sir David was involved I don't know, but we talked over the three names. I told him I was sure he would be recommending the right person in Jimmy Lockhart.

Jimmy was to conduct *Falstaff*, and I was asked to direct the opera as well as sing in it. I'd already had a taste of this in South America and was keen to put into practice the ideas I had for staging Verdi's opera. Visualising a production has never been difficult for me, and I always performed with a stage picture in mind, instinctively adapting to it whatever the circumstances.

Even so, it can be difficult to perform a role and be responsible for the overall production as well. Eyes and ears may need some assistance and I decided I ought to have some help for what had already become known in Wales as 'the investiture opera'. I asked for John Copley, who was working as an assistant producer at Covent Garden (where he had staged the company's first *Così fan tutte* the previous year) and who I thought had tremendous potential.

He was happy to join me in Cardiff for *Falstaff* and I was anxious for him to take some individual responsibility. I asked him to direct the second scene of Act 1, where Falstaff doesn't appear at all, and he did it splendidly. He was such a help in other scenes and in every way that I asked the management to show both our names as co-producers on the programme credits.

We were fortunate to have Carl Toms to design the production, an imaginative artist who was also a practical man of the theatre. I only had to talk things over with him, describing my ideas for the various entrances, for instance, and he would instantly understand and analyse the possibilities for me in terms of the technical stage demands. The result, I believe, was the best-designed and most 'workable' *Falstaff* I've ever played.

To my great joy we had an all-Welsh cast. Elizabeth Vaughan and Joan Davies were Alice and Meg, Margaret Price sang Nanetta, and Helen Watts, Mistress Quickly. Keith Erwen was Fenton and Gwyn Griffiths, Ford, with Edward Byles as Dr Caius and Robert Thomas and David Gwynne as Bardolph and Pistol. Wales had good reason to be proud of its singers, as the Prince of Wales himself appreciated.

His Royal Highness not only came to our opening gala performance at Cardiff, he also watched rehearsals on two occasions. I had first met him at a lunch some months previously, when we discussed the musical plans for his investiture, and I knew that he had a keen interest in music. What I hadn't appreciated was his concern for the practical side of things, such as the way an opera production was brought together on the stage.

He sat in the auditorium during a couple of our piano rehearsals, asking about different aspects of the production, and he came up on to the stage to meet the other singers and the stage staff. I don't know if that was the first time he'd seen how an opera was rehearsed, but his interest extended beyond the opera itself to all the people involved in it.

They were thrilled by this, and even more determined to make the performance a success. With the Bournemouth Symphony Orchestra (who then regularly played for the Welsh opera seasons as part of their regional role) I believe we did make it a memorable production, even if it was the first time the Welsh company had sung in Italian. Indeed I have often wondered why an opera has never been commissioned to be sung in Welsh by the Welsh National Opera Company. After all, we sing in other languages and there are some very interesting Welsh stories which could be adapted.

A few months after the investiture at Caernarvon Castle, I had my second summons to an investiture at Buckingham Palace. Brenda came with me, of course, as did Alun and Huw, the latter then aged six. He kept asking when I would be 'crucified' – how he came to use this word instead of 'invested' I do not know – and was most anxious to know where I would keep my armour. Alun was old enough to share the pride that Brenda and I felt, a pride mixed with excitement and a certain apprehension, rather like a touch of stage-fright, I suppose.

In the Throne Room those receiving awards were grouped in sections according to the honour awarded, just as when I had received the CBE ten years previously. Relatives with children were seated on one side, but by the time Brenda and the boys were ushered in, this was already so full they could only find seats in the corner. Close to them on the wall was a shiny panel of light-switches, and as Huw at that time had an obsession with switches, Brenda and Alun had a rather uncomfortable time, keeping a watchful eye on his every movement.

This reminded me of an earlier occasion, before Huw was born, when Alun accompanied Brenda to see me receive the CBE. When I returned to my seat, next to the footballer Billy Wright, who had received the same award, he remarked that some old man must have fallen asleep as the sounds of snoring could clearly be heard. We chuckled at this, not knowing until later that the culprit was Alun and that Brenda had been terrified to wake him in case he cried out and made a worse disturbance.

My turn came. We had been told where to go and what to do, and when my name was called I walked forward and knelt in front of Her Majesty. It's impossible to separate all the thoughts that pounded through my mind at this moment, but I do remember wishing that my grandparents had been alive to witness it and thinking how proud it would have made them. It also occurred to me, as the sword the Queen used to dub her knights rested a brief instant on each shoulder, that it was a very substantial weapon and must have been very heavy for her to manipulate.

The Queen Mother and the Prince of Wales were present at an emotional occasion at Covent Garden in the summer of 1970, when the Royal Opera staged a gala performance as a tribute to Sir David Webster on his retirement. Nearly forty solo singers took part, as well as seven conductors with the chorus and orchestra, performing excerpts from more than a dozen operas.

Many of the singers had been with the company since its earliest days after the war, some as principals, some in the chorus, and had grown up with it as I did under Sir David's wise guidance. My own share on this occasion included a couple of scenes from *Peter Grimes* with Heather Harper, and a finale of excerpts from *Falstaff* with several close friends and colleagues, including Regina Resnik once more, Elizabeth Vaughan, Elizabeth Robson, Ryland Davies, Kenneth Macdonald, Delme Bryn-Jones and Michael Langdon, with Georg Solti conducting.

At the end the singers and as many of the staff as could be assembled grouped round Sir David on the stage, backed by a deliberate clutter of scenery from various operas. With full hearts we celebrated his quarter-century of achievement in building from nothing a Royal Opera of world repute, and consolidating the reputation of the Royal Ballet.

Although Sir David officially retired at the end of that season, leaving the Royal Opera House in what he knew to be the safe hands of his second-in-command for many years, now Sir John Tooley, he was still often to be seen there, keeping in touch with the next season's activities. It was from his old office that I went to fetch him one February day the next year, to present him with his portrait by David Hockney, which the company subscribed for and commissioned (after finding out which artist he would prefer).

His health had declined greatly since the previous year and I virtually had to talk him into coming down from the office to the Opera House foyer where the singers, musicians and staff were waiting. It fell to me to make the presentation to him and I quote here what I said at the time because it sums up my respect and admiration for the man. I spoke this from my own heart, but I believe it reflected the general sentiment of those around me:

'To see this distinguished gentleman, slow and deliberate of gait, hands in pockets, hat on one side, humming an operatic aria, possibly out of tune, quite unperturbed by the hurry and bustle of the porters of the market at Covent Garden, one would imagine that this was the director of some City bank making his way to his place of business. But, like many of the porters who made way for him with a touch of the cap and a 'Good morning, Guv', we know him to be Sir David Webster of the Royal Opera House, a great administrator, an eloquent speaker, a shy man with a sense of humour, and above all, a person with a deep concern for his fellow men.

'As with many of my colleagues, it has been my privilege to work for him since the beginning of my professional career, and although he has been our unquestioned "boss", I am sure that none of my fellow artists, any more than I, have thought of him as distant or unapproachable. To all of us he has been "D.W.": adviser and friend.

'I wonder how many outside the Opera House realise the number of artists who owe their success to Sir David? He has an almost uncanny gift of being able to see the potential in a singer, and he is not the man to be perturbed or put off by the criticism of others while a singer is still developing. He has a great belief in his own artists, and almost every time he has been proved right. So many of them have said at one time or another, 'If it hadn't been for Sir David ...', knowing that it was his encouragement, his faith in their ability, perhaps at a critical stage in their career, to which they owe their ultimate success.

'We singers are not always the easiest people to deal with, and many of us have gone into his office at some time or another full of grievance, frustration or a sense of injustice, but after talking with him for a while we come out again feeling much better, calmer and at peace with the world, even if, on reflection, we are not always quite sure why. This is a great quality of Sir David's. In his very busy life he always has time to listen, encourage and advise, whether it be about one's professional or private life. He sits back and listens and although he doesn't say very much, what he does say is always very much to the point.

'Indeed, there have been occasions when I have wondered if he was not taking too much time, when I have been waiting anxiously for an answer to an urgent question and he has seemed to procrastinate. But when the answer eventually came, you could be sure that Sir David, having given his word, would never go back on it. This is something which has always been greatly appreciated by all the artists at Covent Garden. It gives a feeling of great security in a precarious profession.

'No doubt there are people who have had only a brief encounter with Sir David, who have gained the impression that he was a man with an air of superiority, divorced from the emotions that beset so many of us. Yet we all know that he is, in reality, an emotional man. No one who has been connected with the Company during his years of administration could ever doubt this. When an artist has a personal success, or a production wins acclaim, he is thrilled and elated. Equally, there are occasions, naturally, when things do not go quite so well. It is at these times when one can count on his sympathy and understanding.

'It has been my privilege to associate with many of the visiting artists who have sung from time to time at the Royal Opera House. So many have told me how much they enjoy coming to "the Garden". In fact, many of the greatest have remarked on the wonderful atmosphere in the House. Apart from the feeling of pride one gets when hearing these things, surely they reflect once again the stability brought to this theatre by the wisdom and guidance of its administrator.

'Naturally we are sad that Sir David is retiring, and we shall miss him tremendously. But what a glorious era to look back upon in the history of this Royal Opera House: an era when so much has been achieved, so many of his artists have become internationally recognised, and the Royal Opera company has taken its place in the forefront of the world's greatest.

'Sir, on behalf of my fellow artists and myself, may I, with the deepest gratitude, thank you for all you have done for us over the years. We all wish you well in your retirement, and express the hope that we may still see you from time to time.'

That last hope did not come to pass because, less than three months later, early in May, Sir David died. His life had been bound up with the Royal Opera House for so long that, afflicted as he was by ill-health, I don't think he had anything else to interest him. A memorial service to give thanks for his life and work was held at the Church of the Holy Sepulchre in Holborn, and again it was my privilege to speak about him. I echoed the sentiments I'd expressed before; I mentioned one or two anecdotes which have also found their way into some earlier pages of this book; I recalled his concern for the wellbeing of artists and staff, his readiness to help in sudden financial distress and his regret that he had not managed then to secure a proper pension scheme at Covent Garden; and I quoted some chorus singers I heard talking about him.

'You were very fond of him, weren't you?' I asked them.

'Fond of him?' one of the men answered. 'We loved him.'

And that, as I said at the time, was the measure of a man who was great enough to leave behind as a memorial to his life's work one of the world's finest opera companies, but human enough also to leave a feeling of emptiness in each of us when we realised that he was no longer there.

A few weeks before Sir David's death there was one more new Mozart role for me at Covent Garden, that of Don Alfonso in *Così fan tutte*, a part which I had sung in my very first operatic performance at the Guildhall School of Music over twenty years previously. At that time I had been decidedly immature for such a sophisticated man of the world as this character represents, but I was eager to find what I could make of it now that I'd acquired the experience, if not necessarily the wisdom.

Paul Schoeffler, himself a great Alfonso, told me some time before this that he thought I was ready for the part and that it would suit me ideally. 'You ought to do it now, whenever you get the chance,' he said. Such a compliment from a singer of his distinction helped to give me confidence when the opportunity did occur.

So also did the director for the Covent Garden production, John Copley. It was, I think, his first important success there, one that established him as a first-class producer. He had staged it originally in 1968, but for the 1971 performances there was a complete change of cast as well as a different conductor: Colin Davis had succeeded Sir Georg Solti as Music Director and he was intending to make the Mozart operas a speciality in the repertory.

Consequently we rehearsed as if it were a new production, with Elisabeth Söderström and Anne Howells the lovelorn sisters, Ryland Davies and Robert Kerns the two officers and, as Despina, my longtime friend and colleague, Graziella Sciutti, whom I was more than glad to have to rely on in the state of confusion I'd put myself in by the first night.

Never have I been quite so mixed up as I was then because, at the same time as I was rehearsing and singing Alfonso at Covent Garden, I was also making a gramophone recording as Guglielmo, the other baritone role in *Così*, which I'd previously sung so many times. This was recorded with another cast of singers and with Klemperer conducting. Sometimes, when I set out from home, I wasn't sure if I was supposed to be going to the Opera House or the recording studio.

Having both sets of lines and music in my mind at one time didn't help. There is a lot of ensemble singing in *Così*, and I had to concentrate fiercely. I wouldn't have committed myself to both engagements if the dates could possibly have been different but I had accepted the Covent Garden performances first. When I was offered the recording, I knew that another chance to record Guglielmo wasn't likely to come my way, so I had to cope with both.

There were two people I was dependent on for Alfonso at Covent Garden. Graziella was one: she knew the Despina role so well that if I did go wrong in our recitatives, she would quickly be able to put me right. The other was Robin Stapleton in the prompter's box, who cued me with the first few words for practically each of Alfonso's entries. I doubt I would have got through without his help.

Even so, I had to hold myself tightly in check so that I didn't answer Guglielmo's cues instead of Alfonso's, and I had to watch my stage movements carefully. I think I only slipped once, starting a few notes of Guglielmo's music at the same time as Robert Kerns before shutting my mouth and letting him continue. Apart from this identity problem, which I brought on myself, it was a happy and successful production for all of us involved in it.

It led quite naturally later the same year to a new staging of *The Marriage of Figaro*, also directed by John Copley, and the first new production for which Colin Davis had charge after his appointment as the Royal Opera's Music Director. Again we worked as a team, and although Colin had very much his own ideas he would often ask me if I felt comfortable with this or that way of doing things.

Visually, I thought it looked quite lovely, in the settings designed by Stefanos Lazaridis, with costumes by Michael Stennett. After all the *Figaro* productions with which I'd been involved over the years, I shall remember this as one of the most satisfying for the artists. They included Kiri te Kanawa making her debut as the Countess, and giving us all reason to hope that she was a singer with a future. Victor Braun was the Count, and for Susanna and Cherubino there were the delightful Reri Grist and Patricia Kern, each a vividly assured character. I maintain that Pat Kern sang the best Cherubino I ever heard.

I didn't envy John Copley this particular assignment. He took it on after Peter Hall and John Bury had withdrawn from an earlier arrangement, by which the former was due to become the Royal Opera's Director of Productions. I wonder at times how the company would have developed with Davis and Hall in tandem, but that's somebody else's story.

As it was, John went about staging *Figaro* in his own way, and with great confidence. He asked my advice about one or two incidents and I tried to help, but they were small matters and I was very touched that he should take the trouble to send me a letter afterwards, thanking me.

I certainly had no cause for complaint from the reviews. Some were written as if the critic had just seen me for the first time, which was very flattering to me in the circumstances, when the question uppermost in my own mind was whether I was still singing a familiar role as well as I had done when younger.

At the end of that season, in 1972, John Tooley reminded me that the following year would be my twenty-fifth anniversary at Covent Garden. 'What opera would you like to do for it?' he asked, indicating that it could be something not in the repertory. One that came to mind was Donizetti's *Don Pasquale*, which I first sang at Buenos Aires in 1965 and with the Welsh National Opera the following year. I liked its comedy character, thought it was right for me then and it was agreed to put it on.

My hope was that it could be, as far as possible, a wholly British affair. I asked if John Pritchard would conduct it and suggested Colin Graham to direct, with various other ideas for the singers. Happily John was free, but not Colin. John then suggested Jean-Pierre Ponnelle, whom I'd often met and talked with in Salzburg and whose work I knew from operas he had directed there. He seemed an excellent choice to me and it was arranged that he would design the production as well as direct it.

It was a very successful production except for a couple of details. There were thirty-two stuffed cats placed about the stage in the first scene. I thought that was overdoing it a bit, especially as I was somewhat allergic to cats anyway, having suffered from asthma when I was younger. But Ponnelle asked me to try to put up with them and to look upon Pasquale as a bachelor whose only interests, before his sudden desire to get married, had been his cats and his books.

If one could have trained a live cat it would have made more sense, I thought, but I went along with the idea for the sake of the production, although in later performances I managed to get their numbers reduced by about half.

The set also had a double staircase curving up to a balcony, and it worried me that my first entry was from the upper level and down the stairs, so that my face was cut off from the audiences in the upper levels by the top of the proscenium arch.

Elizabeth Harwood and Ryland Davies were the soprano and tenor, and for Malatesta I suggested Sesto Bruscantini, an old friend with whom I'd sung in the same opera at Buenos Aires. Unfortunately he wasn't available, and Gabriel Bacquier took the role, but we persuaded Ponnelle to adopt one of Bruscantini's ideas. This was to sing the fast patter-duet between Pasquale and Malatesta in Act 2 in front of a drop-curtain.

The device had a double advantage: it brought us closer to the audience and helped a quick scene-change behind us. It worked excellently, and for the first time in many years at Covent Garden there were vociferous demands for an encore. We'd hoped there might be, and were quite ready to provide it!

Halfway through the evening I had something of a shock when I was told that the audience included two bus-loads of people from Wales who'd travelled up specially for the performance and were going back home immediately afterwards. I couldn't let them go without greeting them and offering some refreshments, but how to organise it?

While I was off-stage I spoke to John Tooley about the problem. He called the house manager, who understood my predicament and responded valiantly. I arranged for the canteen staff to stay on and sandwiches and wine were made ready for my visitors, who all came round to the stage door after the performance.

By the time we'd shepherded them inside, they overflowed from the canteen and packed the Green Room as well. But I was thrilled to see them, old and young, family groups, and many I hadn't seen for years. They were ample reason for me to be glad the performance had gone well.

Another three hundred or so 'Friends of Covent Garden' were at the Savoy Hotel a few days later when I was given a jubilee lunch. Their President then was Marion, Countess of Harewood, who was supported by the Earl of Drogheda, Chairman of the Royal Opera House Board of Directors at that time. As far back as the 1950s, before he became Chairman, he often came backstage to talk about my performances. I had in mind his interest and encouragement when I replied to his kind tribute on this occasion, and I also told the Friends how much their support had meant in all that I'd done at Covent Garden.

For the Edinburgh Festival in 1973 Peter Diamand, the festival director, assembled a special opera company instead of engaging a foreign company to visit. He invited Daniel Barenboim to conduct *Don Giovanni* and Peter Ustinov to direct it, and Danny asked if I would sing Leporello.

I felt I'd done enough summer festivals and wanted more time at home. My sons were growing up and soon they would want their own summer holidays, without me around, but Danny paid me a compliment which greatly touched me: 'I'd feel much happier to know that you were in the cast,' he said. For all his experience in the Mozart repertory as pianist and orchestral conductor, I knew this would be his operatic debut and was proud to take part.

Danny and his wife, Jacqueline du Pré, were a devoted couple and we had a great deal of fun together. It was at about this time that she began to feel some pain in her arm, making it difficult to continue playing her 'cello. We teased her that it was only the Scottish mist getting into her bones, little realising the tragedy of multiple sclerosis that was soon to cut short her brilliant career and change her whole life.

When we came to rehearsals and performances, I was flabbergasted to see that Danny was conducting the entire opera without a score. I'd worked with conductors who knew the music backwards, who could have dispensed with a score if necessary, but I doubt they would have known from memory the words of every single part as well, as Danny did. He may have been new to opera, but he had absolute confidence in what he was doing.

I was much less impressed by the set. It was in three sections, like stalls in a gents' toilet, which is what we called it. It bore little relation to the subject matter of each scene, and a painted drop-cloth decorated with bosomy women looked to me a waste of money.

Ustinov is the nicest person and I enjoyed being in his company. He is a raconteur without equal and has an abundance of wit and humour, but he could be desperately indecisive. Several times in this production I could not figure out what he wanted. Neither could the rest of the cast, which included Heather Harper and Luigi Alva, with Roger Soyer as the Don.

Some ideas we thought wildly out-of-keeping. During the ball-room scene at the end of Act 1, we were startled to see a priest hurrying a couple of girls across the stage in front of us. It disrupted the musical interest as much as the dramatic tension, but Ustinov explained: 'He's taking them somewhere else to seduce them, because that's what it's all about. It's about seduction.'

So much for Mozart, and Mozart's intentions.

Several times I've been involved with opera producers who have no experience of the medium, and little idea of the differences between musical and spoken drama, yet they are given large budgets while others who start from the bottom and learn their craft in operatic stage management, working their way up, are denied the opportunities their experience deserves. Very often the directors with little or no operatic experience needed more help from the singers than we did from them and, in many instances, it was only the help we gave them that saved them from falling flat on their faces.

The following year we were invited to take our Edinburgh production of *Don Giovanni* to Israel, but there was some concern over the expense of shipping out the sets. I mentioned to Danny that we might perform it without them, like Glyndebourne first did at the London Promenade concerts, with the cast dressing according to their status in the opera, coming and going according to cue, and creating some kind of dramatic illusion by the way each responded to the others.

In the event we did it this way, in Jerusalem, Tel Aviv and Caesarea, accompanied by the Israel Philharmonic Orchestra, and it was most successfully received. I often wonder how much we need cumbersome stage productions to make an opera successful in the theatre?

Shortly before going to Israel, I had one or two warning signs that all wasn't well with me physically. Our neighbour, Robin Crellin, an orthopaedic surgeon, called in one day on a social visit and noticed I was subconsciously massaging my chest from time to time. In answer to his question I said I felt a little pain now and again, and he left without saying anything further. But inside half an hour he was back, telling me he was taking me to hospital for an X-ray.

Apparently all was not quite as it should be and I was admitted for observation and tests, then told to go home and rest completely. This meant cancelling everything before the trip to Israel, after which we were due to go back to the Edinburgh Festival to repeat *Don Giovanni* there for a second year.

As Brenda well knows, I'm not good at being idle. I enjoy a few days' rest, but if it's two or three weeks I get very irritable. All the same, I think we performers sometimes need more rest from the tensions of a career than we usually take. These tensions are not always obvious to us, and they are difficult to explain. They become part of our lives and we often fail to make enough allowances for them. Even when our bodies send out warning signals, we don't always take as much notice of them as we should. I had my own warning that summer but the next year, 1975, found me working twice as hard. I went to Poland in February, then from March to July at Covent Garden I sang successively in *Wozzeck, La forza del destino*, *Falstaff* and a new production of *Peter Grimes*. After that I went to Edinburgh to direct my own production of *The Marriage of Figaro* at the festival; on to Paris for Leporello in *Don Giovanni* and back to Covent Garden for *L'elisir d'amore* before Christmas.

It's true that I mostly enjoyed every minute of it, the exception being *Peter Grimes*. It was done on a limited budget, and none the worse for that. The critics admired it and the audience enjoyed it, but that was because of what we, the singers and the chorus, achieved by working out for ourselves where to move and what to do, for lack of adequate direction. We wanted it to be successful for our own sakes, and we made a fine co-operative venture of it.

When I went to the Paris Opéra for *Don Giovanni* a little while later, I encountered more stage confusion. Not all the scenery would always be in place, and movements would have to be improvised accordingly. There were so many stage staff that a simple request could be self-defeating. I needed the Don's sword for the graveyard scene, but by the time my request had been passed from one to another among about ten people, and then come back to the one I first asked, I was already on stage without it.

Musically the Paris performances went well, and there was a strong British contingent taking part. Charles Mackerras conducted and the cast included Stuart Burrows, Margaret Price, Kiri te Kanawa and Richard van Allan. One day we were all invited by

President Giscard d'Estaing to a late-afternoon reception at the Elysée Palace, which was something of an honour for us as guest performers.

Of all my engagements that year I think I derived most pleasure from the new production of *L'elisir d'amore* at Covent Garden. The quack 'doctor', Dulcamara, with his elixirs, his love-potions, I had first sung some years before in Chicago, but the stage-within-a-stage, on which that production relied, wasn't very interesting and did little for the mostly frivolous comedy and Donizetti's musical sparkle.

The Covent Garden production had more of a pantomime style which I thought better suited to the subject. It was directed by John Copley, and Beni Montresor's designs evoked an Italianate warmth and exuberance of colour, while John Pritchard's conducting kept the musical spirits bubbling. We had a new Japanese soprano, Yasuko Hayashi, as Adina, with José Carreras an eloquent Nemorino, and Thomas Allen, who has since gone on to still greater successes, was a splendid Belcore, the swaggering recruiting sergeant.

Nearly ten years later I decided on this opera for my farewell performances at Covent Garden in 1984 because I wanted to end on a happy note, and what could be better than handing out love-potions to everybody?

During that first run at Covent Garden, we were visited one night by the Queen Mother and the Prince of Wales, who showed a lively interest in the 'love-potion' bottles Dulcamara distributes from slots in the inside of his cloak.

There were still a couple of bottles left in place when I went to be presented to HRH. He asked me what they were and I handed him one to look at: a gin bottle overpainted in blue and with a decorated cork. As I held out my hand to take it back, he said he'd like it for a keepsake. Who was I to refuse? But as there had been rumours of his possible engagement flying about for a long time, I reminded him that it was a 'love-potion' and said, 'I hope it brings you luck, Sir!'

Later, when his engagement to Lady Diana Spencer was announced, I sent him a somewhat cheeky telegram:

'VERY GLAD THE ELIXIR OF LOVE HAS TAKEN EFFECT.'

Not expecting a reply, I was delighted when the Prince wired back:

'THE ELIXIR WORKED BUT IT WAS RATHER SLOW TO ACT.'

The following year after the Donizetti production, the Royal Opera made one of its increasingly rare sorties abroad, on an exchange visit with the company of La Scala, Milan. Although we were no longer a company wholly under contract, as we were when we went on tour in my early years at Covent Garden, I still much enjoyed the company spirit that came about when we travelled together.

As well as the Berlioz opera *Benvenuto Cellini*, and our latest Mozart production, *La clemenza di Tito*, we took *Peter Grimes* with Jon Vickers, Heather Harper and myself. We certainly made the Italian audiences sit up and take notice. The ovations were quite something, not at all what we'd been warned to expect at La Scala, where it is often said that the audience sits on one hand and applauds with the other.

On the management side, the organisation was superbly carried out by Paul Findlay, who has since been named assistant director to Sir John Tooley. He organised us so well that everything went without a hitch, and three years later he took equally good charge of us when the Royal Opera went to the Far East for performances in Korea and Japan. Again I went as Balstrode in *Peter Grimes*, having this time grown a beard (and moustache) to save having to stick one on at every performance.

This time nearly 350 people were transported, including our own orchestra as well as the stage staff, the children involved in the Britten opera, *Tosca* and *The Magic Flute*, and some forty-five tons of scenery, most of it sent by sea. The costs were shared between the British Council (for *Peter Grimes*) and by business undertakings in Japan and, in Korea, an influential newspaper, *Dong a Ilbo*, whose chairman, Dr Kim, was a prominent Anglophile and had underwritten the Royal Ballet's visit there two years before.

The South Koreans in Seoul showed us a wonderful warmth and hospitality, although it seemed tragic to me that there was such a barrier with North Korea. Our hotel was only a short distance from the border, and our rooms faced in that direction, but the windows in each room were shielded by a louvred effect which totally prevented us from seeing beyond it.

Our shopping expeditions took us down streets where there were clusters of the same kind of shops: furniture shops, brass shops and so on. Time and again Brenda and I would linger and then find ourselves being persuaded to take coffee with the hospitable shopkeeper at the back of his narrow little shop. Of course we succumbed to this or that purchase. Who wouldn't? I bought a lacquered table and a small lacquered chest. Others bought bedroom suites in white lacquer and the like. What we hadn't quite realised was that it would take about eighteen months before the goods we bought actually arrived in Britain as part of a ship's cargo, and I believe some things never arrived at all.

In Japan we were welcomed to Tokyo by a family who had become opera fans in London, and who were wonderfully hospitable to Brenda, Stuart Burrows and me when we visited them at home. Another occasion found us invited with some other members of the cast to a special Mandarin meal which we had the utmost difficulty in eating because so much of it, the octopus and the sharks' fins for example, was unfamiliar to us and frankly unappealing. Only later did we learn that it had cost more than a hundred pounds a head!

At this reception the young Japanese lady who acted as interpreter to our host asked where we came from. I explained we were Welsh and came from a small town called Pontypridd which I am sure she had never heard of. It transpired, however, that she had studied at the Polytechnic College in Pontypridd: the world we live in grows smaller indeed.

Our three operas were also performed in Osaka and Yokohama, to enthusiastic receptions in each city. With time to spare between performances, the whole company made the most of our opportunities for sightseeing, including one temple with row upon row of statues, all looking thoroughly mournful. We were gazing in what I thought was quiet appreciation, with only the odd hushed comment from one or the other of us, when suddenly the mood was shattered by the deep bass of Forbes Robinson: 'My God! They look like the crowd at Cardiff Arms Park when England have scored a try!'

The sense of being together as a company seemed to me very strong on this tour, and we made the long flight home in high spirits. They were soon dissipated after we landed at Gatwick, though, where that morning, as I remember, only one, or perhaps two, customs officers were on duty to handle our special flight with more than three hundred of us.

We were tired. Families and friends were waiting. We felt we had been a national export for Britain, flying the flag, if you like, yet we were treated with a total lack of consideration. Other flights from the continent were being allowed through but it was about two hours before any more customs officers appeared, and we were nearly four hours on the ground before the last of our party was passed through. Sir John Tooley was so embarrassed by this that he himself organised and helped to serve tea and sandwiches to us.

A few days later I flew out again to Chicago, there to take part in the longest gala performance I've ever known. It was organised to celebrate the twenty-fifth anniversary of the Chicago Lyric Opera and with it, of course, the achievement of Carol Fox in forming and managing the company over this time. The solo singers alone read like a roll-call of international celebrities. Imagine Carlo Cossutta, Alfredo Kraus, Luciano Pavarotti and Jon Vickers as tenors together in one house, just as an example.

By the time these and all the others had sung their say or, in the case of retired artists like Gobbi, Elisabeth Schwarzkopf, Giulietta Simionato and Eleanor Steber, spoken their tributes, more than four hours had gone by. There was certainly wonderful singing to be heard, but I shall never forget how Margaret Price came on, almost at the end of the long programme, and made the occasion something still more special.

She sang Desdemona's 'Willow Song' and prayer from *Otello* so ravishingly that I almost cried with delight and affection. The audience went wild with their applause, but so did the artists who had sung earlier and were now waiting around in the wings to come on stage at the end of the gala. Every one of them applauded to give Margaret her own personal triumph, and I couldn't have been more pleased.

My contribution was to sing the patter-duet from *Don Pasquale* with the American baritone, Richard Stilwell. We'd sung the opera together in Chicago the year before, and I thought this would make a good contrast to the rather grand arias that most of the others were singing, as indeed it proved.

Carol Fox had long wanted the Lyric Opera to show itself as a company somewhere other than Chicago, and she had a plan to take the *Don Pasquale* production to Palm Springs, the Californian resort, with the best cast she could arrange. It soon became clear, however, that this would be too expensive, even for Palm Springs, so Carol had to think again.

She then had the idea of staging it there with the Lyric Opera's scholarship students who were working at the opera studio in Chicago, talented singers acquiring professional coaching and experience before embarking upon their individual careers. She asked if I would sing Pasquale with them and direct the opera as well.

I felt that I owed it to Carol for all the opportunities she had given me, and I knew that the venture meant a tremendous amount to her even though she was then not well enough to be there herself. So I took it on.

We had a lengthy and useful period of rehearsal in Chicago first, and when we got to Palm Springs the students were marvellous. I thoroughly enjoyed myself and I gather the audience did too. We had borrowed props to dress the stage more elaborately than in Chicago, and the garden scene had tropical plants in profusion obtained from the local park.

Much of this was made possible through the good offices of Lee Freeman and his wife Brena. He had funded the opera's original production at Chicago, and at Palm Springs I had the luxury of staying in a penthouse apartment at a hotel he owned. Never have I been better looked after.

I seemed to be doing a run of Pasquale performances for two or three years, taking me to Seattle, Portland and back to San Francisco as well. After twenty-one years going back and back again to that lovely city it was time to exit gracefully, and for some time I had determined that the *Don Pasquale* performances there in 1980 would be my last.

To say goodbye is always sad, and I was beginning to experience what it would be like. After so long, a part of my heart was in San Francisco, and I wanted to take my leave while I was still on top form. I sang well at those performances and I began to wish I wasn't finishing after all. But there it was. After the last performance I heard some moving and very flattering things said about me by Mrs Watt Miller and Kurt Adler, and to crown everything I was presented with the San Francisco Opera Medal for 'appreciation of his exceptional contributions to the San Francisco Opera since 1958', a rare honour I treasured greatly.

Fate nevertheless ordained that I wasn't quite finished with San Francisco. A longtime friend of mine, Terry McEwan, succeeded Adler as general director and at first he tried to talk me into going back on my decision. I had prepared myself for my retirement, though, and wouldn't go back on my word as far as actual performances went, but I did agree to go there again in 1983 to give master-classes for the students at the opera studio run by the company, like that in Chicago.

A week before I was due there I had an agitated call from Terry at about one o'clock in the morning. Tragedy had struck with the sudden death from a heart attack of Donald Gramm, who was to rehearse and sing Alfonso in *Così fan tutte*. Now Terry asked me, as a favour to him, to take on the performances as I would be there anyway, and it would only mean my leaving home a week earlier.

I felt I could hardly refuse, since I'd arranged to be there, and so I gave the master-classes and sang six performances as Don Alfonso. There were more farewell speeches afterwards and I started to feel embarrassed in case people might say I was 'doing a Sinatra'. But let's just say it was a little bonus, and definitely not one I shall repeat.

As it happened, Don Alfonso was the role I'd planned for my last appearance at Chicago later that year. This time Graziella Sciutti was to direct it, and for old times' sake I looked forward to our association once more. Besides, nobody knew more about *Così* than she did, and I reckoned I could still get new ideas about it from her.

Fate now turned the other way and sent me tumbling from a ladder at home in Aberaeron a few weeks before I was due to leave for Chicago. I'd broken a rib a couple of times before, playing rugby on one occasion, and even during a performance of *Wozzeck* at Covent Garden, when I was caught off-balance during a fight with Edgar Evans, who was playing the Drum-major. But the pain of those accidents was as nothing compared to what I now suffered with three broken ribs.

It put me out of commission for several months and forced me to cancel all hopes of getting to Chicago, where I knew another farewell occasion had been arranged for me. Ardis Krainik, Carol Fox's successor, begged me to come later, offering me dates for the next season, but with great regret I held firm. Chicago had become almost as much of a second home company to me as San Francisco, but I knew that, once my resolution to finish was broken, I might be lured into going on, and on . . .

Some years previously I'd signed a contract for some further performances of *Falstaff* at Covent Garden in 1978, not knowing then that these would also be my last in that role. Just before they were due, I had another warning about my health.

This time my doctor advised that if I were to do those performances, I should change the way I went about them. He considered the amount of energy I expended was dangerous and suggested that I should be less energetic on stage, avoid climbing up and down stairs and, above all, cut down the weight of costume and padding I wore.

To me, all this was so much a part of the role I had created, which had grown with me over the years, that to compromise my interpretation of the character was something I couldn't accept. If these were to be my last performances of Falstaff, at least I would go out in glory.

I was delighted that Solti came back to conduct them: with his exuberance and with the excellent cast, I felt I was right on top of the role, singing as well as I ever had.

The last performance was wonderfully exhilarating, even though it was the only time I remember putting on a forced smile to lead off the final joyful chorus, 'Tutto nel mondo è burla'. Underneath I was truly sad to leave Sir John, the character who had given me such tremendous satisfaction, the greatest acclamation and taken me all over the world. But it was a great way to bow out from the Verdi repertoire.

When it came to Covent Garden's new production of *The Magic Flute* I was disappointed to learn that it would be given in German, and that was one reason I didn't sing Papageno again. I always believed that this opera should be given in English here, and became even more convinced of this after the Klemperer performances in German, years before. Where was the point in spoken comedy, in comedy dependent on words, if most of the audience couldn't understand them?

At the same time, I was concerned that Thomas Allen should have the chance of taking the role because I knew he would be an ideal Papageno, as good as, if not better than anybody from outside the country. In the event, Tom did sing it, and a splendid Papageno he made.

Another factor was the increasing embarrassment caused to the family by the fact that I was still playing juvenile leads. Brenda had firm views on Papageno being played by a man now past fifty, and Alun was already about the age that Figaro was supposed to be – I knew I couldn't go on pretending to be other than what I was. I'd finished with Papageno; Figaro would have to be the next one to go.

With all this in mind I cast about for some other role that would be new for me at Covent Garden but less out of keeping with my advancing years, and that's how I came to take on Claggart in *Billy Budd*. There had been some first-rate Claggarts at Covent Garden, of course: Frederick Dalberg, Mike Langdon (who both televised and recorded it) and Forbes Robinson, but I was glad to follow them even though I wished I'd been able to do it sooner.

To give up Figaro was the greatest wrench from a sentimental point of view. After all, it had been my first big role at Covent Garden, thirty years before, and the hundreds of performances I'd given of it in different parts of the world were part of the fabric of my life. Each one had been a challenge. Each time I had tried to improve on the one before.

It's absolutely necessary to do this, or else performances soon become dull, routine affairs, but as Churchill once said: 'You have to grow old and try to improve at the same time, and that is very difficult.'

Now there were extra wrinkles on my face which could no longer be covered under make-up, and the cummerbund was telling its own tale further down. I didn't announce any 'last performances' because it wasn't my practice to do so, and once more I felt they were as good as any I'd done. I enjoyed John Copley's production and Colin Davis, over the years since we first worked together in

Mozart, had matured in a way that was difficult to explain but which gave the opera a dignity, style and spirit that added up to a kind of musical magic.

Even the critics were enthusiastic, and from one or two you might have thought that I'd only then come into my own with Figaro and shown what it was all about. Perhaps I had!

Once again the last performance came around and, as I embraced Susanna, a new one this time in Helen Donath, I thought of the number of wonderful Susannas I'd embraced over the years in the ensemble of happy reconciliation at the end of the opera. There was a feeling of great sadness inside me, but not unmixed with relief that one more 'assignation' was over.

I had intended to finish my operatic career with Beckmesser at Covent Garden in 1983, coming back in a full circle to the opera in which I'd begun my career as the Nighwatchman all those years before. Yet when I talked this over with Sir John Tooley he didn't want me to finish.

'You're singing so well,' he said.

'That's why I want to stop,' I replied. 'Before the rot sets in.'

Anyway we thought that Beckmesser was perhaps rather a sad kind of role on which to finish.

'What would you like to do?' he asked.

'Something like Dulcamara,' I said. 'Then I could pass out all the love-potions as a wish for their happiness, and a thankyou for mine.'

He liked the idea of my bowing out on *L'elisir d'amore* and, as there was a suitable gap in the repertory schedule for 1984, that is what I planned to do, letting myself finish on a very happy note indeed.

Throughout our long acquaintance at Covent Garden, after he became assistant to David Webster, I had nothing but encouragement from John Tooley, and I'm grateful for all the support he gave me. His kind disposition showed in many ways, and nobody should underestimate the problems he has had as general director in keeping a company together in the face of increasing financial problems. A few days after my sixtieth birthday in 1982, after I sang Beckmesser in *Die Meistersinger*, he made a surprise presentation to me on the stage of an 1868 first edition of the opera score, and I could have wished for no more splendid gift from what was still my 'home' company.

Nearly all my concert engagements for the last five years were for charitable causes I was glad to support, but I have never found concert singing greatly enjoyable. I'd already decided not to do any more when I was asked by the National Eisteddfod of Wales, for whom I'd sung a couple of years previously, if I would again take part in the 1982 concert at Swansea.

This I agreed to do, casually remarking that it would have to be the last one. Somehow this was taken up and repeated all around so that, almost before I knew what was happening, not only had it become a radio and television occasion but the Press were labelling it my 'farewell concert', which indeed it was.

Elizabeth Vaughan and Stuart Burrows were also taking part, along with the Welsh National Opera Chorus and the BBC Welsh Orchestra, and with Robin Stapleton conducting. The occasion turned out to be not only wonderfully and warmly emotional so far as I was concerned, but also a more dramatic evening backstage than anybody expected.

The night was hot. The auditorium even hotter. By the time we'd sung our operatic items in the first half, my voice was still in good shape although I thought I must be feeling the effects of the heat. When Brenda came to my dressing-room in the interval to say how well the concert was going, she was startled to see me with trousers rolled up and a St John's Ambulance lady vigorously massaging my legs.

'What on earth's the matter?' she asked.

'It's not my voice,' I answered, 'It's my legs. I can hardly move them . . .'

My masseuse, Mair Davies, now asked me how long I'd been diabetic, and this was news to me indeed. She assured me that was the cause of my trouble and wanted me to take something to alleviate the problem. I refused at that moment, because I still had the second part of the concert with all its Welsh music to perform, and I was afraid that swallowing any medication might affect my voice.

I'm told that when I appeared for the second half I looked as if I might have had a tot or two. The fact was that my legs had become so weak they were threatening to give way. I had to be helped both on and off the stage, as circumspectly as possible, although the condition wasn't so bad when I stood still and braced myself to sing.

Happily the voice wasn't affected, and I was able to sing the Welsh items with all my usual fervour. Stuart and Elizabeth helped me to and fro for the calls, and when I saw six thousand people standing to applaud, it affected me deeply. Brenda now joined me on the platform for the presentation of my portrait painted by David Griffiths, and given by the National Eisteddfod as 'a sign of their appreciation of his services to music and to Wales.'

Like the accolade of knighthood, this was a moment when my

heart was so full of gratitude, happiness and a sense of fulfilment, mingling with an inescapable dash of pride, that I can only recall a few details. I've no idea how coherently I replied to the president of the National Eisteddfod, Emrys Evans, who presented the portrait, nor do I remember what kind of a figure I cut with the physical ill-effects I was suffering.

Brenda stayed so close to me on the platform it must have looked as if she was hanging on to me for dear life, when in fact she was physically helping me to stay upright. Somebody had called an ambulance at the stage door, but I was content and relieved to be taken back in a car to the hotel, where I could have further treatment for a diabetic condition I now had to accept and cope with.

As artists we are seen and heard by the public, but the degree of our success depends to a very great extent on the way we are looked after backstage. I've always been indebted to my dressers who anticipate most of our needs before we're even conscious of them. They always seem to be calm and patient, and these qualities are to be found all over the world.

We also depend on the work of craftsmen like the wigmakers, in my case Albert Sargood in the early days, and later Ron Freeman, who made my wigs so well that I could be assured of looking right *and* feeling comfortable – not always the same thing. They were so good at it that I never went anywhere in the world without taking along, for whatever role, a wig made for me by one or other of them.

The stage hands and the administrative staff, in their various ways, also contribute to the wellbeing of a performer, both on and off the stage, and I have enjoyed valued friendships with many musicians in the splendid Royal Opera House Orchestra. To all those I have worked with I owe my own personal debt of gratitude for the support they have given me in performance at home and abroad.

I count myself lucky to have had such a career and such opportunities, and amid what I believe were more ups than downs, there's little I haven't enjoyed. I used to say that Brenda would be the first to tell me when the voice was no longer what it was, but I think I already knew when the time had come to bow out, to exit in good order, consoled for any regrets by all the fulfilment my career has brought me.

I won't attempt to teach singing, not in the way of voice production. It's never appealed to me, and I've always been nervous of imposing methods of technique on something as fragile as a young voice. Maybe I can give hints here and there. Maybe I can coach some singers in particular roles, like I've enjoyed doing in the master-classes. A lot of letters come to me from aspiring singers wondering if they're good enough to go on with it. Maybe I can take an interest, and perhaps help them with some advice.

This could be one way of putting something back into a profession that has given me a happiness beyond anything I could possibly have dreamed.

Otherwise, apart from keeping an interest in music and the theatre generally, I'll probably have more time than ever to enjoy Aberaeron. Brenda and I will share it together. We have our family. We can follow our interests. I'd like to take up painting again, which I enjoyed a lot in my 'teens. I want to catch up with life and do things there has been little time to do. Simple things, like going for walks and reading.

We have the mountains there. We have the sea. I have my boat. And when I take it out from the little harbour, and I'm a fair way offshore and out of earshot . . .

I might even sing a little.

CHRONOLOGY OF ROLES

First performances of roles, for theatre productions and new television operas.
* Created role at premiere.

Date	Role	Opera	Location
1948			
21 January	Nightwatchman	The Mastersingers of Nuremberg	Covent Garden
1 April	Second Priest	The Magic Flute	Covent Garden
1 April	Armed Man	The Magic Flute	Covent Garden
6 April	Marquis d'Obigny	La traviata	Covent Garden
12 May	Police Officer	Boris Godunov	Covent Garden
8 October	Nikitich	Boris Godunov	Covent Garden
14 October	Count Ceprano	Rigoletto	Covent Garden
15 October	Schaunard	La Bohème	Covent Garden
1949			
22 January	Figaro	The Marriage of Figaro	Covent Garden
15 April	Baron Douphol	La traviata	Birmingham (Covent Garden Opera)
29 October	Escamillo	Carmen	Covent Garden
11 November	Second Soldier	Salome	Covent Garden
1950			
18 May	Lescaut	Manon (Massenet)	Covent Garden
29 June	Melot	Tristan and Isolde	Covent Garden
19 July	Guglielmo	Così fan tutte	Glyndebourne
18 November	Sacristan	Tosca	Covent Garden
1951			
26 April	Herald*	The Pilgrim's Progress (Vaughan Williams)	Covent Garden
11 July	Masetto	Don Giovanni	Glyndebourne
1 December	Mr Flint*	Billy Budd	Covent Garden
1952			
8 March	Leporello	Don Giovanni	Sadler's Wells
28 October	Speaker	The Magic Flute	Covent Garden
30 December	Shchelkalov	Boris Godunov	Covent Garden

1953

16 January	Papageno	*The Magic Flute*	Covent Garden
8 June	Mountjoy*	*Gloriana*	Covent Garden
14 November	Balstrode	*Peter Grimes*	Covent Garden

1954

7 January	Prince Afron	*Le Coq d'or*	Covent Garden
1 March	Sharpless	*Madama Butterfly*	Croydon (Covent Garden Opera)
16 March	Kilian	*Der Freischütz*	Cardiff (Covent Garden Opera)
6 May	Marullo	*Rigoletto*	Covent Garden
25 June	Abbate Cospicuo	*Arlecchino* (Busoni)	Glyndebourne
25 June	Music Master	*Ariadne auf Naxos*	Glyndebourne
26 October	Spalanzani	*The Tales of Hoffmann*	Covent Garden
3 December	Antenor*	*Troilus and Cressida* (Walton)	Covent Garden
20 December	Amonasro	*Aïda*	Covent Garden
22 December	Ottokar	*Der Freischütz*	Covent Garden

1955

26 October	Ping	*Turandot*	Covent Garden
28 November	Kruschina	*The Bartered Bride*	Covent Garden

1957

28 January	Beckmesser	*The Mastersingers of Nuremberg*	Covent Garden
29 June	Falstaff	*Falstaff*	Glyndebourne
27 October	Sergeant Sulpizio	*La figlia del reggimento*	Wexford Festival
23 November	Count Almaviva	*The Marriage of Figaro*	Covent Garden

1958

29 January	Ned Keene	*Peter Grimes*	Covent Garden
25 February	Valens	*Theodora*	St Pancras (Handel Opera Society)
October	Don Giovanni	*Don Giovanni*	Dublin (Grand Opera Society

1959

17 February	Enrico	*Lucia di Lammermoor*	Covent Garden
22 April	Rodrigo	*Don Carlos*	Covent Garden
16 December	Tonio	*I pagliacci*	Covent Garden

1960

16 January	Lindorf/ Coppelius/ Dr Miracle/ Dapertutto	*Les Contes d'Hoffmann*	Covent Garden
27 September	Paolo	*Simon Boccanegra*	San Francisco
4 October	Wozzeck	*Wozzeck*	San Francisco
17 October	Gianni Schicchi	*Gianni Schicchi*	San Francisco

1961

2 February	Bottom	*A Midsummer Night's Dream*	Covent Garden
25 November	Lemuel*	*The Harvest* (Giannini)	Chicago Lyric Opera

1964

7 February	Rigoletto	*Rigoletto*	Covent Garden
8 October	Kečal	*The Bartered Bride*	San Francisco
13 October	Pizarro	*Fidelio*	San Francisco

1965

23 June	Saul	*Saul*	Sadler's Wells (Handel Opera Society)
13 August	Don Pasquale	*Don Pasquale*	Buenos Aires (Teatro Colón)

1967

22 March	Dr Bartolo	*Il barbiere di Siviglia*	Covent Garden

1968

22 March	Scarpia	*Tosca*	Covent Garden
19 May	Betumain*	*The Rose Affair* (Kay)	BBC TV

1970

6 November	Claggart	*Billy Budd*	Chicago Lyric Opera

1971

24 March	Alfonso†	*Così fan tutte*	Covent Garden

† Alfonso in *Così fan tutte* previously performed at Guildhall School of Music, Summer 1948, followed by Arts Theatre, Cambridge.

1974

26 March	Case*	*The Beach at Falesá* (Hoddinott)	Cardiff (Welsh National Opera)

1975

26 May	Fra Melitone	*La forza del destino*	Covent Garden
18 December	Dulcamara	*L'elisir d'amore*	Covent Garden

1976

11 February	Sesto*	*Murder, the Magician* (Hoddinott)	Harlech TV
20 October	Prus	*The Makropoulos Case* (Janáček)	San Francisco

1977

27 July	Old Man*	*What the Old Man does is always right* (Hoddinott)	Fishguard

1978

25 December	Scrooge*	*A Christmas Carol* (Kay)	Harlech TV

1979

24 November	Jack Vandeleur*	*The Rajah's Diamond* (Hoddinott)	BBC TV

APPENDIX B

DEBUT PERFORMANCES

Major companies and festivals.

Location	Date	Role	Opera
Covent Garden	21 January 1948	Nightwatchman	*The Mastersingers of Nuremberg*
Glyndebourne	19 July 1950	Guglielmo	*Cosi fan tutte*
Edinburgh Festival	23 August 1951	Masetto	*Don Giovanni* (Glyndebourne Opera)
Sadler's Wells	8 March 1952	Leporello	*Don Giovanni*
Wexford Festival	27 October 1957	Sergeant Sulpizio	*La figlia del reggimento*
San Francisco	18 September 1959	Beckmesser	*Die Meistersinger von Nürnberg*
Milan (La Scala)	6 May 1960	Figaro	*Le nozze di Figaro*
Vienna Staatsoper	6 March 1961	Schaunard	*La Bohème*
Chicago Lyric Opera	25 November 1961	Lemuel	*The Harvest*
Salzburg Festival	26 July 1962	Figaro	*Le nozze di Figaro*
Buenos Aires (Teatro Colón)	30 August 1963	Falstaff	*Falstaff*
New York (Metropolitan Opera)	25 March 1964	Falstaff	*Falstaff*
Scottish Opera	6 May 1966	Falstaff	*Falstaff*
Welsh National Opera	26 September 1966	Don Pasquale	*Don Pasquale*

DISCOGRAPHY

Notes: The individual role is noted in brackets after the title of the opera or oratorio. The year in brackets after the record number(s) is that of first issue in the UK, or of reissue where this is noted.

(m) – Monaural recording.   (s) – Stereo recording.

BACH: *St Matthew Passion* (Priest)
Philharmonia/Klemperer
Columbia 33CXS 1799, 33CX 1800–03 (m) (1962)
SAXS 2446, SAX 2447–50 (s) (1962)
Reissue: HMV SLS 827 (s) (1972).

BRITTEN: *Peter Grimes* (Ned Keene)
Covent Garden Opera/Britten
Decca SXL 2150–52 (s)
Tape K71K33 (1959).

BUSONI: *Arlecchino* (Abbate Cospicuo)
Glyndebourne Festival/Pritchard
HMV ALP 1223 (m)
Tape HTA 14 (1955).

DONIZETTI: *L'elisir d'amore* (Dulcamara)
Royal Opera House/Pritchard
CBS 79210 (s)
Tape 40-79210 (1977).

MAHLER: *Des Knaben Wunderhorn*, Nos 1–10, 13, 14, with Janet Baker
London Philharmonic/Morris
Delysé ECB 3177 (m)
DS 6077 (s) (1966)
Reissue: Decca Ace of Diamonds SDD R326 (1972).

MATHIAS: *Elegy for a Prince*
New Philharmonia/Atherton
included in Argo ZRG 882 (s) (1978).

MOZART: *Così fan tutte* (Guglielmo)
New Philharmonia/Klemperer
HMV SLS 961 (s) (1972).

Le nozze di Figaro (Figaro)
New Philharmonia/Klemperer
HMV SLS 955 (s) (1971).

Le nozze di Figaro (Figaro)
English Chamber Orchestra/Barenboim
HMV SLS 995 (s) (1977).

MOZART (continued):
Vocal trios, with Emmerentia Scheepers, Monica Sinclair
Notturni: *Luci care, luci belle* (K346); *Ecco quel fiero istante* (K436); *Mi lagnerò tacendo* (K437); *Se lontan, ben mio, tu sei* (K438); *Due pupille amabile* (K439);
Canzonetta: *Più non si trovano* (K549)
London Baroque Ensemble/Haas
Parlophone R20622 (78 rpm)
PMB 1008 (m) (1954).

SULLIVAN: *The Gondoliers* (Duke of Plaza-Toro)
Pro Arte Orchestra/Sargent
HMV ALP 1504–5 (m) (1957)
ASD 265–6 (s) (1959)
Reissue: HMV SXDW 3027 (s)
Tape TC2-SXDW 3027 (1976).

The Mikado (Ko-Ko)
Pro Arte Orchestra/Sargent
HMV ALP 1485–86 (m) (1957)
ASD 256–7 (s) (1958)
Reissue: HMV SXDW 3019 (s)
Tape TC2-EXE 1021 (1976).

The Yeomen of the Guard (Jack Point)
Pro Arte Orchestra/Sargent
HMV ALP 1601–2 (m) (1958); ASD 364–5 (1960)
Reissue: HMV SXDW 3033
Tape TC2-SXDW 3033 (1977).

VERDI: *Falstaff* (Falstaff)
RCA Italiana/Solti
Decca 2BB 104–6 (s)
Tape K110K32 (1964).

La forza del destino (Fra Melitone)
Royal Philharmonic/Gardelli
HMV SLS 948 (s) (1970).

WAGNER: *Die Meistersinger von Nürnberg* (Beckmesser)
Dresden State Opera/von Karajan
HMV SLS 957 (s) (1971).

COLLECTIONS

'GERAINT EVANS SINGS IN LLANDAFF CATHEDRAL'

Mendelssohn/*Elijah*: Lord God of Abraham; Cast thy burden; Is not His word like fire?; Thanks be to God. **Handel**/*Judas Maccabeus*: Arm, arm ye brave; *Messiah*: The trumpet shall sound; Anthem – Zadok the Priest. **Brahms**/*A German Requiem*: Lord, let me know mine end
Shelly, Lyrian and Glendower Singers/BBC Welsh Orchestra/Thomas
Delysé ECB 3163 (m)
DS 6063 (s) (1962).

OPERATIC ARIAS

Handel/*Berenice*: Si trai ceppi; *Semele*: Leave me, radiant light. **Mozart**/*Le nozze di Figaro*: Non più andrai; *Don Giovanni*: Madamina!; *Die Zauberflöte*: Der Vogelfänger; *L'oca del Cairo*: Ogni momento. **Beethoven**/*Fidelio*: Ha! Welch' ein Augenblick! **Leoncavallo**/*I pagliacci*: Si può. **Donizetti**/*Don Pasquale*: Un fuoco insolito. **Verdi**/*Otello*: Credo in un Dio crudel; *Falstaff*: Ehi! Paggio! . . . L'onore, ladri!. **Britten**/*A Midsummer Night's Dream*: Bottom's Dream. **Mussorgsky**/*Boris Godunov*: Ye Muscovites

Suisse Romande Orchestra/Balkwill
Decca LXT 6262 (m); SXL 6262 (s) (1967)
Reissue: Decca 'Jubilee' JB60 (s)
Tape – KJBC 60 (1979).

ROYAL OPERA HOUSE 21ST ANNIVERSARY ALBUM

Verdi/*Falstaff*: Ehi! Taverniere! (from Act 3)
Covent Garden Orchestra/Downes
Included in Decca MET 392–3 (m); SET 392–3 (s) (1968).

APPENDIX D

HONOURS AND AWARDS

Knight Bachelor   1969
Commander, Order of the British Empire (CBE)   1959
Freeman of the City of London   1984

Fellow, Guildhall School of Music and Drama   1960
Fellow, University College, Cardiff   1976
Fellow, Royal Northern College of Music   1978
Fellow, Jesus College, University of Oxford   1979
Fellow, Royal College of Music   1981
Fellow, Royal Society of Arts   1984

Hon DMus University of Wales   1963
Hon DMus University of Leicester   1969
Hon RAM Royal Academy of Music   1969
Hon DMus Council for National Academic Awards   1980
Hon DMus University of London   1983

Sir Charles Santley Memorial Award (Worshipful Company of Musicians)   1963
Harriet Cohen International Music Award: Opera Medal   1967
San Francisco Opera Medal ('with appreciation of his exceptional contributions to
   the San Francisco Opera since 1958')   1980
Fidelio Medal (International Association of Opera Directors)   1980

INDEX